NELSON
MANDELA
THE UNCONQUERABLE SOUL
1918 – 2013

CAMPFIRE®

D1254674

KALYANI NAVYUG MEDIA PVT LTD

"No one is born hating another person because of the color of his skin, or his background, or his religion. People must learn to hate, and if they can learn to hate, they can be taught to love, for love comes more naturally to the human heart than its opposite."

Nelson Mandela

NELSON MANDELA

Sitting around the Campfire, telling the story, were:

ILLUSTRATOR **SANKHA BANERJEE**

COLORISTS **PRADEEP SHERAWAT & DEBU PAYEN**

LETTERER **BHAVNATH CHAUDHARY**

EDITOR **ASWATHY SENAN**

PRODUCTION CONTROLLER **VISHAL SHARMA**

COVER ART **SANKHA BANERJEE**

DESIGNER **JAYAKRISHNAN K. P.**

CAMPFIRE®

www.campfire.co.in

Mission Statement

To entertain and educate young minds by creating unique illustrated books
that recount stories of human values, arouse curiosity in the world around us,
and inspire with tales of great deeds of unforgettable people.

Published by Kalyani Navyug Media Pvt. Ltd.
101 C, Shiv House, Hari Nagar Ashram, New Delhi 110014, India

ISBN: 978-93-80741-16-1

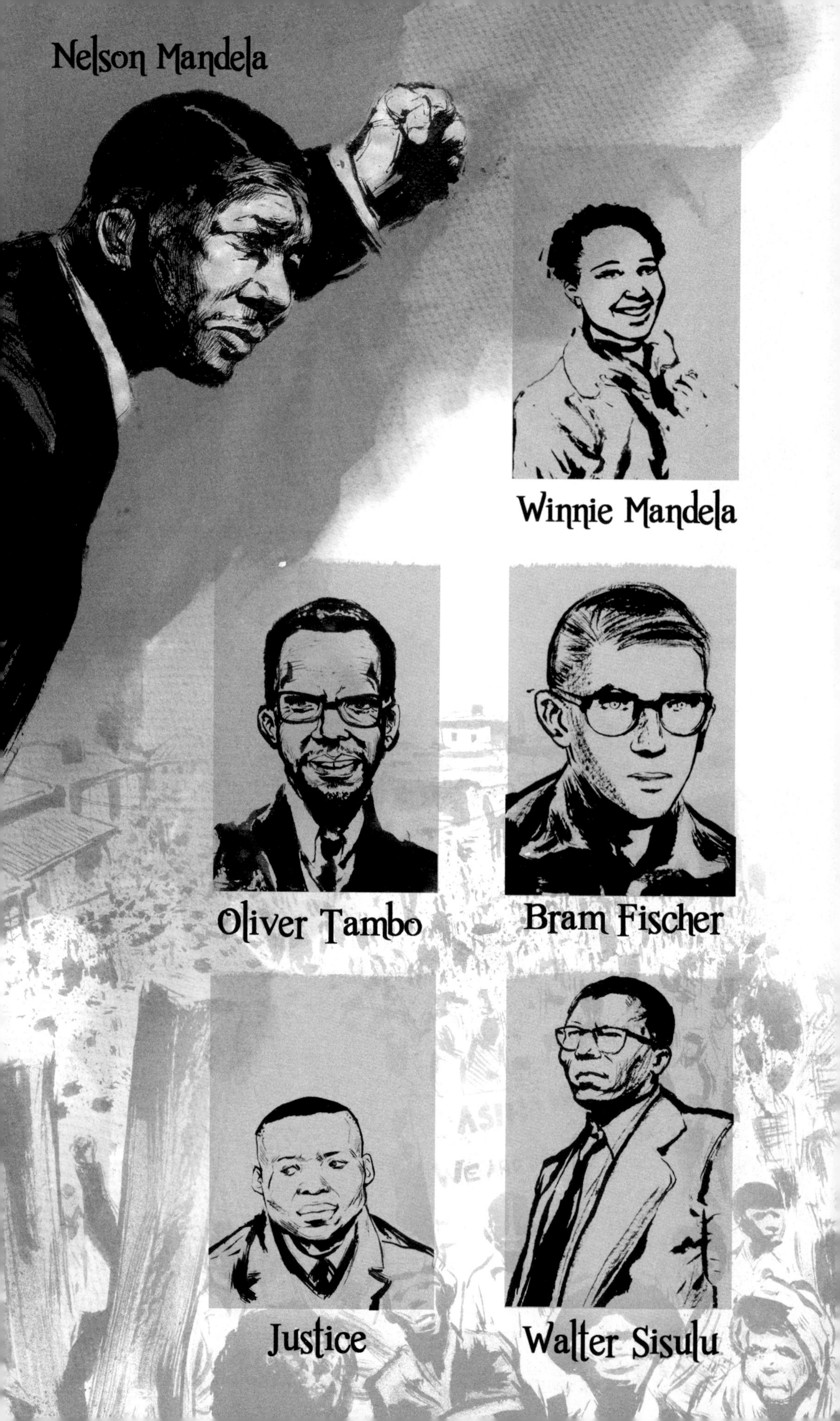
Nelson Mandela
Winnie Mandela
Oliver Tambo
Bram Fischer
Justice
Walter Sisulu

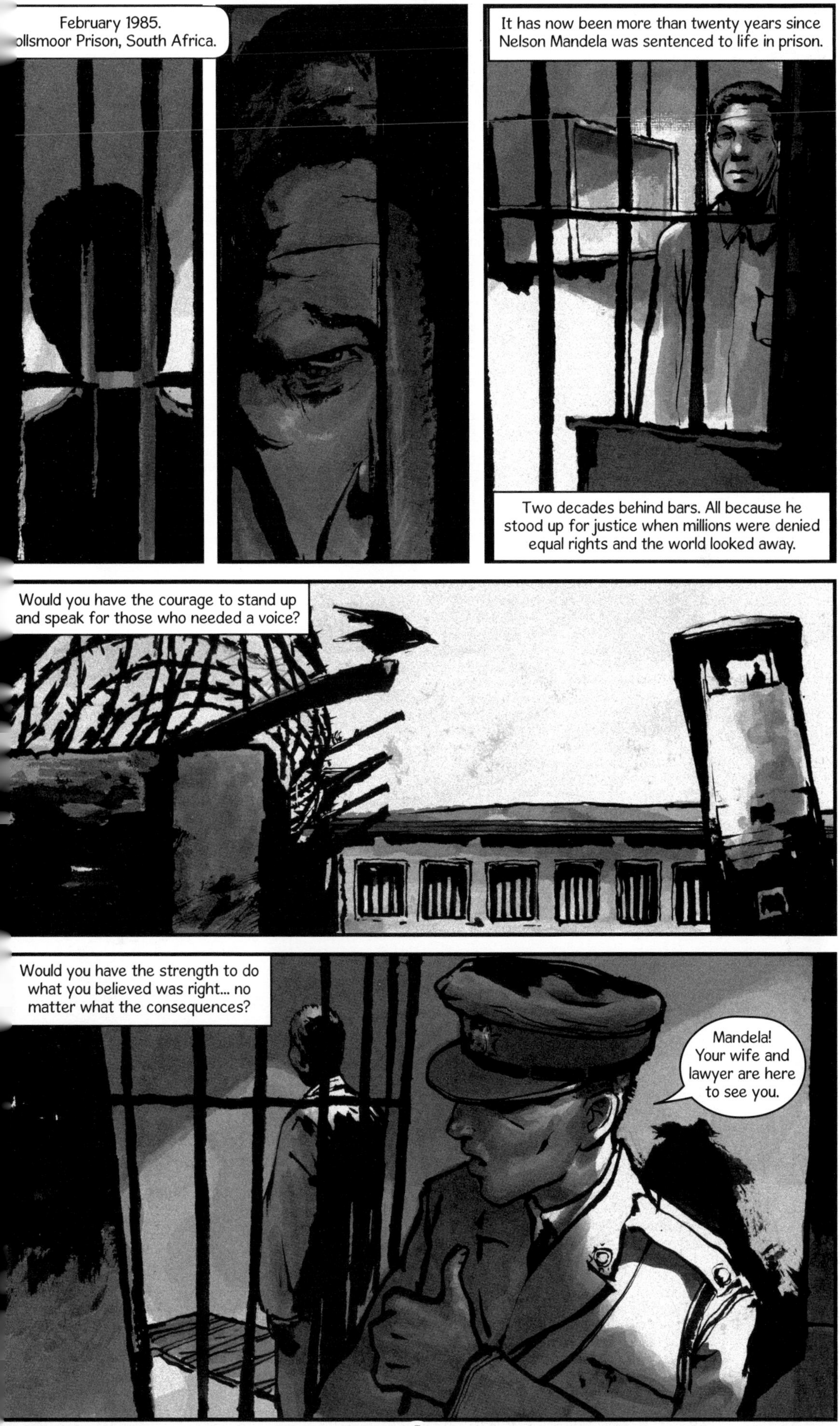
February 1985.
ollsmoor Prison, South Africa.
It has now been more than twenty years since Nelson Mandela was sentenced to life in prison.
Two decades behind bars. All because he stood up for justice when millions were denied equal rights and the world looked away.
Would you have the courage to stand up and speak for those who needed a voice?
Would you have the strength to do what you believed was right... no matter what the consequences?
Mandela! Your wife and lawyer are here to see you.

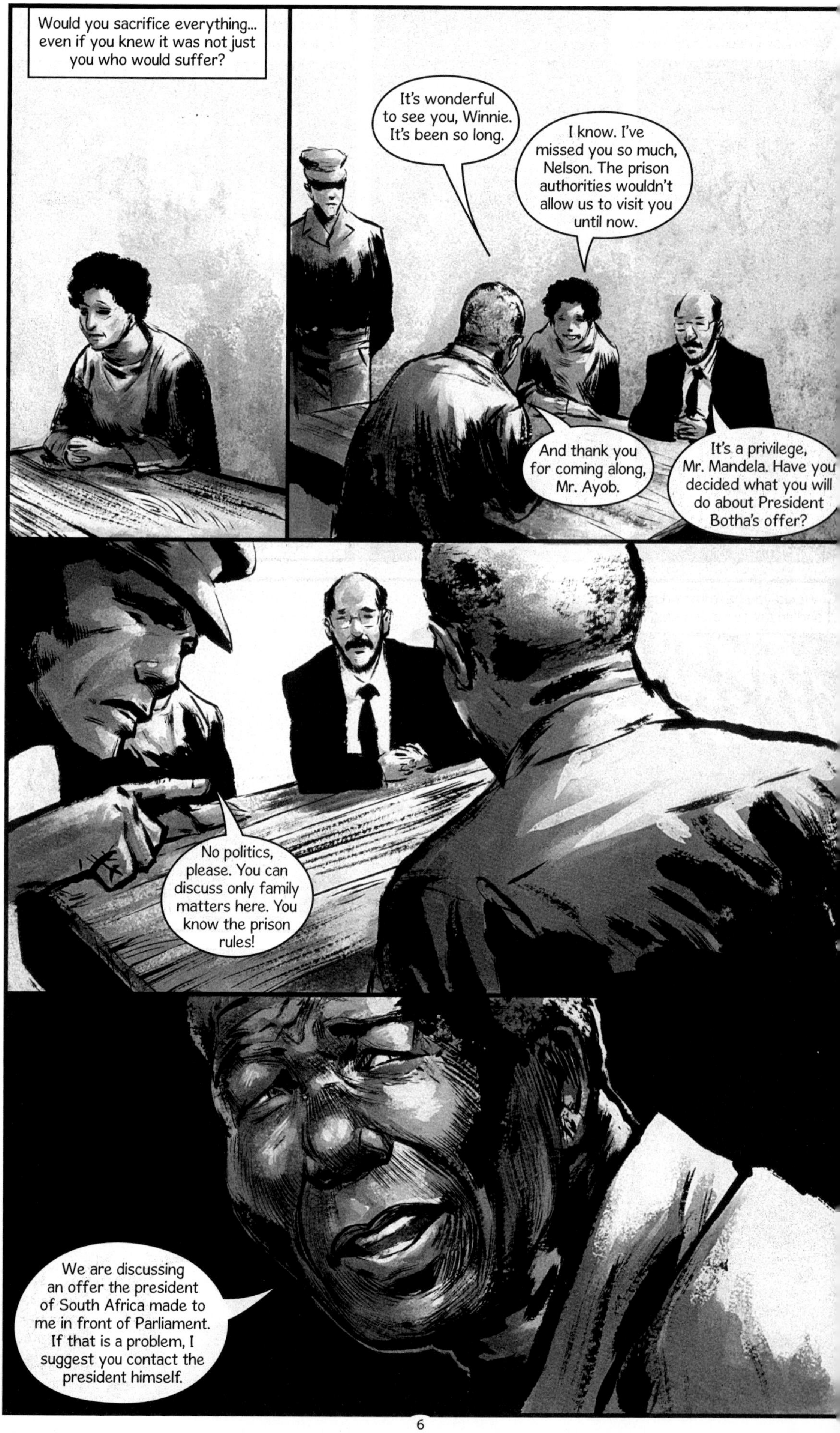

Would you sacrifice everything... even if you knew it was not just you who would suffer?
It's wonderful to see you, Winnie. It's been so long.
I know. I've missed you so much, Nelson. The prison authorities wouldn't allow us to visit you until now.
And thank you for coming along, Mr. Ayob.
It's a privilege, Mr. Mandela. Have you decided what you will do about President Botha's offer?
No politics, please. You can discuss only family matters here. You know the prison rules!
We are discussing an offer the president of South Africa made to me in front of Parliament. If that is a problem, I suggest you contact the president himself.

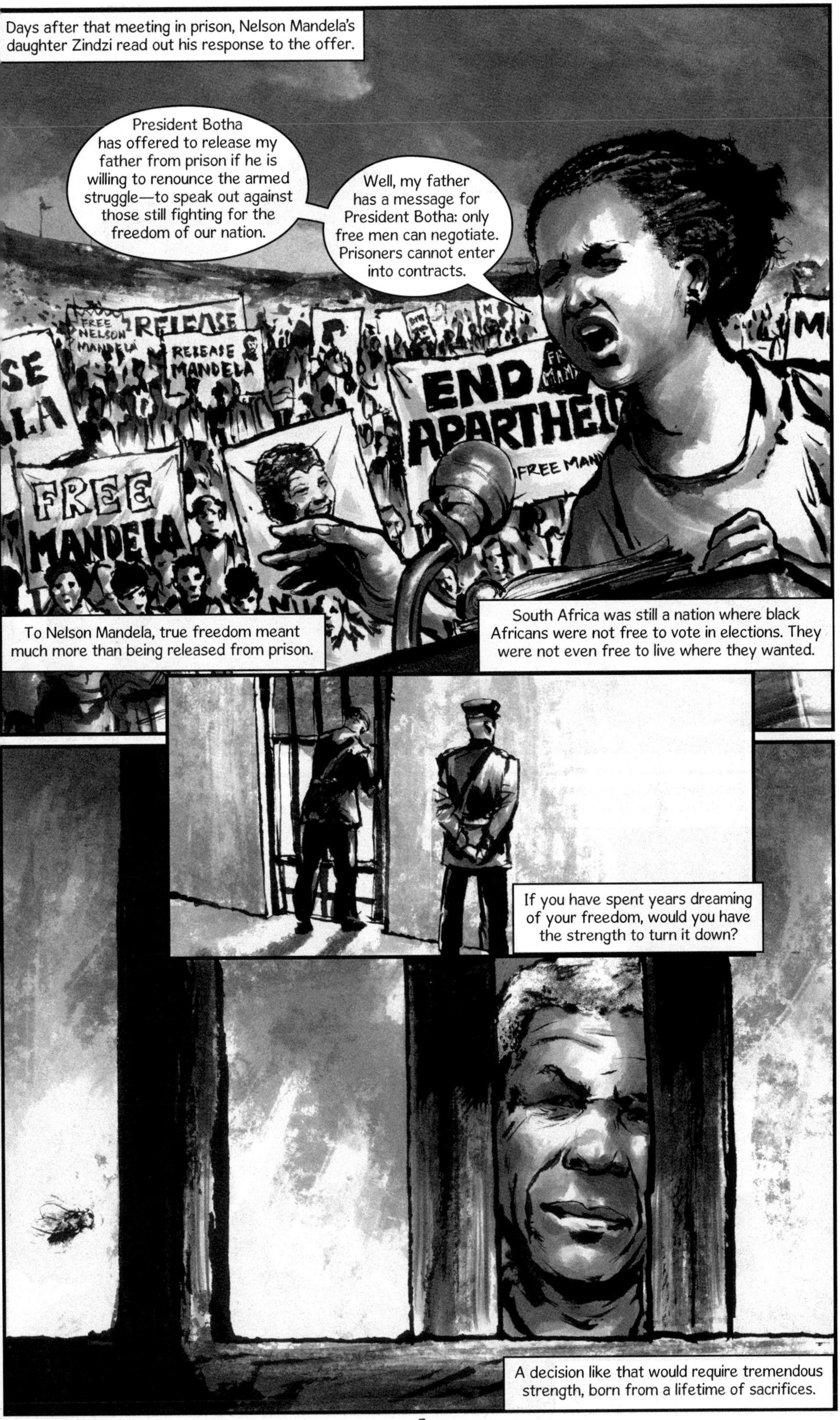

Days after that meeting in prison, Nelson Mandela's daughter Zindzi read out his response to the offer.
President Botha has offered to release my father from prison if he is willing to renounce the armed struggle—to speak out against those still fighting for the freedom of our nation.
Well, my father has a message for President Botha: only free men can negotiate. Prisoners cannot enter into contracts.
FREE NELSON MANDELA
RELEASE
RELEASE MANDELA
END APARTHEID
FREE MAN
FREE MANDELA
To Nelson Mandela, true freedom meant much more than being released from prison.
South Africa was still a nation where black Africans were not free to vote in elections. They were not even free to live where they wanted.
If you have spent years dreaming of your freedom, would you have the strength to turn it down?
A decision like that would require tremendous strength, born from a lifetime of sacrifices.

Mandela's lessons about strength and sacrifice had begun in Mvezo, South Africa. It was a small village located hundreds of kilometers from the cities of Cape Town and Johannesburg.

Born in the Madiba clan of the Xhosa nation on July 18, 1918, Mandela was given the name Rolihlahla, which roughly means 'troublemaker'.

Little did they know what kind of 'trouble' he would go on to cause.

His father, Gadla Henry Mphakanyiswa, never went to school and did not know how to read or write.

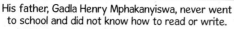

But he was a brilliant speaker, and was soon given a high rank by a local king.

Do you know that I am the new chief of Mvezo, Rolihlahla? It is my job to serve as a counselor to the kings. That will be your job, too, someday.

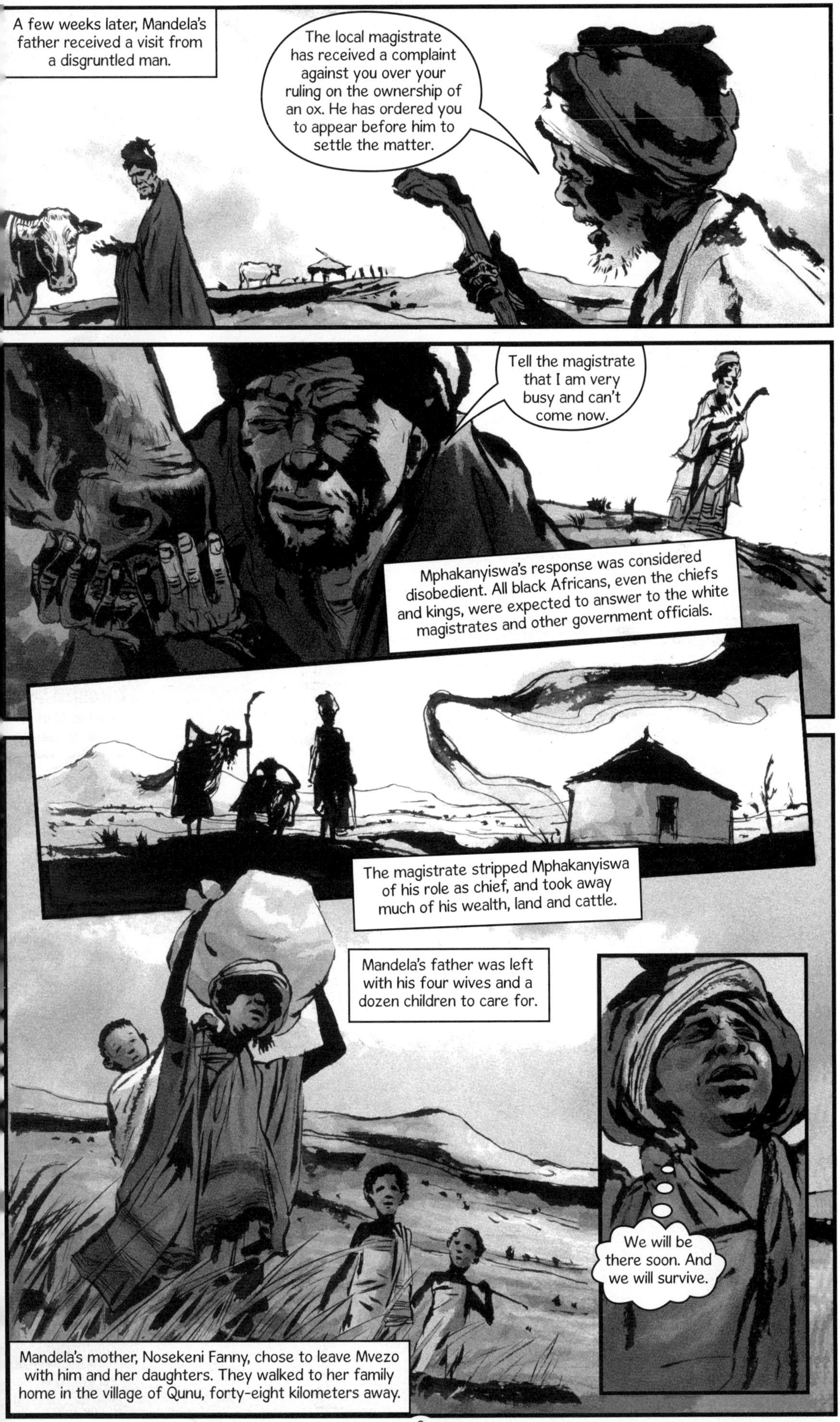

A few weeks later, Mandela's father received a visit from a disgruntled man.
The local magistrate has received a complaint against you over your ruling on the ownership of an ox. He has ordered you to appear before him to settle the matter.
Tell the magistrate that I am very busy and can't come now.
Mphakanyiswa's response was considered disobedient. All black Africans, even the chiefs and kings, were expected to answer to the white magistrates and other government officials.
The magistrate stripped Mphakanyiswa of his role as chief, and took away much of his wealth, land and cattle.
Mandela's father was left with his four wives and a dozen children to care for.
We will be there soon. And we will survive.
Mandela's mother, Nosekeni Fanny, chose to leave Mvezo with him and her daughters. They walked to her family home in the village of Qunu, forty-eight kilometers away.

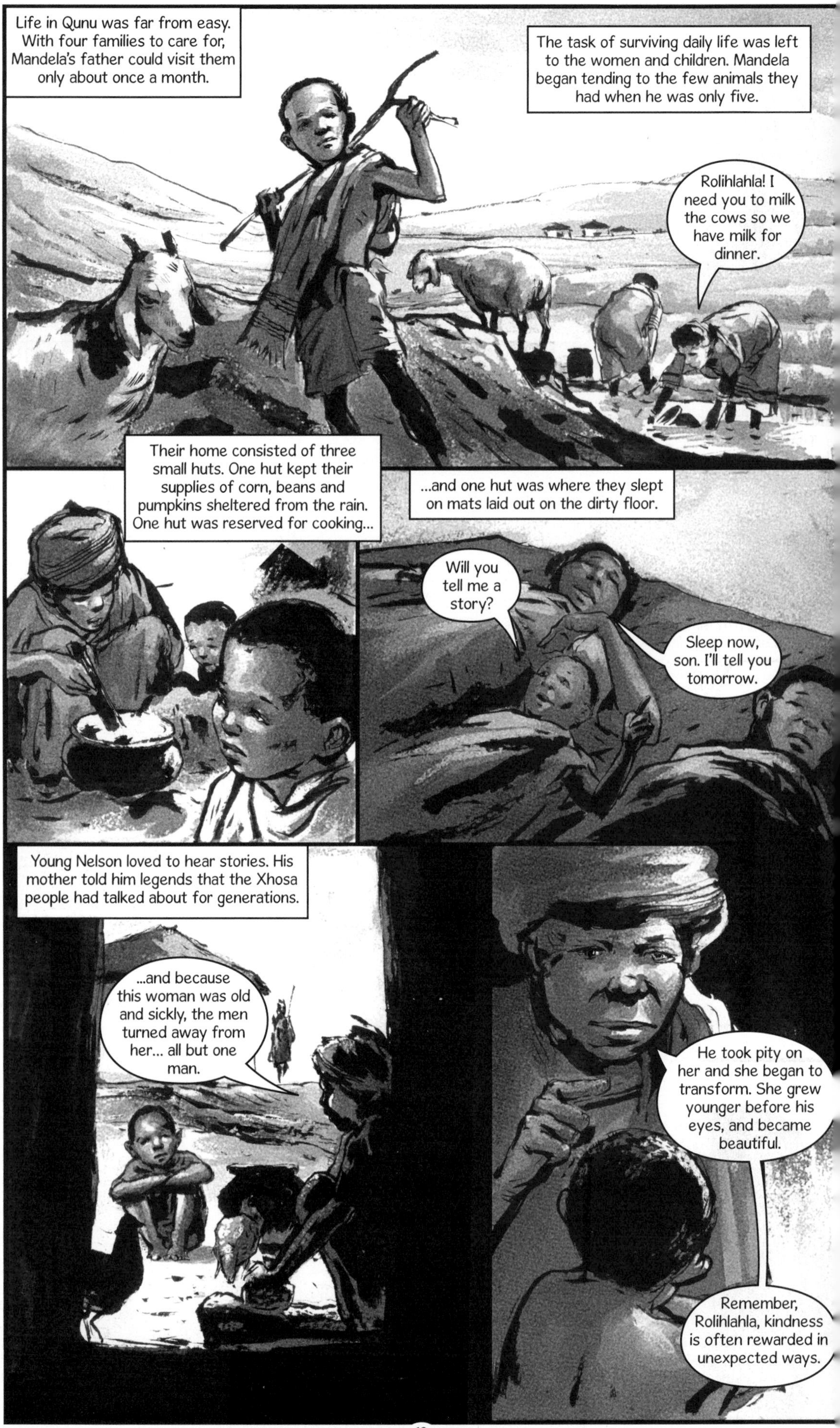
Life in Qunu was far from easy. With four families to care for, Mandela's father could visit them only about once a month.
The task of surviving daily life was left to the women and children. Mandela began tending to the few animals they had when he was only five.
Rolihlahla! I need you to milk the cows so we have milk for dinner.
Their home consisted of three small huts. One hut kept their supplies of corn, beans and pumpkins sheltered from the rain. One hut was reserved for cooking...
...and one hut was where they slept on mats laid out on the dirty floor.
Will you tell me a story?
Sleep now, son. I'll tell you tomorrow.
Young Nelson loved to hear stories. His mother told him legends that the Xhosa people had talked about for generations.
...and because this woman was old and sickly, the men turned away from her... all but one man.
He took pity on her and she began to transform. She grew younger before his eyes, and became beautiful.
Remember, Rolihlahla, kindness is often rewarded in unexpected ways.

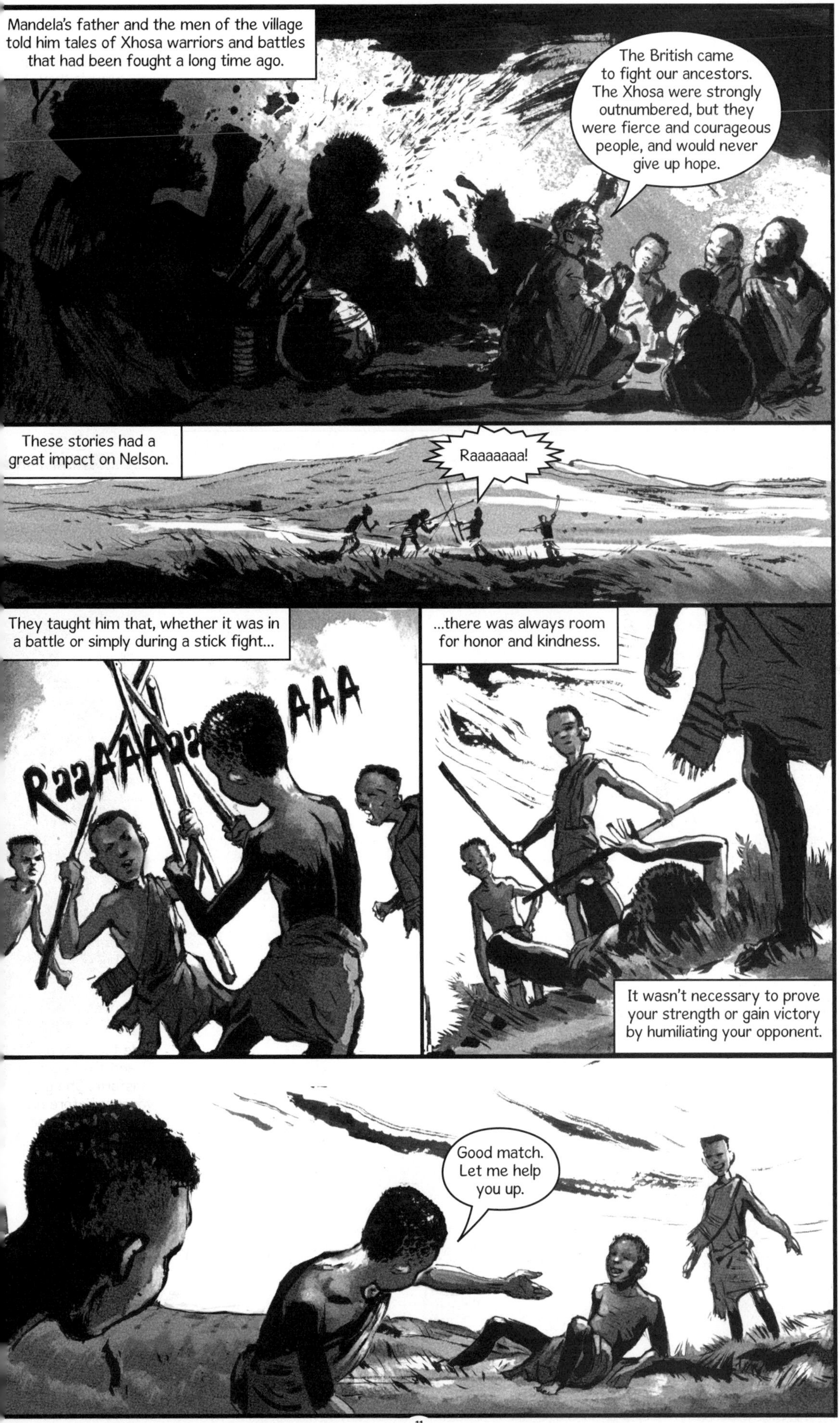
Mandela's father and the men of the village told him tales of Xhosa warriors and battles that had been fought a long time ago.
The British came to fight our ancestors. The Xhosa were strongly outnumbered, but they were fierce and courageous people, and would never give up hope.
These stories had a great impact on Nelson.
Raaaaaaa!
They taught him that, whether it was in a battle or simply during a stick fight...
AAA
...there was always room for honor and kindness.
It wasn't necessary to prove your strength or gain victory by humiliating your opponent.
Good match. Let me help you up.

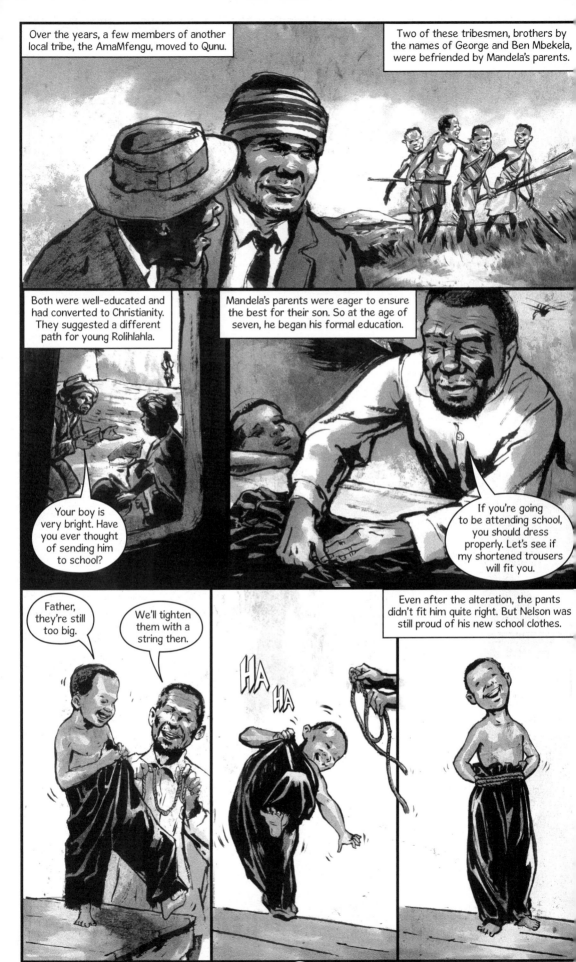

Over the years, a few members of another local tribe, the AmaMfengu, moved to Qunu.

Two of these tribesmen, brothers by the names of George and Ben Mbekela, were befriended by Mandela's parents.

Both were well-educated and had converted to Christianity. They suggested a different path for young Rolihlahla.

Mandela's parents were eager to ensure the best for their son. So at the age of seven, he began his formal education.

Your boy is very bright. Have you ever thought of sending him to school?

If you're going to be attending school, you should dress properly. Let's see if my shortened trousers will fit you.

Father, they're still too big.

We'll tighten them with a string then.

HA HA

Even after the alteration, the pants didn't fit him quite right. But Nelson was still proud of his new school clothes.

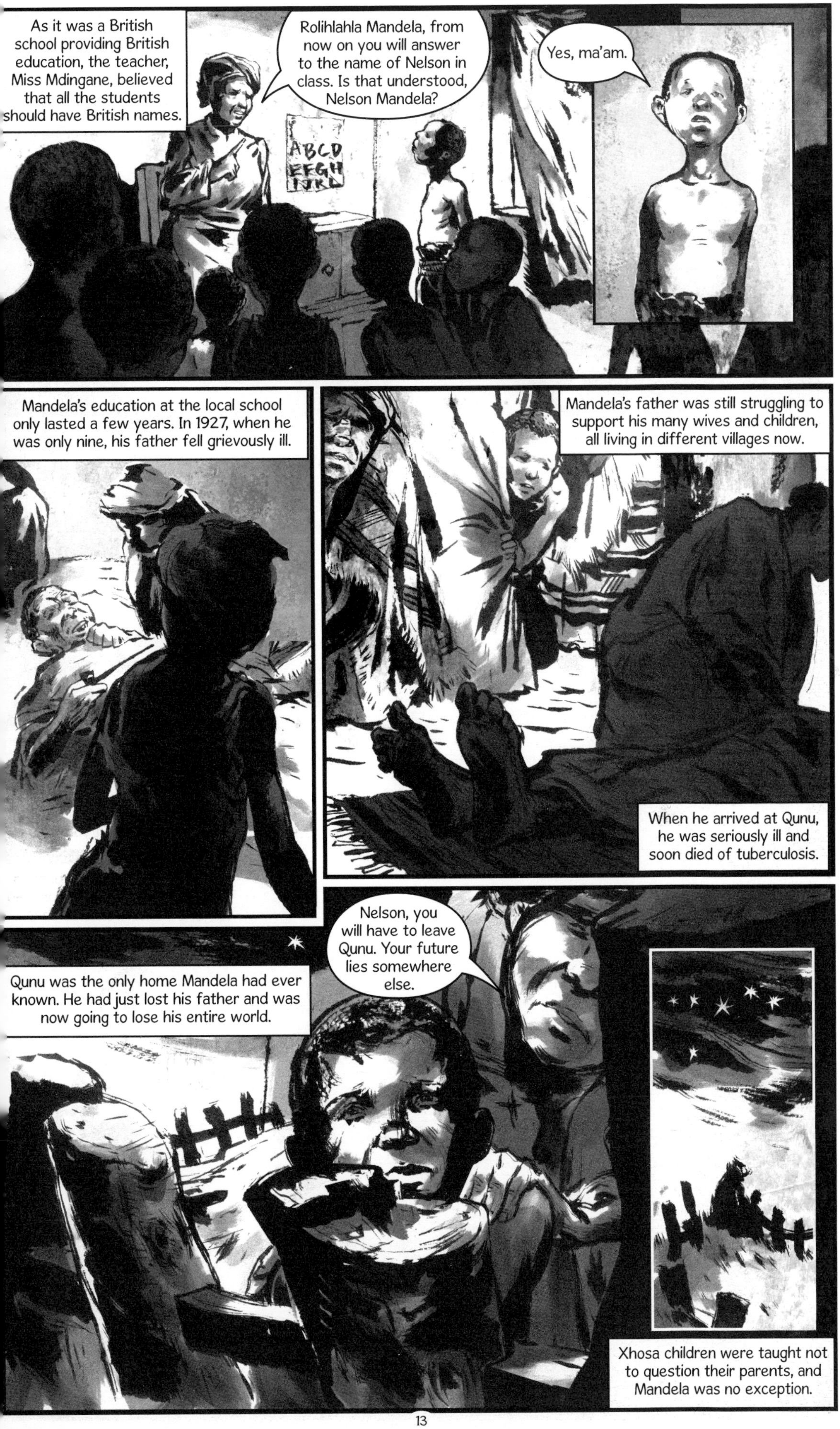
As it was a British school providing British education, the teacher, Miss Mdingane, believed that all the students should have British names.
Rolihlahla Mandela, from now on you will answer to the name of Nelson in class. Is that understood, Nelson Mandela?
ABCD EFGH IJKL
Yes, ma'am.
Mandela's education at the local school only lasted a few years. In 1927, when he was only nine, his father fell grievously ill.
Mandela's father was still struggling to support his many wives and children, all living in different villages now.
When he arrived at Qunu, he was seriously ill and soon died of tuberculosis.
Qunu was the only home Mandela had ever known. He had just lost his father and was now going to lose his entire world.
Nelson, you will have to leave Qunu. Your future lies somewhere else.
Xhosa children were taught not to question their parents, and Mandela was no exception.

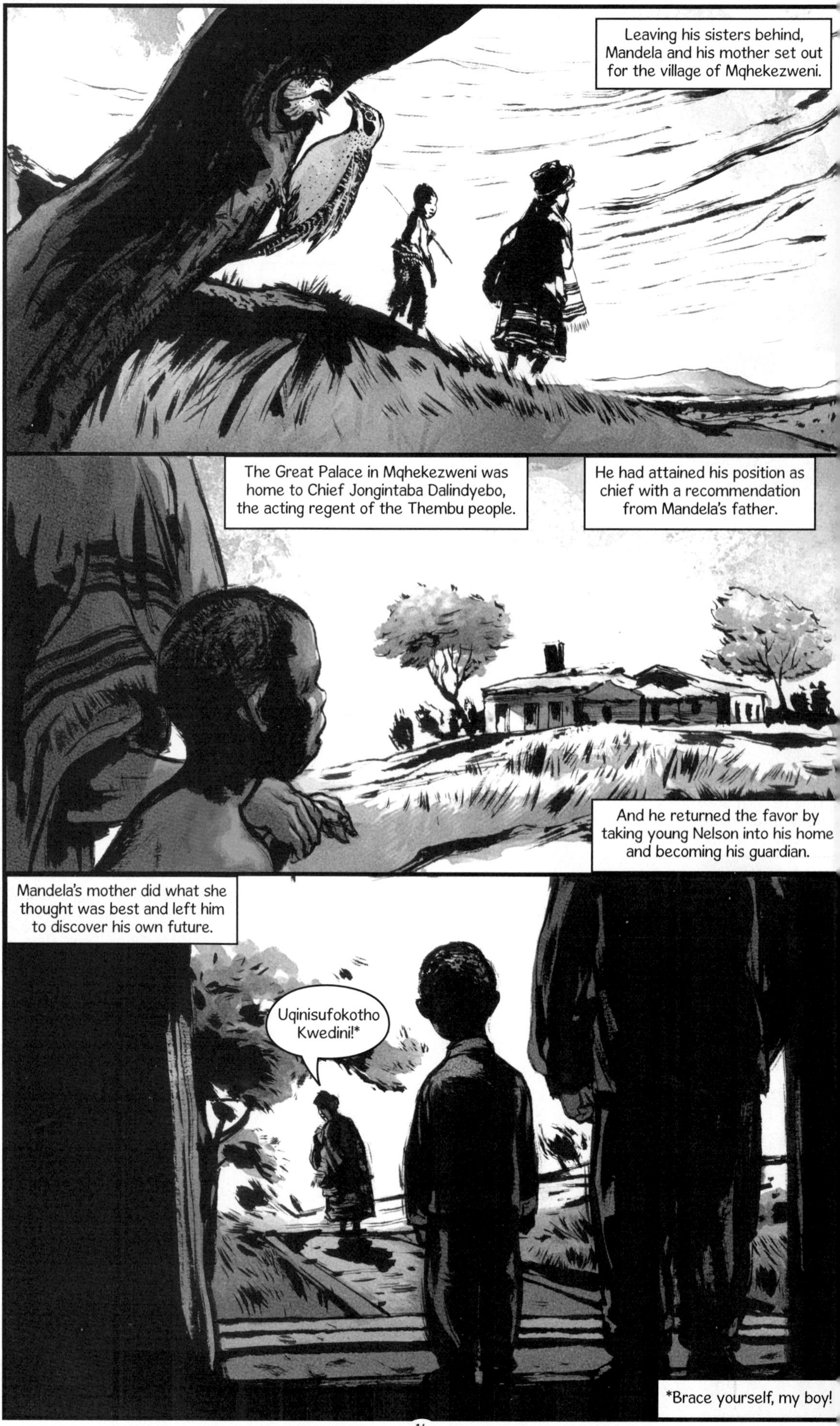
Leaving his sisters behind, Mandela and his mother set out for the village of Mqhekezweni.
The Great Palace in Mqhekezweni was home to Chief Jongintaba Dalindyebo, the acting regent of the Thembu people.
He had attained his position as chief with a recommendation from Mandela's father.
And he returned the favor by taking young Nelson into his home and becoming his guardian.
Mandela's mother did what she thought was best and left him to discover his own future.
Uqinisufokotho Kwedini!*
*Brace yourself, my boy!

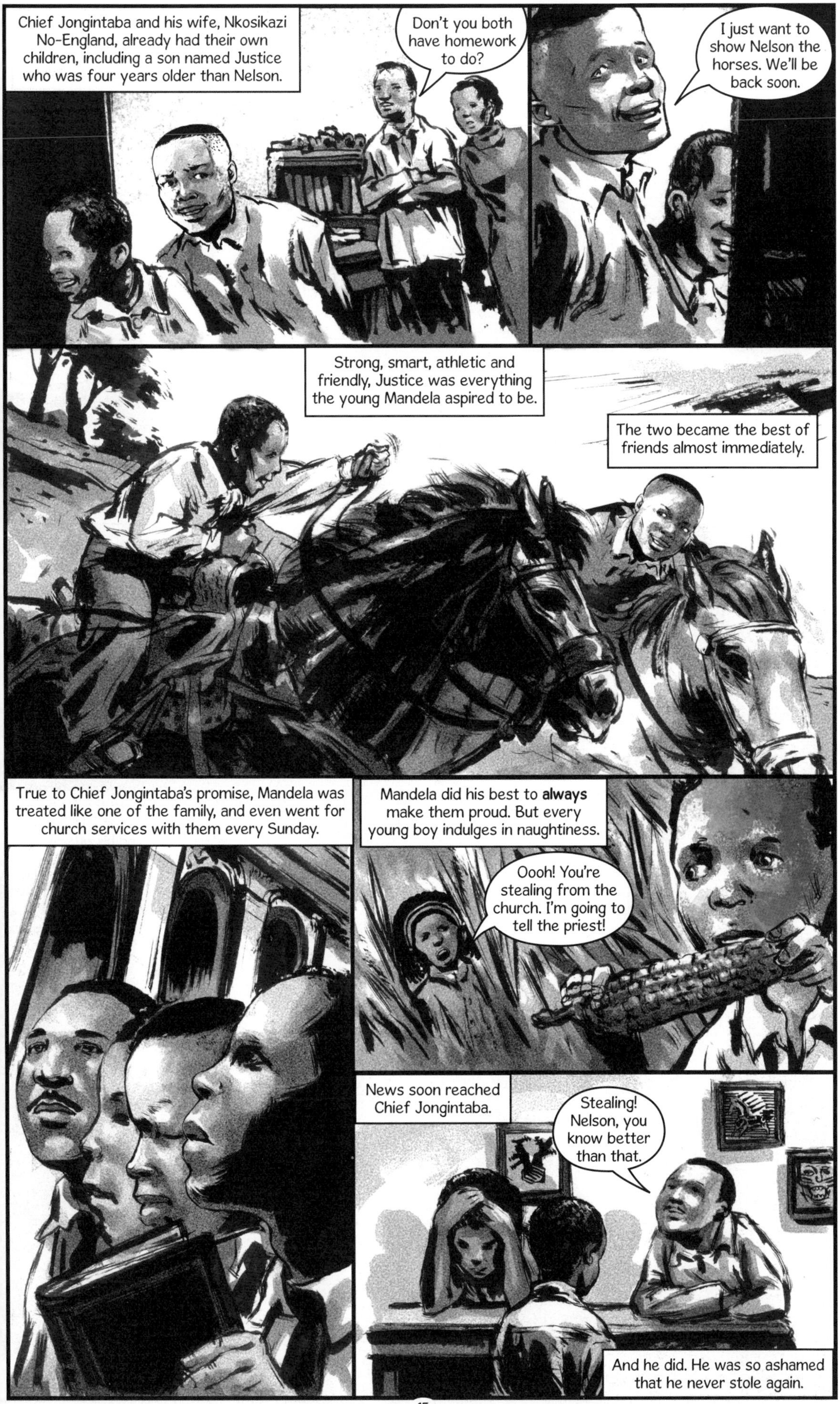
Chief Jongintaba and his wife, Nkosikazi No-England, already had their own children, including a son named Justice who was four years older than Nelson.
Don't you both have homework to do?
I just want to show Nelson the horses. We'll be back soon.
Strong, smart, athletic and friendly, Justice was everything the young Mandela aspired to be.
The two became the best of friends almost immediately.
True to Chief Jongintaba's promise, Mandela was treated like one of the family, and even went for church services with them every Sunday.
Mandela did his best to **always** make them proud. But every young boy indulges in naughtiness.
Oooh! You're stealing from the church. I'm going to tell the priest!
News soon reached Chief Jongintaba.
Stealing! Nelson, you know better than that.
And he did. He was so ashamed that he never stole again.

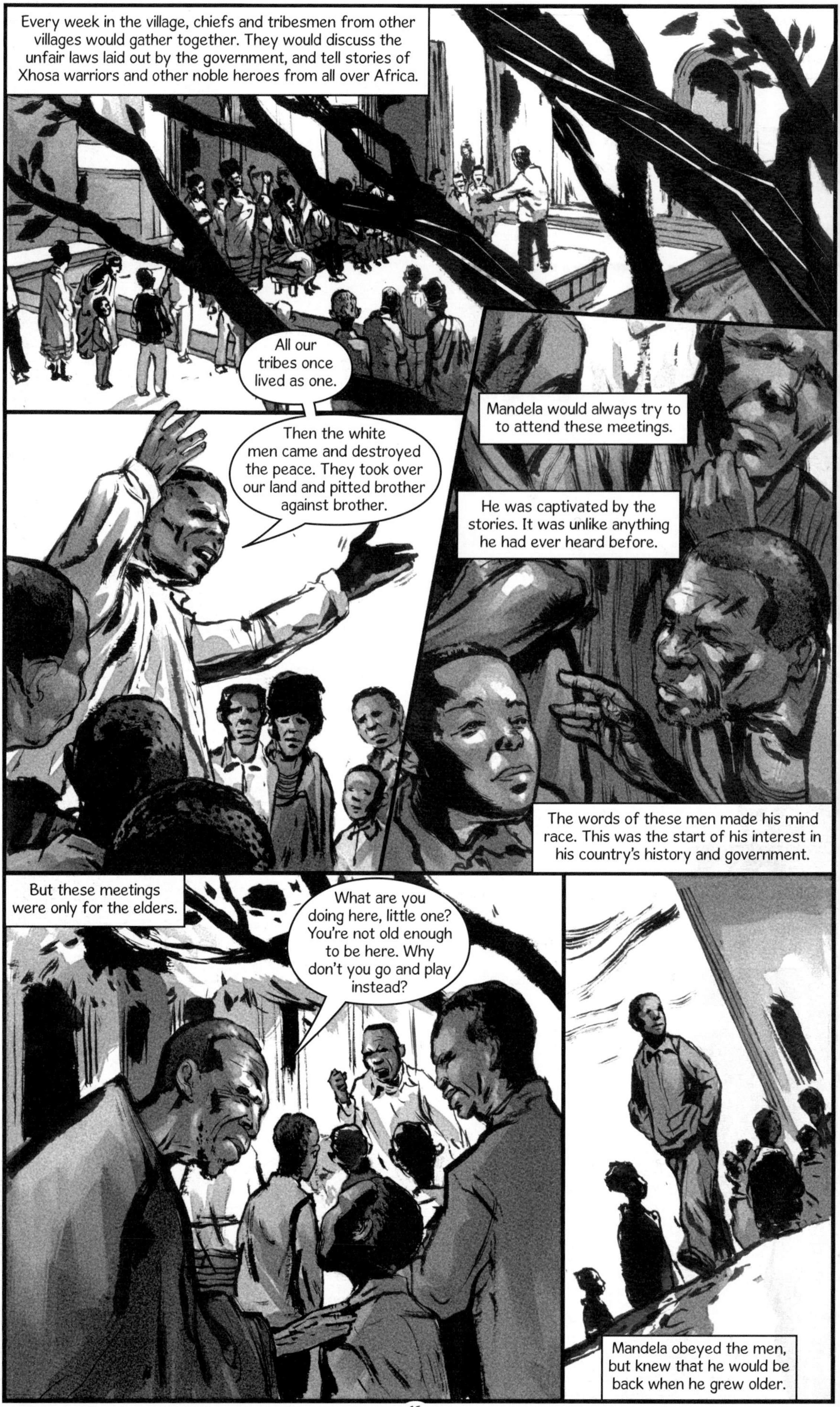
Every week in the village, chiefs and tribesmen from other villages would gather together. They would discuss the unfair laws laid out by the government, and tell stories of Xhosa warriors and other noble heroes from all over Africa.
All our tribes once lived as one.
Then the white men came and destroyed the peace. They took over our land and pitted brother against brother.
Mandela would always try to to attend these meetings.
He was captivated by the stories. It was unlike anything he had ever heard before.
The words of these men made his mind race. This was the start of his interest in his country's history and government.
But these meetings were only for the elders.
What are you doing here, little one? You're not old enough to be here. Why don't you go and play instead?
Mandela obeyed the men, but knew that he would be back when he grew older.

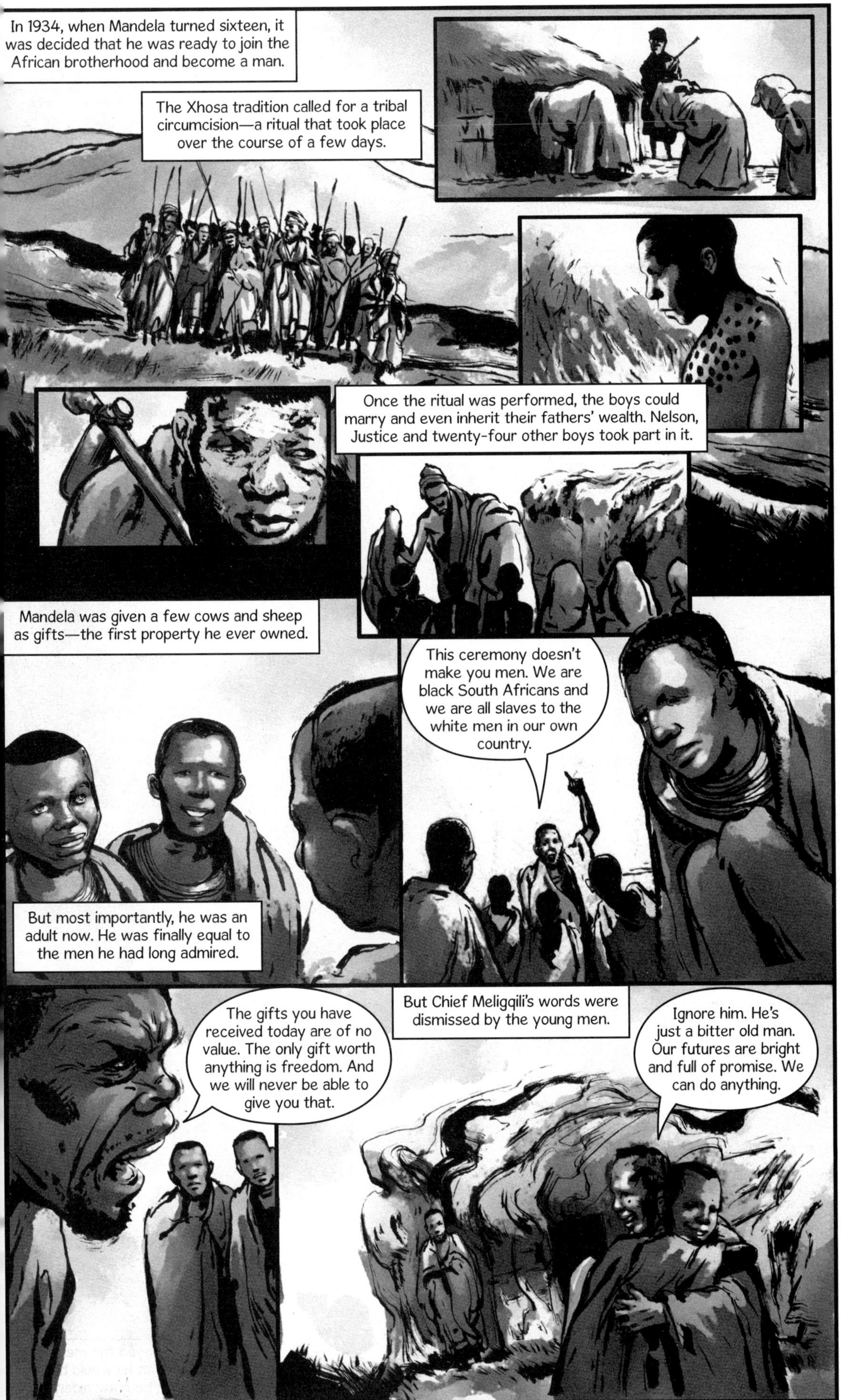

In 1934, when Mandela turned sixteen, it was decided that he was ready to join the African brotherhood and become a man.
The Xhosa tradition called for a tribal circumcision—a ritual that took place over the course of a few days.
Once the ritual was performed, the boys could marry and even inherit their fathers' wealth. Nelson, Justice and twenty-four other boys took part in it.
Mandela was given a few cows and sheep as gifts—the first property he ever owned.
But most importantly, he was an adult now. He was finally equal to the men he had long admired.
This ceremony doesn't make you men. We are black South Africans and we are all slaves to the white men in our own country.
The gifts you have received today are of no value. The only gift worth anything is freedom. And we will never be able to give you that.
But Chief Meligqili's words were dismissed by the young men.
Ignore him. He's just a bitter old man. Our futures are bright and full of promise. We can do anything.

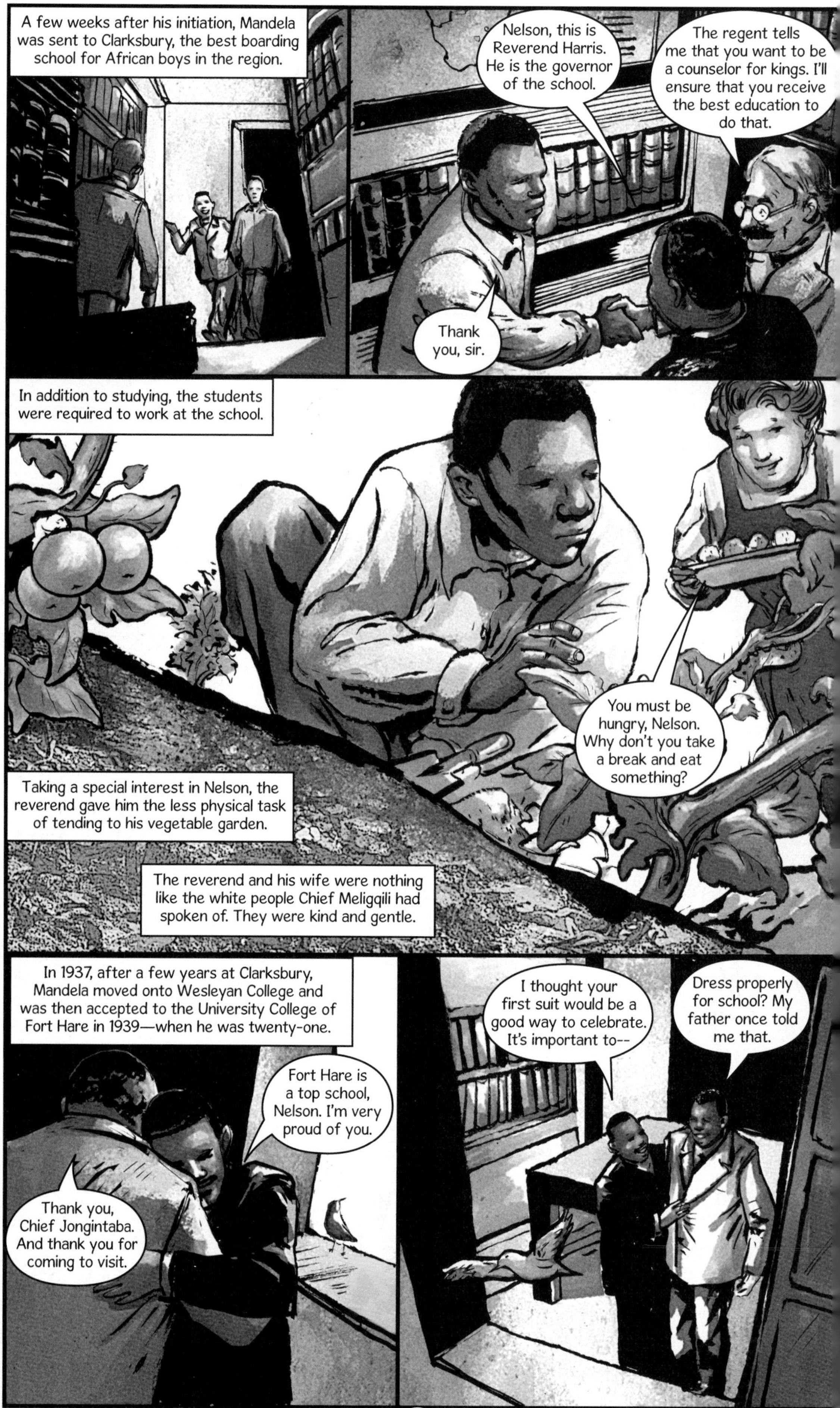
A few weeks after his initiation, Mandela was sent to Clarksbury, the best boarding school for African boys in the region.
Nelson, this is Reverend Harris. He is the governor of the school.
The regent tells me that you want to be a counselor for kings. I'll ensure that you receive the best education to do that.
Thank you, sir.
In addition to studying, the students were required to work at the school.
You must be hungry, Nelson. Why don't you take a break and eat something?
Taking a special interest in Nelson, the reverend gave him the less physical task of tending to his vegetable garden.
The reverend and his wife were nothing like the white people Chief Meligqili had spoken of. They were kind and gentle.
In 1937, after a few years at Clarksbury, Mandela moved onto Wesleyan College and was then accepted to the University College of Fort Hare in 1939—when he was twenty-one.
Fort Hare is a top school, Nelson. I'm very proud of you.
Thank you, Chief Jongintaba. And thank you for coming to visit.
I thought your first suit would be a good way to celebrate. It's important to--
Dress properly for school? My father once told me that.

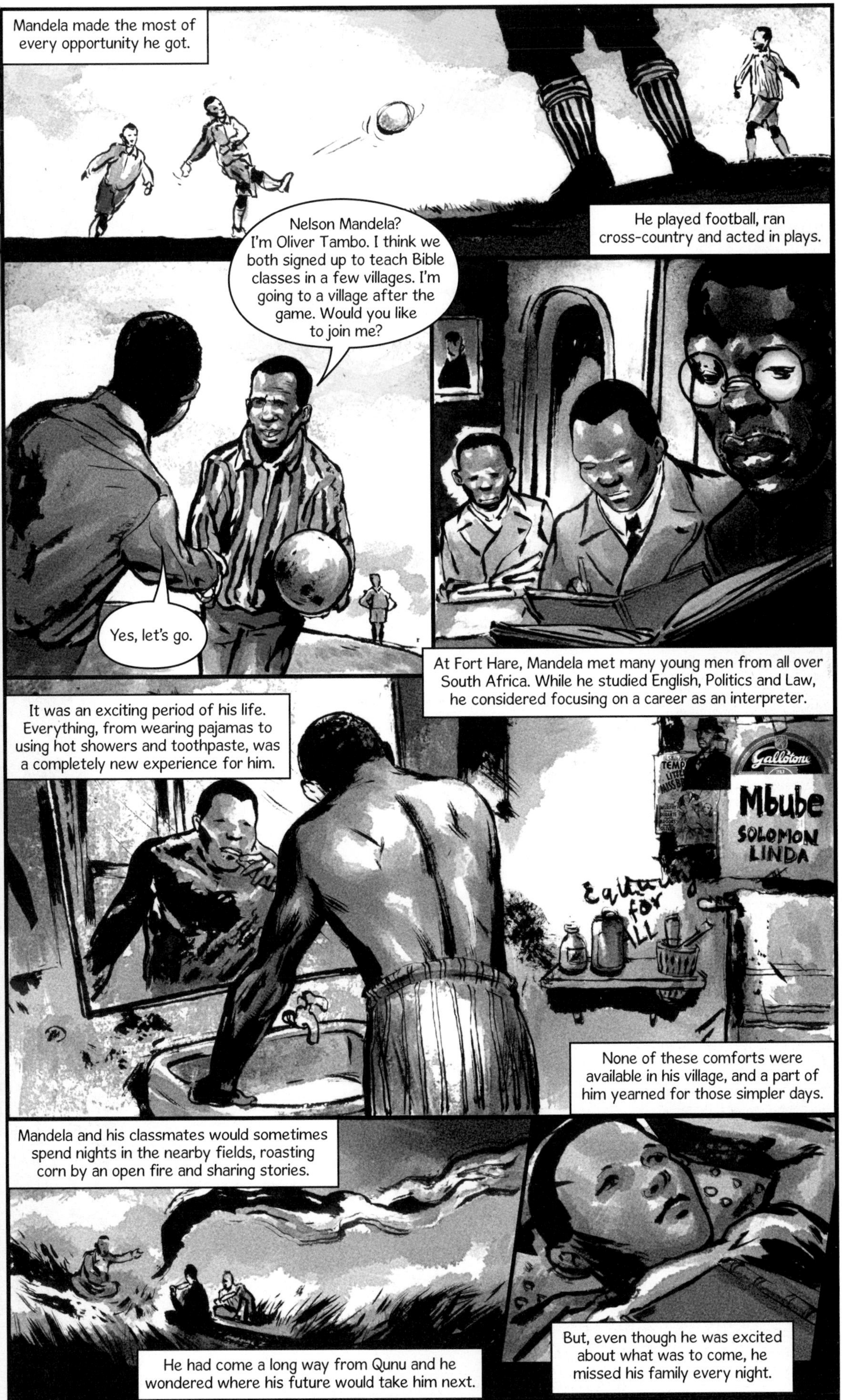

Mandela made the most of every opportunity he got.
He played football, ran cross-country and acted in plays.
Nelson Mandela? I'm Oliver Tambo. I think we both signed up to teach Bible classes in a few villages. I'm going to a village after the game. Would you like to join me?
Yes, let's go.
At Fort Hare, Mandela met many young men from all over South Africa. While he studied English, Politics and Law, he considered focusing on a career as an interpreter.
It was an exciting period of his life. Everything, from wearing pajamas to using hot showers and toothpaste, was a completely new experience for him.
Gallotone
Mbube
SOLOMON LINDA
None of these comforts were available in his village, and a part of him yearned for those simpler days.
Mandela and his classmates would sometimes spend nights in the nearby fields, roasting corn by an open fire and sharing stories.
He had come a long way from Qunu and he wondered where his future would take him next.
But, even though he was excited about what was to come, he missed his family every night.

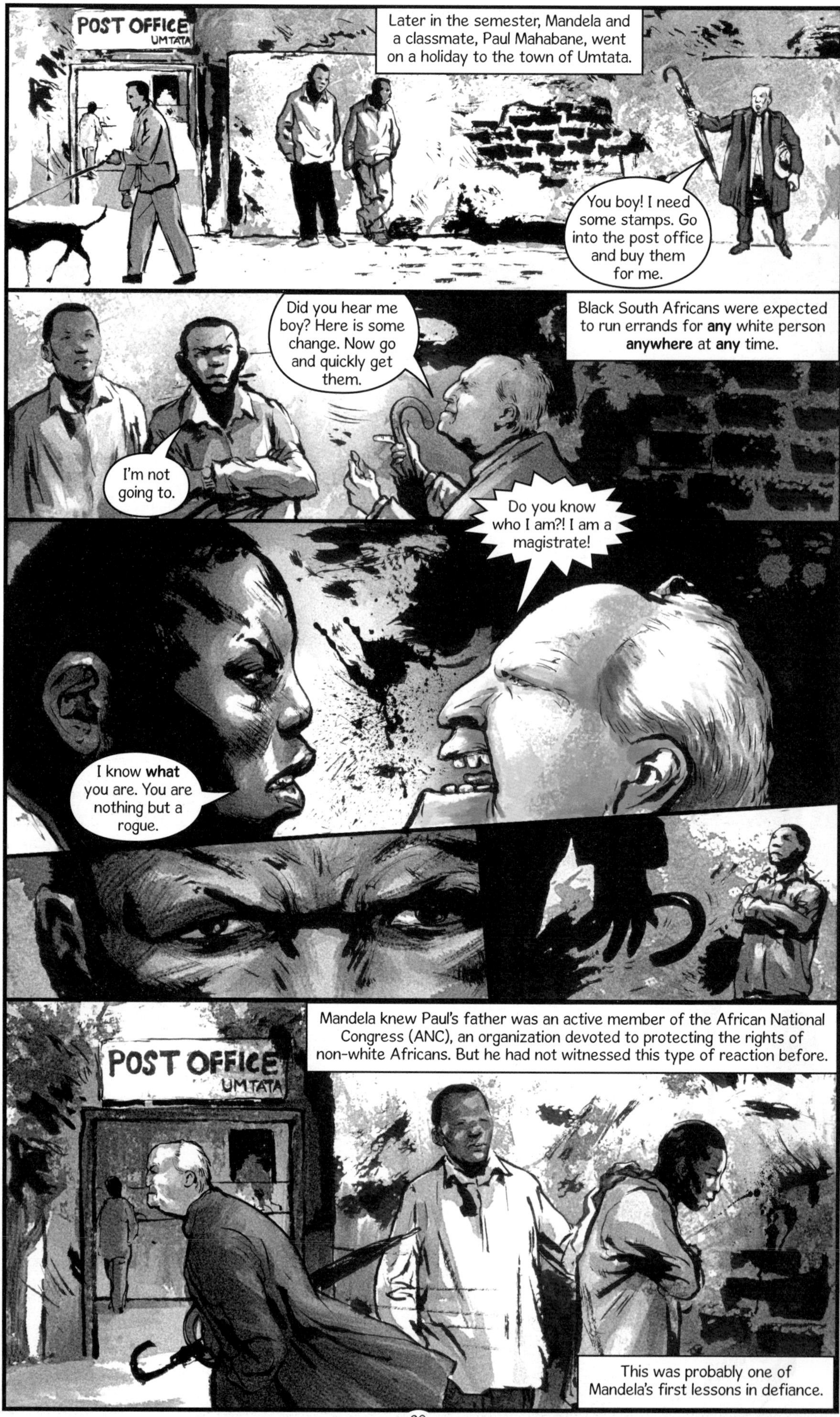
POST OFFICE
UMTATA
Later in the semester, Mandela and a classmate, Paul Mahabane, went on a holiday to the town of Umtata.
You boy! I need some stamps. Go into the post office and buy them for me.
Did you hear me boy? Here is some change. Now go and quickly get them.
Black South Africans were expected to run errands for **any** white person **anywhere** at **any** time.
I'm not going to.
Do you know who I am?! I am a magistrate!
I know **what** you are. You are nothing but a rogue.
Mandela knew Paul's father was an active member of the African National Congress (ANC), an organization devoted to protecting the rights of non-white Africans. But he had not witnessed this type of reaction before.
POST OFFICE
UMTATA
This was probably one of Mandela's first lessons in defiance.

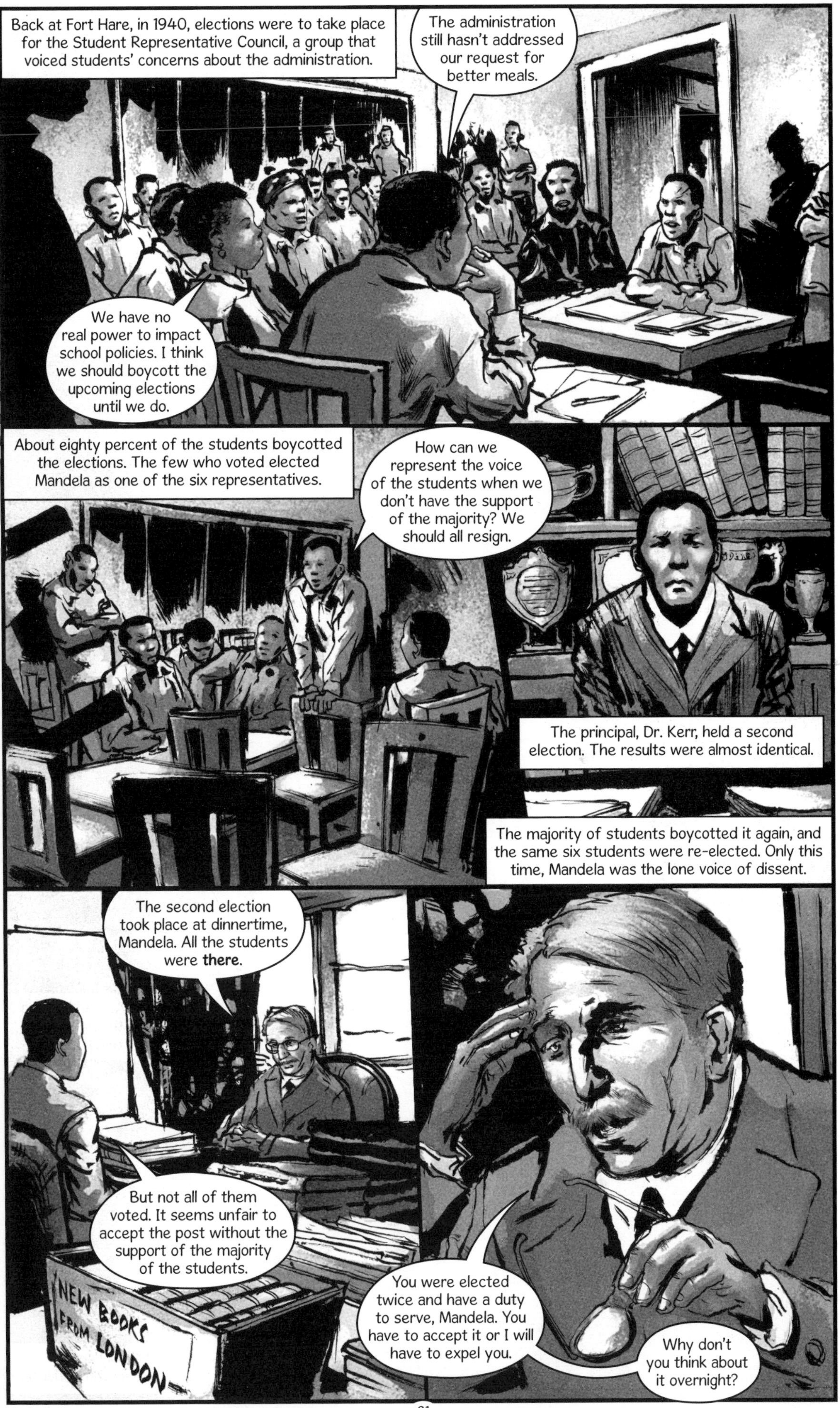
Back at Fort Hare, in 1940, elections were to take place for the Student Representative Council, a group that voiced students' concerns about the administration.
The administration still hasn't addressed our request for better meals.
We have no real power to impact school policies. I think we should boycott the upcoming elections until we do.
About eighty percent of the students boycotted the elections. The few who voted elected Mandela as one of the six representatives.
How can we represent the voice of the students when we don't have the support of the majority? We should all resign.
The principal, Dr. Kerr, held a second election. The results were almost identical.
The majority of students boycotted it again, and the same six students were re-elected. Only this time, Mandela was the lone voice of dissent.
The second election took place at dinnertime, Mandela. All the students were **there**.
But not all of them voted. It seems unfair to accept the post without the support of the majority of the students.
NEW BOOKS FROM LONDON
You were elected twice and have a duty to serve, Mandela. You have to accept it or I will have to expel you.
Why don't you think about it overnight?

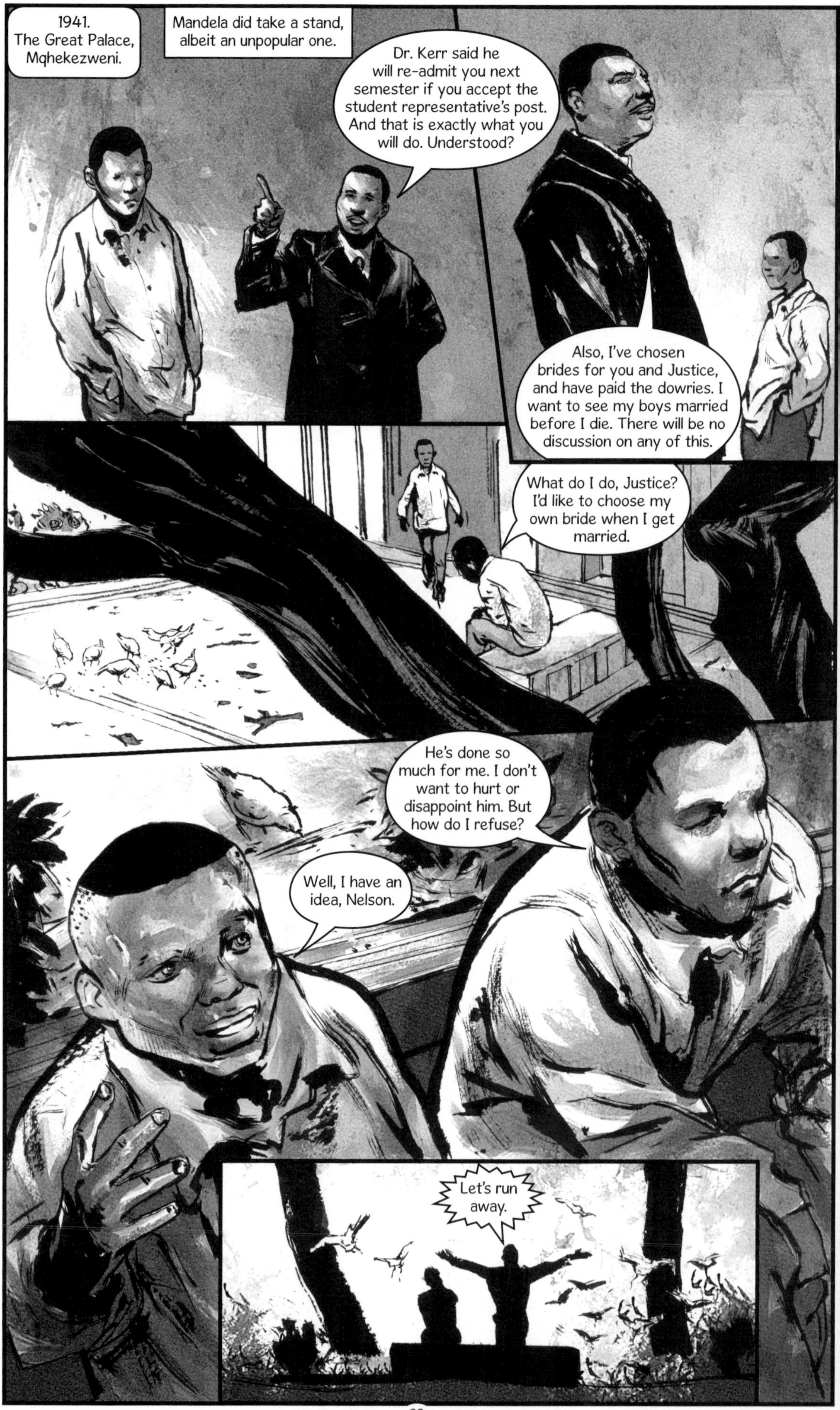
1941.
The Great Palace,
Mqhekezweni.
Mandela did take a stand, albeit an unpopular one.
Dr. Kerr said he will re-admit you next semester if you accept the student representative's post. And that is exactly what you will do. Understood?
Also, I've chosen brides for you and Justice, and have paid the dowries. I want to see my boys married before I die. There will be no discussion on any of this.
What do I do, Justice? I'd like to choose my own bride when I get married.
He's done so much for me. I don't want to hurt or disappoint him. But how do I refuse?
Well, I have an idea, Nelson.
Let's run away.

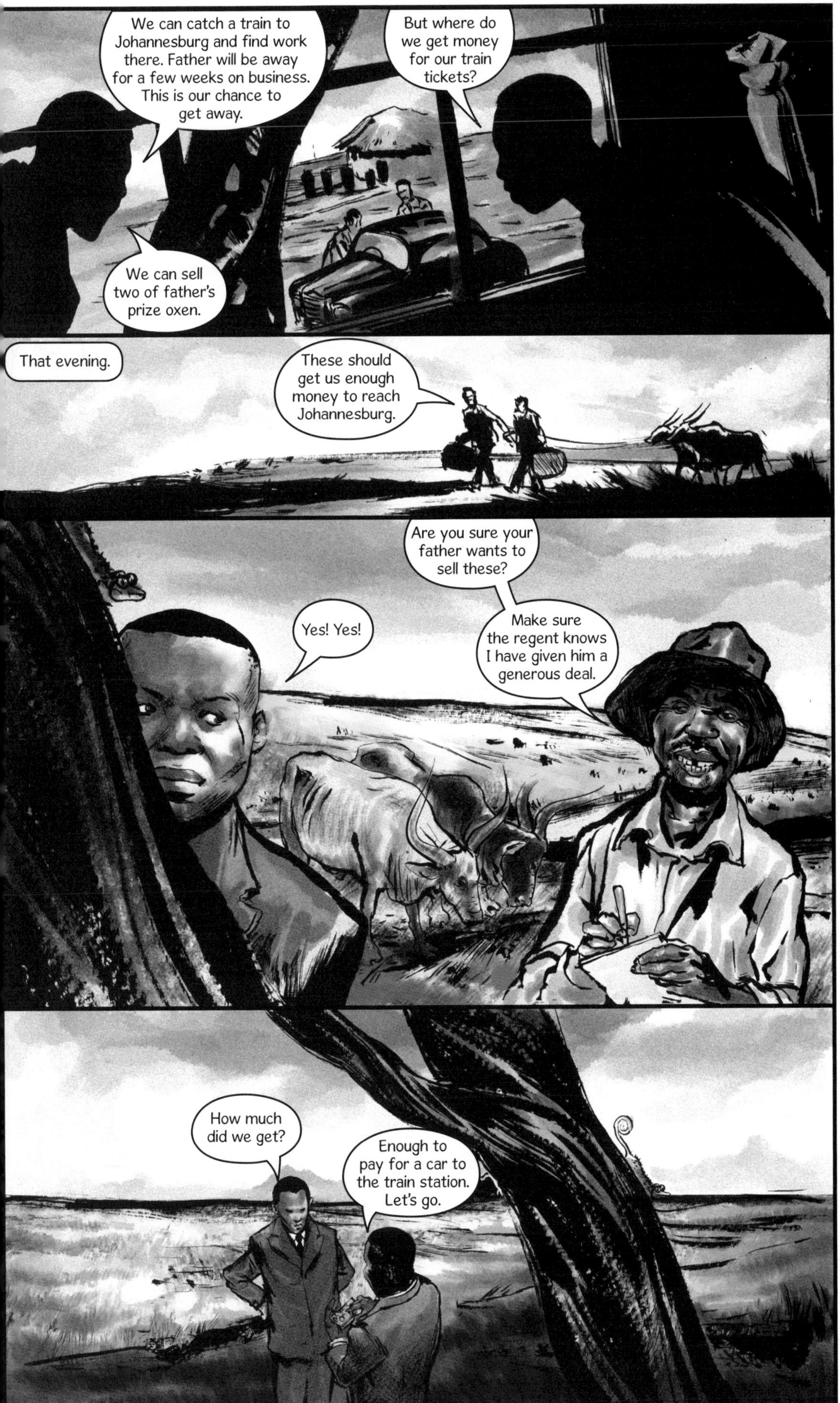

We can catch a train to Johannesburg and find work there. Father will be away for a few weeks on business. This is our chance to get away.
But where do we get money for our train tickets?
We can sell two of father's prize oxen.
That evening.
These should get us enough money to reach Johannesburg.
Are you sure your father wants to sell these?
Yes! Yes!
Make sure the regent knows I have given him a generous deal.
How much did we get?
Enough to pay for a car to the train station. Let's go.

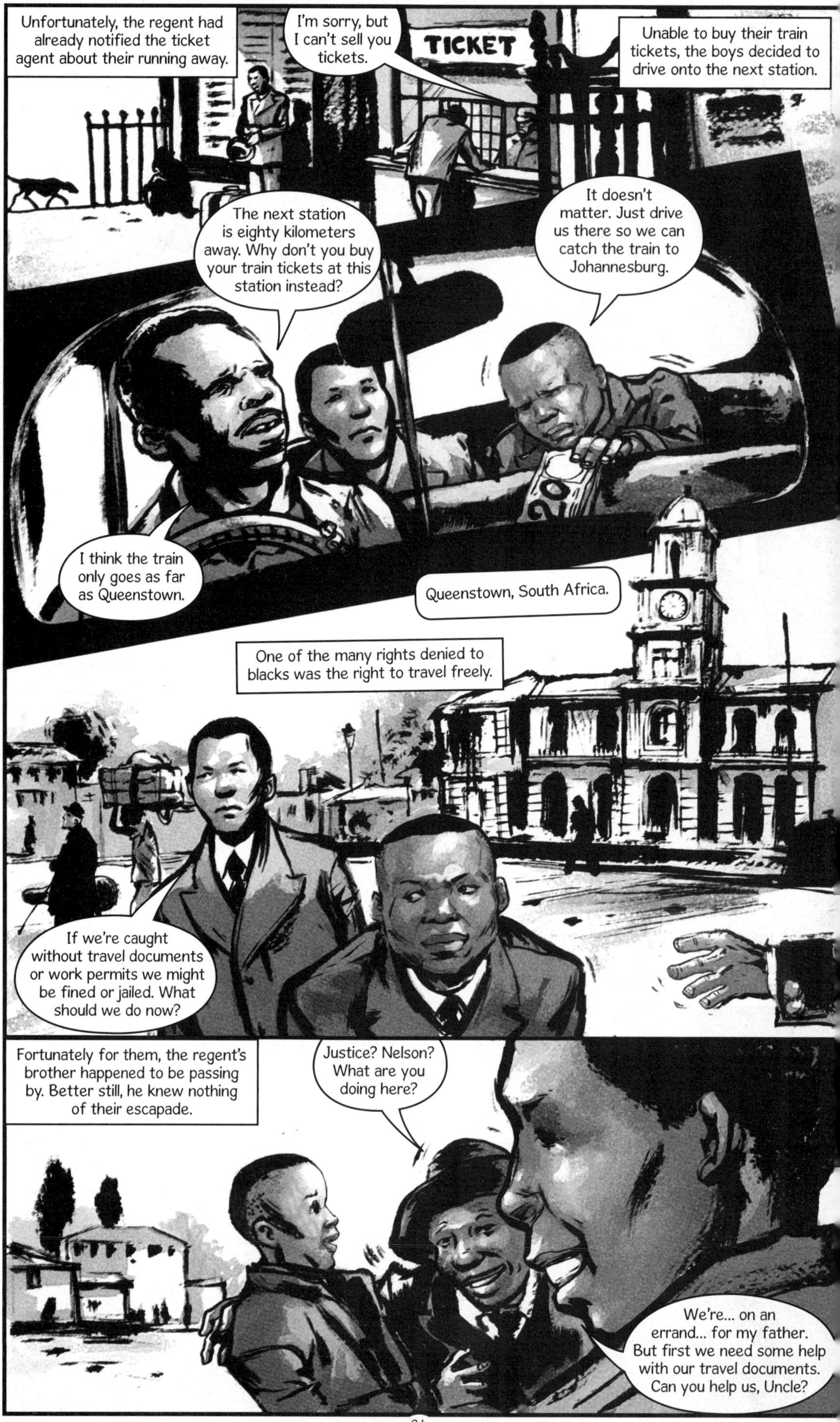
Unfortunately, the regent had already notified the ticket agent about their running away.
I'm sorry, but I can't sell you tickets.
TICKET
Unable to buy their train tickets, the boys decided to drive onto the next station.
The next station is eighty kilometers away. Why don't you buy your train tickets at this station instead?
It doesn't matter. Just drive us there so we can catch the train to Johannesburg.
I think the train only goes as far as Queenstown.
Queenstown, South Africa.
One of the many rights denied to blacks was the right to travel freely.
If we're caught without travel documents or work permits we might be fined or jailed. What should we do now?
Fortunately for them, the regent's brother happened to be passing by. Better still, he knew nothing of their escapade.
Justice? Nelson? What are you doing here?
We're... on an errand... for my father. But first we need some help with our travel documents. Can you help us, Uncle?

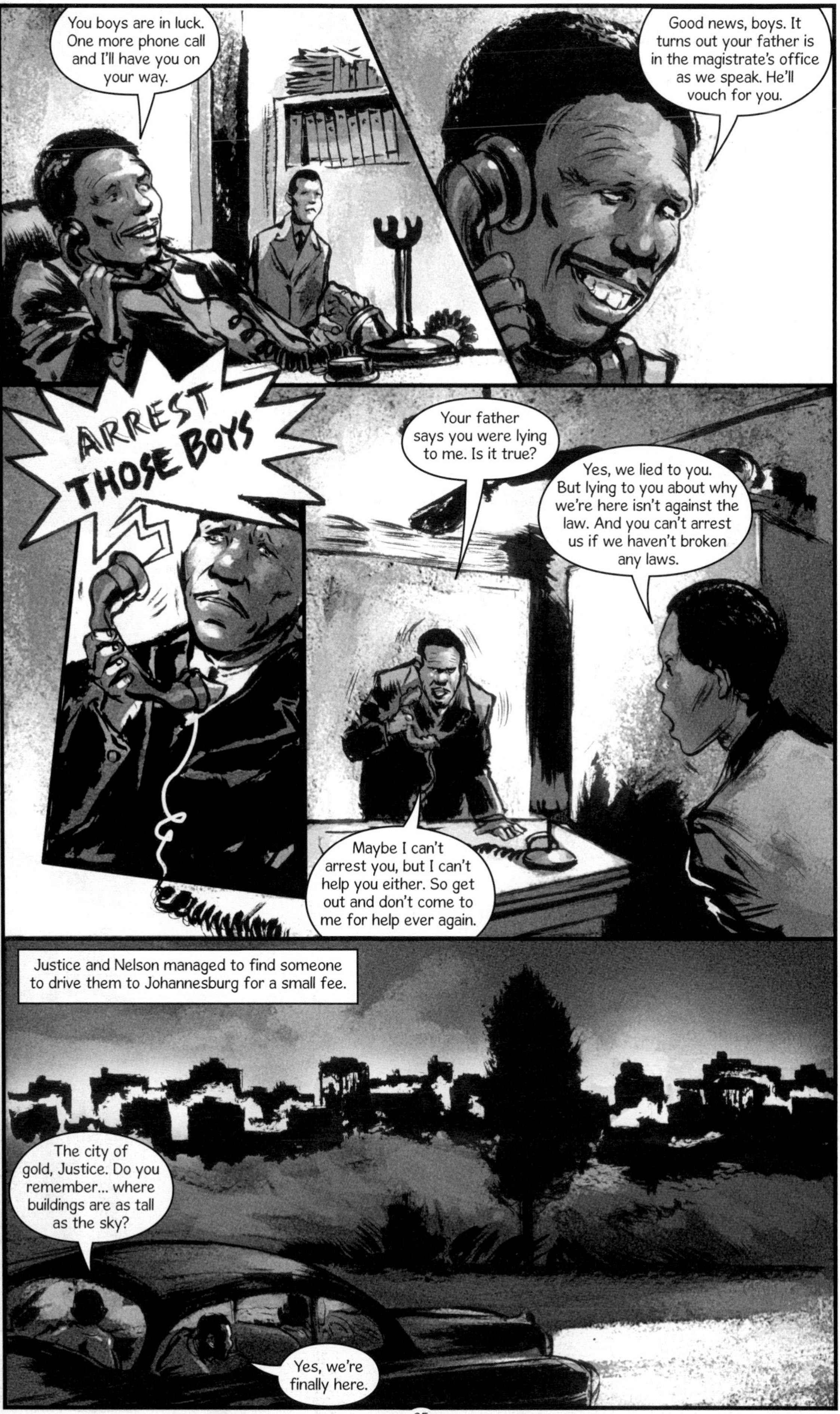

You boys are in luck. One more phone call and I'll have you on your way.
Good news, boys. It turns out your father is in the magistrate's office as we speak. He'll vouch for you.
ARREST THOSE BOYS
Your father says you were lying to me. Is it true?
Yes, we lied to you. But lying to you about why we're here isn't against the law. And you can't arrest us if we haven't broken any laws.
Maybe I can't arrest you, but I can't help you either. So get out and don't come to me for help ever again.
Justice and Nelson managed to find someone to drive them to Johannesburg for a small fee.
The city of gold, Justice. Do you remember... where buildings are as tall as the sky?
Yes, we're finally here.

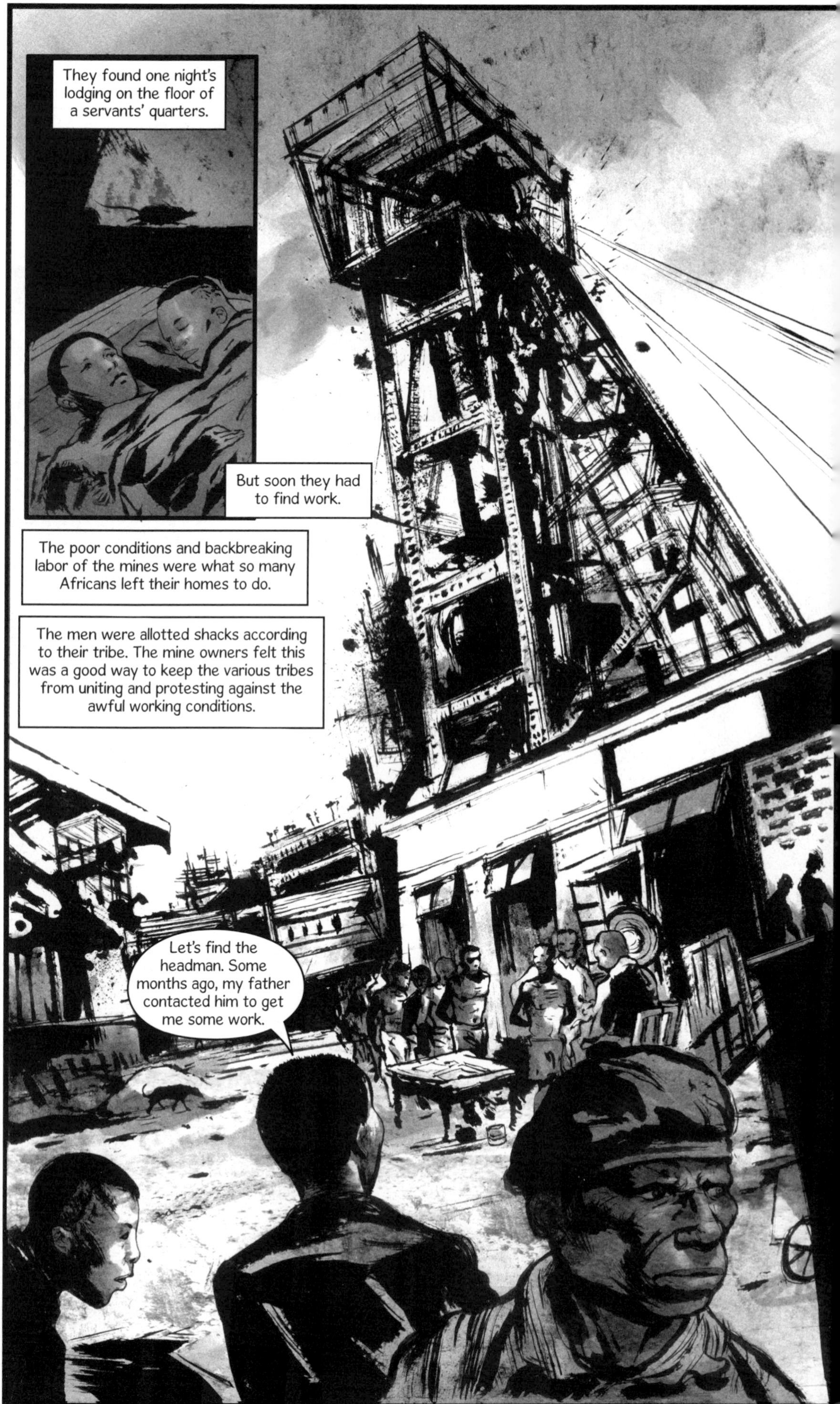
They found one night's lodging on the floor of a servants' quarters.
But soon they had to find work.
The poor conditions and backbreaking labor of the mines were what so many Africans left their homes to do.
The men were allotted shacks according to their tribe. The mine owners felt this was a good way to keep the various tribes from uniting and protesting against the awful working conditions.
Let's find the headman. Some months ago, my father contacted him to get me some work.

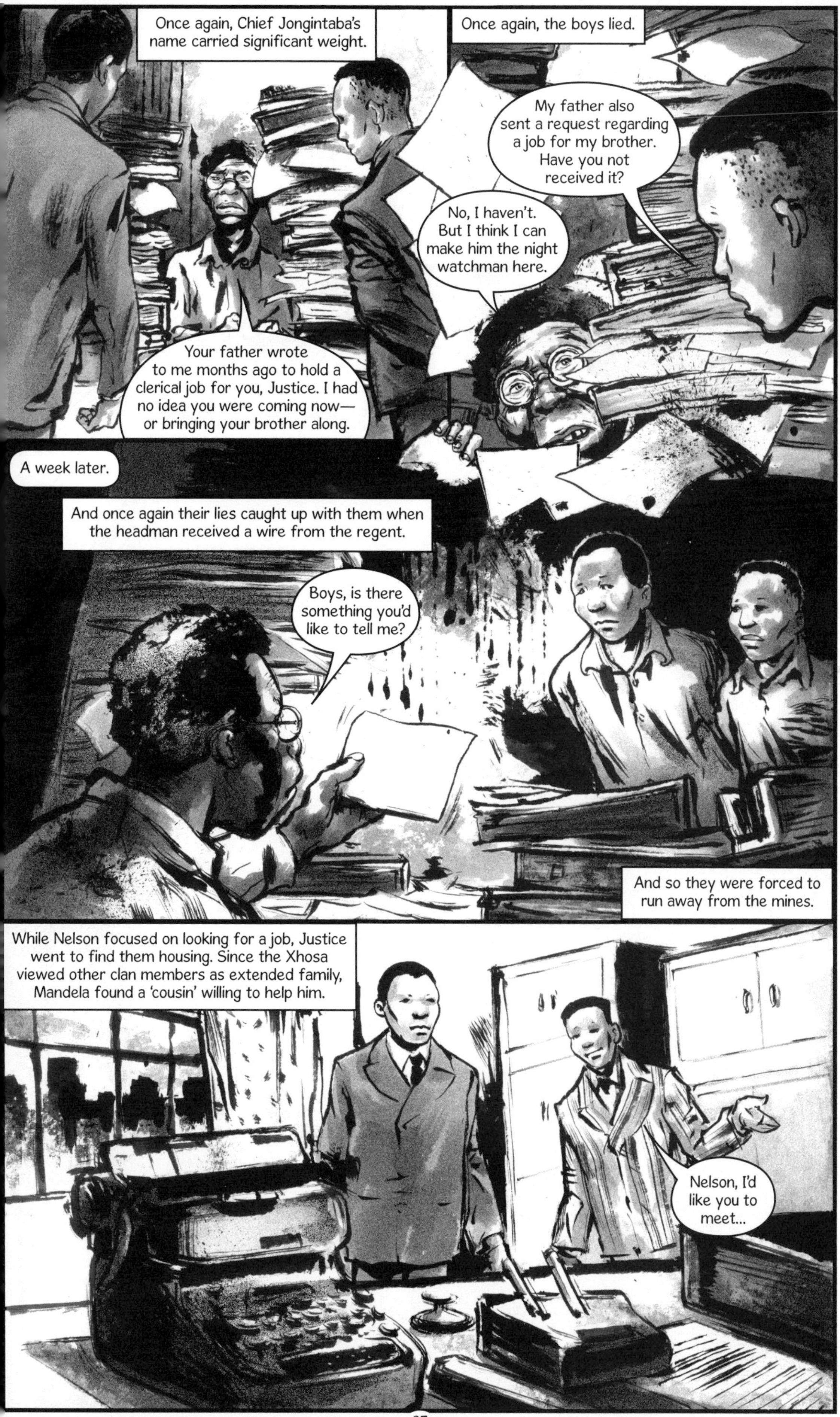

Once again, Chief Jongintaba's name carried significant weight.
Your father wrote to me months ago to hold a clerical job for you, Justice. I had no idea you were coming now—or bringing your brother along.
Once again, the boys lied.
My father also sent a request regarding a job for my brother. Have you not received it?
No, I haven't. But I think I can make him the night watchman here.
A week later.
And once again their lies caught up with them when the headman received a wire from the regent.
Boys, is there something you'd like to tell me?
And so they were forced to run away from the mines.
While Nelson focused on looking for a job, Justice went to find them housing. Since the Xhosa viewed other clan members as extended family, Mandela found a 'cousin' willing to help him.
Nelson, I'd like you to meet...

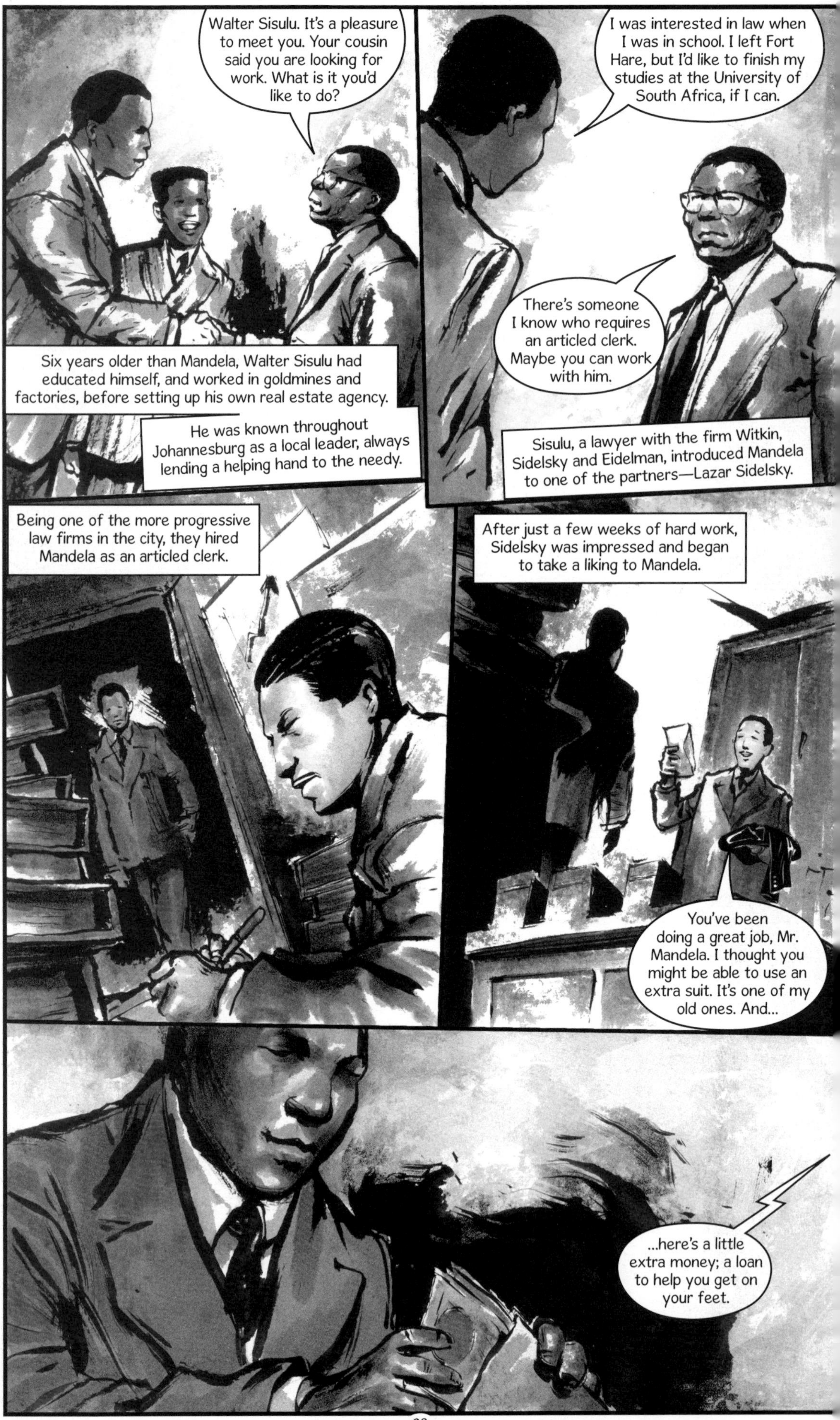
Walter Sisulu. It's a pleasure to meet you. Your cousin said you are looking for work. What is it you'd like to do?
Six years older than Mandela, Walter Sisulu had educated himself, and worked in goldmines and factories, before setting up his own real estate agency.
He was known throughout Johannesburg as a local leader, always lending a helping hand to the needy.
I was interested in law when I was in school. I left Fort Hare, but I'd like to finish my studies at the University of South Africa, if I can.
There's someone I know who requires an articled clerk. Maybe you can work with him.
Sisulu, a lawyer with the firm Witkin, Sidelsky and Eidelman, introduced Mandela to one of the partners—Lazar Sidelsky.
Being one of the more progressive law firms in the city, they hired Mandela as an articled clerk.
After just a few weeks of hard work, Sidelsky was impressed and began to take a liking to Mandela.
You've been doing a great job, Mr. Mandela. I thought you might be able to use an extra suit. It's one of my old ones. And...
...here's a little extra money; a loan to help you get on your feet.

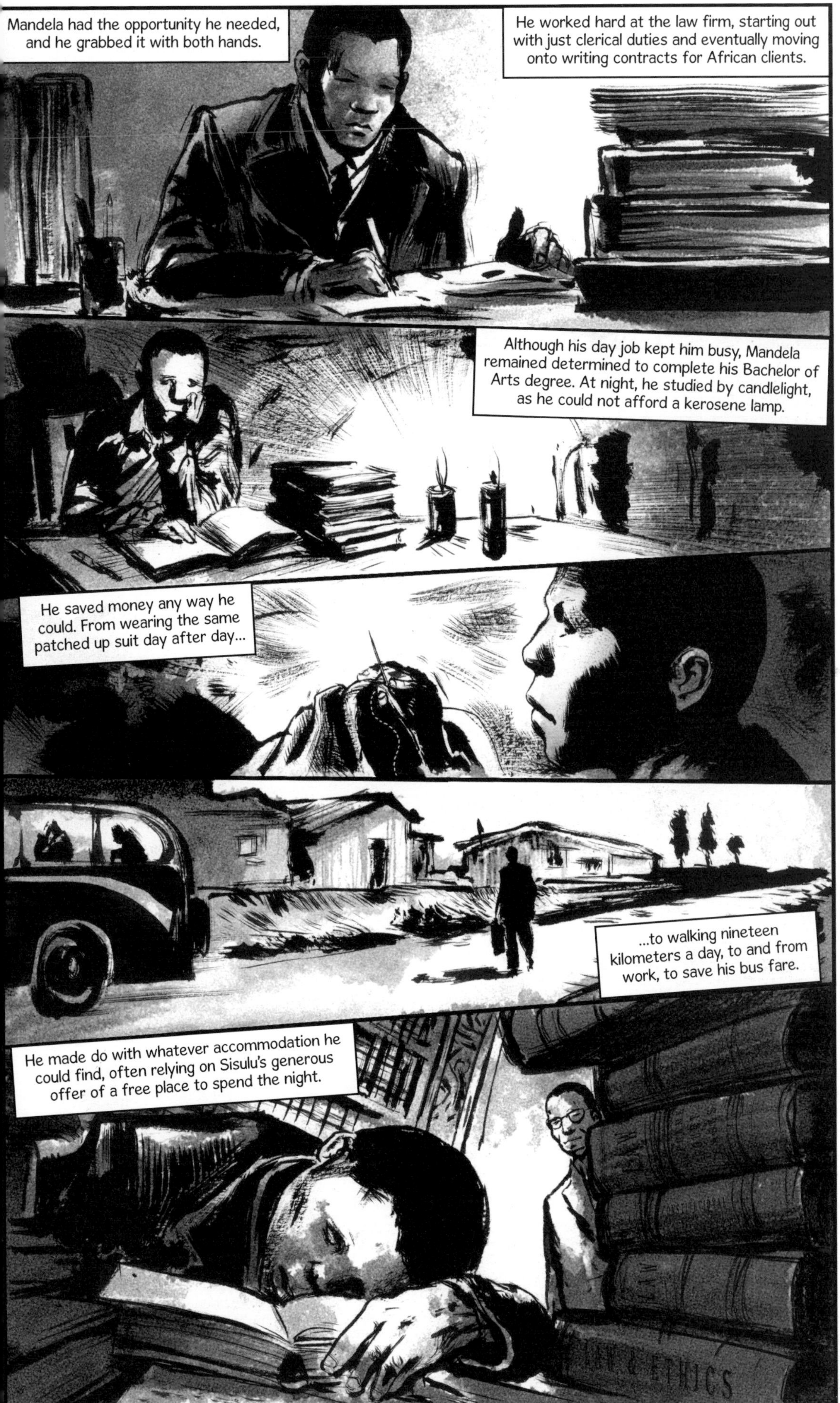
Mandela had the opportunity he needed, and he grabbed it with both hands.
He worked hard at the law firm, starting out with just clerical duties and eventually moving onto writing contracts for African clients.
Although his day job kept him busy, Mandela remained determined to complete his Bachelor of Arts degree. At night, he studied by candlelight, as he could not afford a kerosene lamp.
He saved money any way he could. From wearing the same patched up suit day after day...
...to walking nineteen kilometers a day, to and from work, to save his bus fare.
He made do with whatever accommodation he could find, often relying on Sisulu's generous offer of a free place to spend the night.

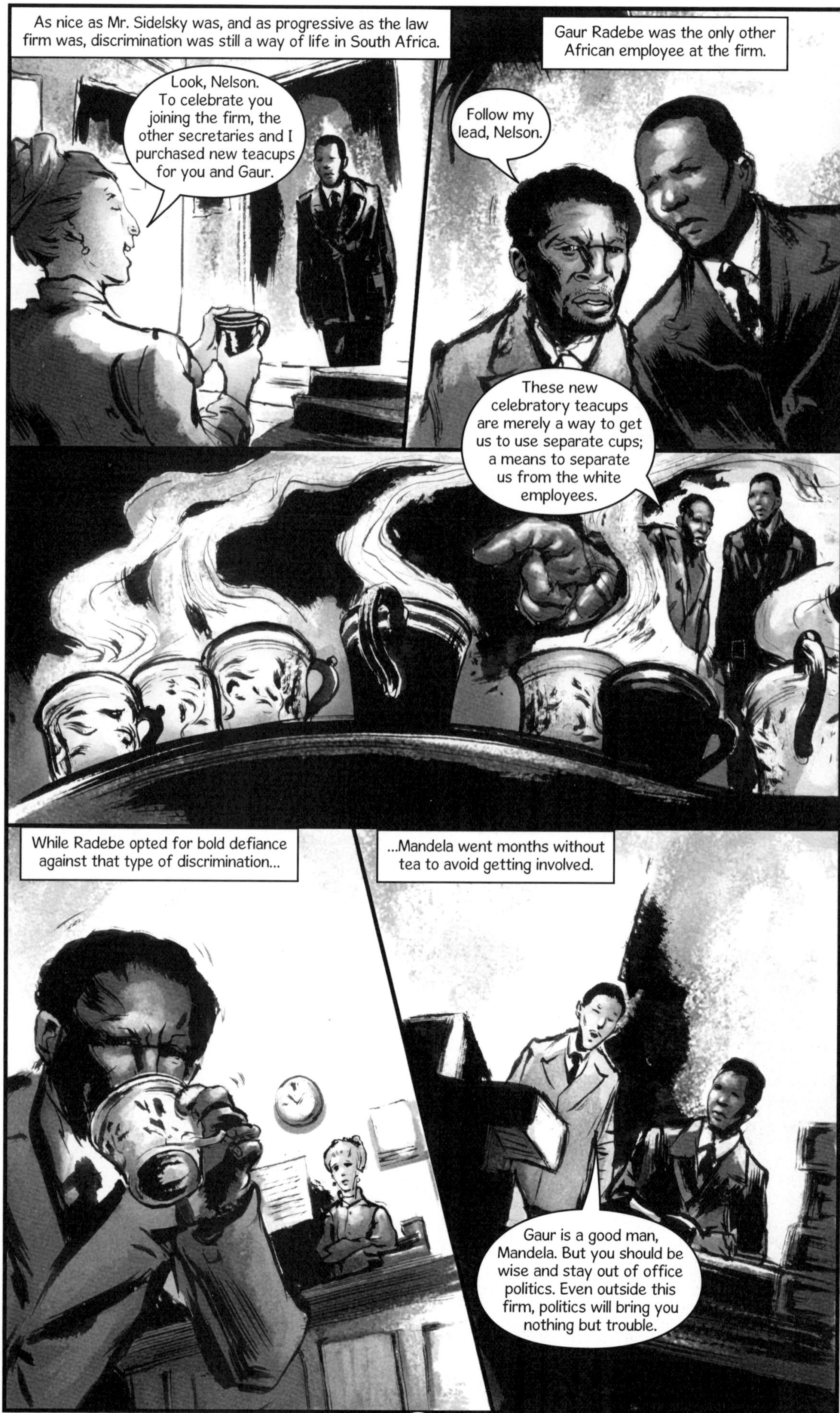

As nice as Mr. Sidelsky was, and as progressive as the law firm was, discrimination was still a way of life in South Africa.
Look, Nelson. To celebrate you joining the firm, the other secretaries and I purchased new teacups for you and Gaur.
Gaur Radebe was the only other African employee at the firm.
Follow my lead, Nelson.
These new celebratory teacups are merely a way to get us to use separate cups; a means to separate us from the white employees.
While Radebe opted for bold defiance against that type of discrimination...
...Mandela went months without tea to avoid getting involved.
Gaur is a good man, Mandela. But you should be wise and stay out of office politics. Even outside this firm, politics will bring you nothing but trouble.

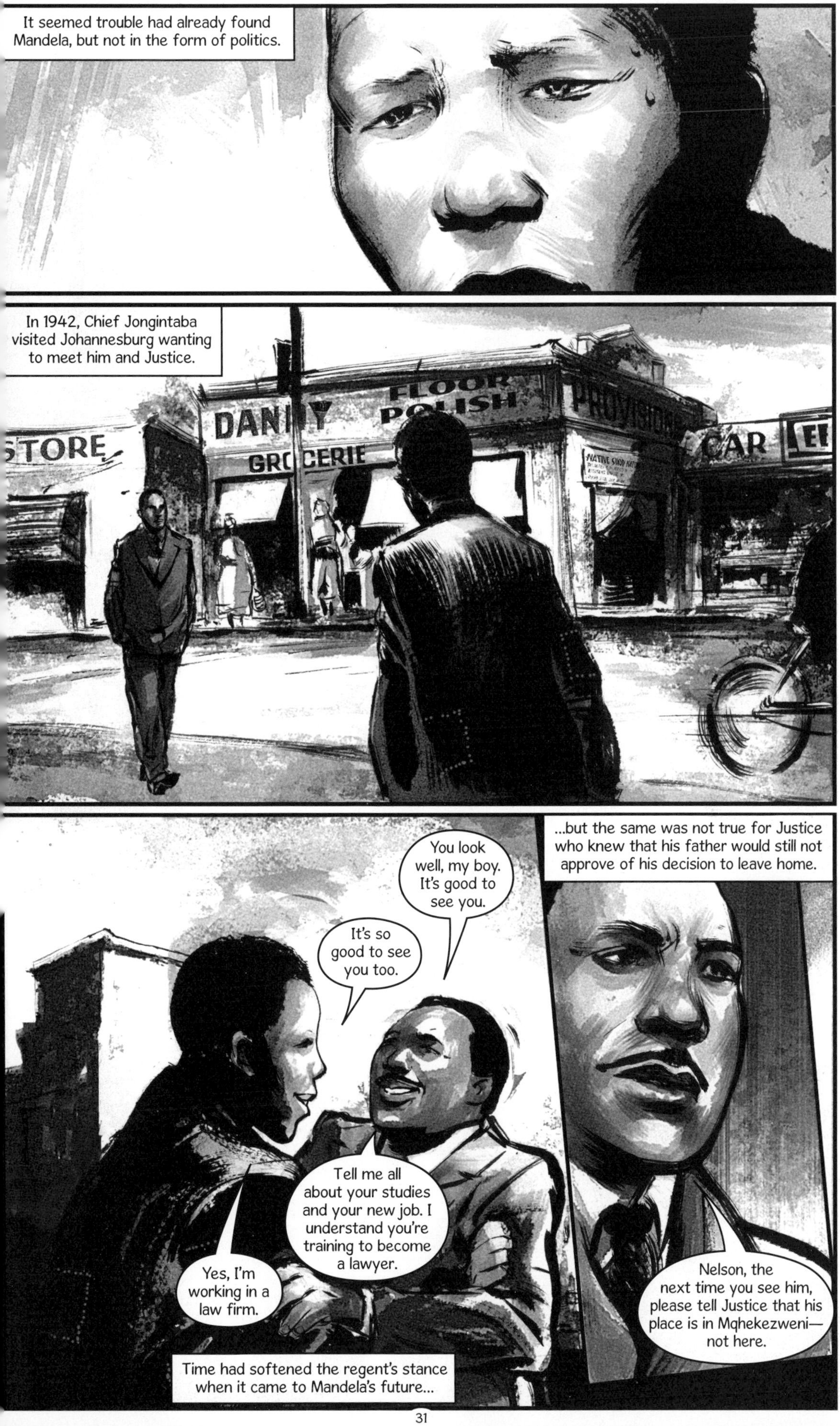
It seemed trouble had already found Mandela, but not in the form of politics.
In 1942, Chief Jongintaba visited Johannesburg wanting to meet him and Justice.
STORE
DAN Y
GRO CERIE
FLOOR POLISH
PROVISION
NATIVE SHOP
CAR
You look well, my boy. It's good to see you.
It's so good to see you too.
Tell me all about your studies and your new job. I understand you're training to become a lawyer.
Yes, I'm working in a law firm.
Time had softened the regent's stance when it came to Mandela's future...
...but the same was not true for Justice who knew that his father would still not approve of his decision to leave home.
Nelson, the next time you see him, please tell Justice that his place is in Mqhekezweni— not here.

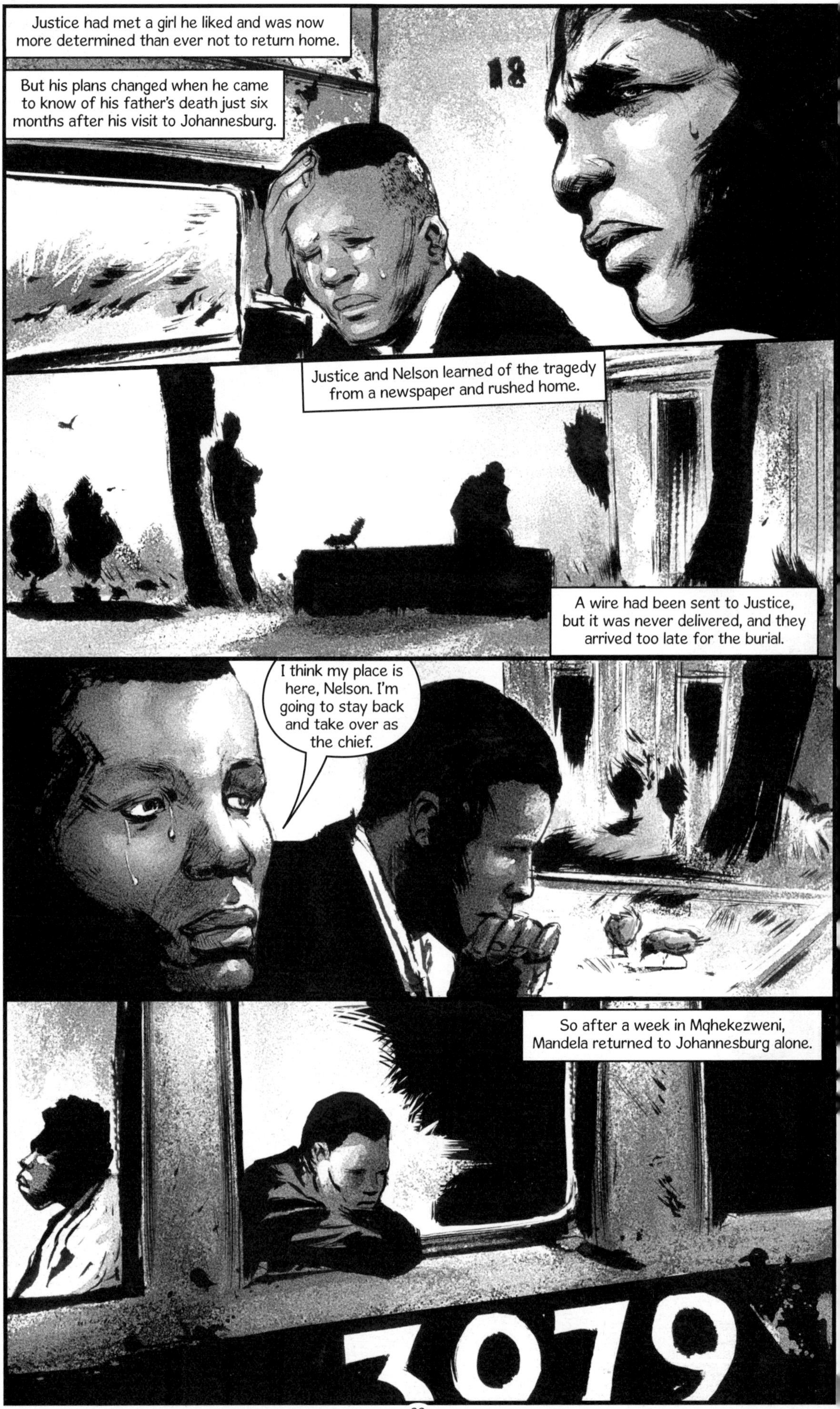
Justice had met a girl he liked and was now more determined than ever not to return home.
But his plans changed when he came to know of his father's death just six months after his visit to Johannesburg.
18
Justice and Nelson learned of the tragedy from a newspaper and rushed home.
A wire had been sent to Justice, but it was never delivered, and they arrived too late for the burial.
I think my place is here, Nelson. I'm going to stay back and take over as the chief.
So after a week in Mqhekezweni, Mandela returned to Johannesburg alone.
3079

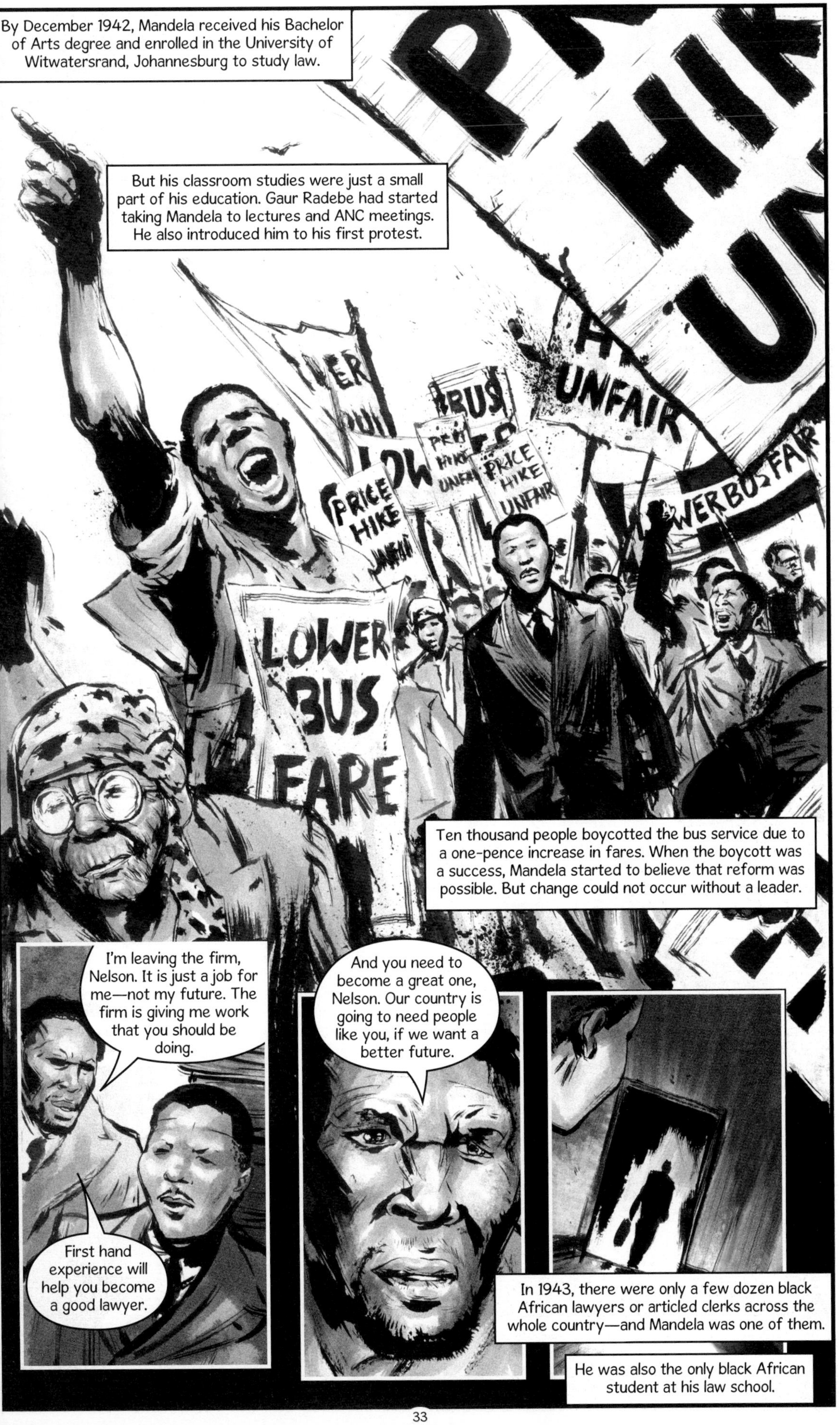
By December 1942, Mandela received his Bachelor of Arts degree and enrolled in the University of Witwatersrand, Johannesburg to study law.
But his classroom studies were just a small part of his education. Gaur Radebe had started taking Mandela to lectures and ANC meetings. He also introduced him to his first protest.
UNFAIR
PRICE HIKE UNFAIR
LOWER BUS FARE
Ten thousand people boycotted the bus service due to a one-pence increase in fares. When the boycott was a success, Mandela started to believe that reform was possible. But change could not occur without a leader.
I'm leaving the firm, Nelson. It is just a job for me—not my future. The firm is giving me work that you should be doing.
First hand experience will help you become a good lawyer.
And you need to become a great one, Nelson. Our country is going to need people like you, if we want a better future.
In 1943, there were only a few dozen black African lawyers or articled clerks across the whole country—and Mandela was one of them.
He was also the only black African student at his law school.

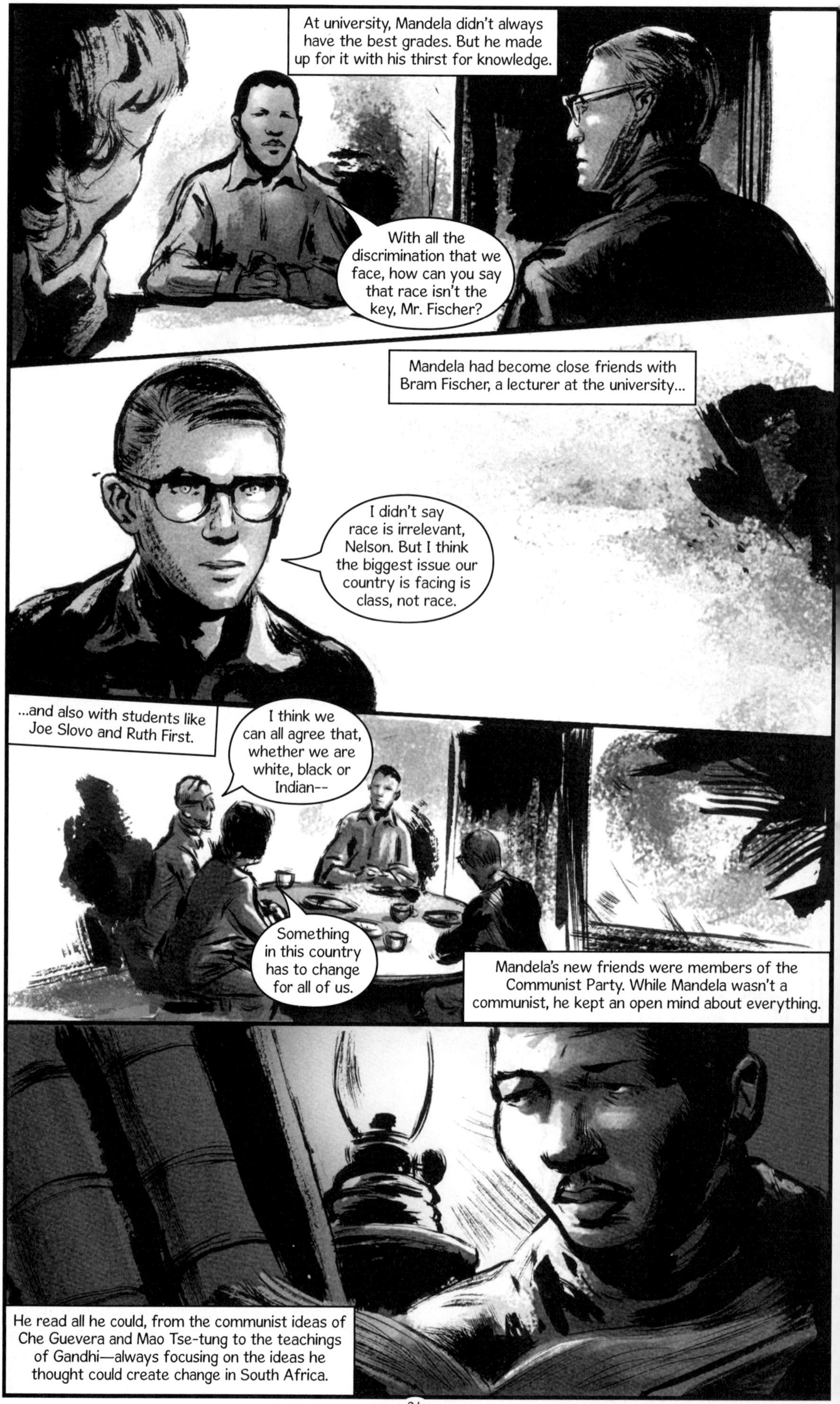

At university, Mandela didn't always have the best grades. But he made up for it with his thirst for knowledge.
With all the discrimination that we face, how can you say that race isn't the key, Mr. Fischer?
Mandela had become close friends with Bram Fischer, a lecturer at the university...
I didn't say race is irrelevant, Nelson. But I think the biggest issue our country is facing is class, not race.
...and also with students like Joe Slovo and Ruth First.
I think we can all agree that, whether we are white, black or Indian--
Something in this country has to change for all of us.
Mandela's new friends were members of the Communist Party. While Mandela wasn't a communist, he kept an open mind about everything.
He read all he could, from the communist ideas of Che Guevera and Mao Tse-tung to the teachings of Gandhi—always focusing on the ideas he thought could create change in South Africa.

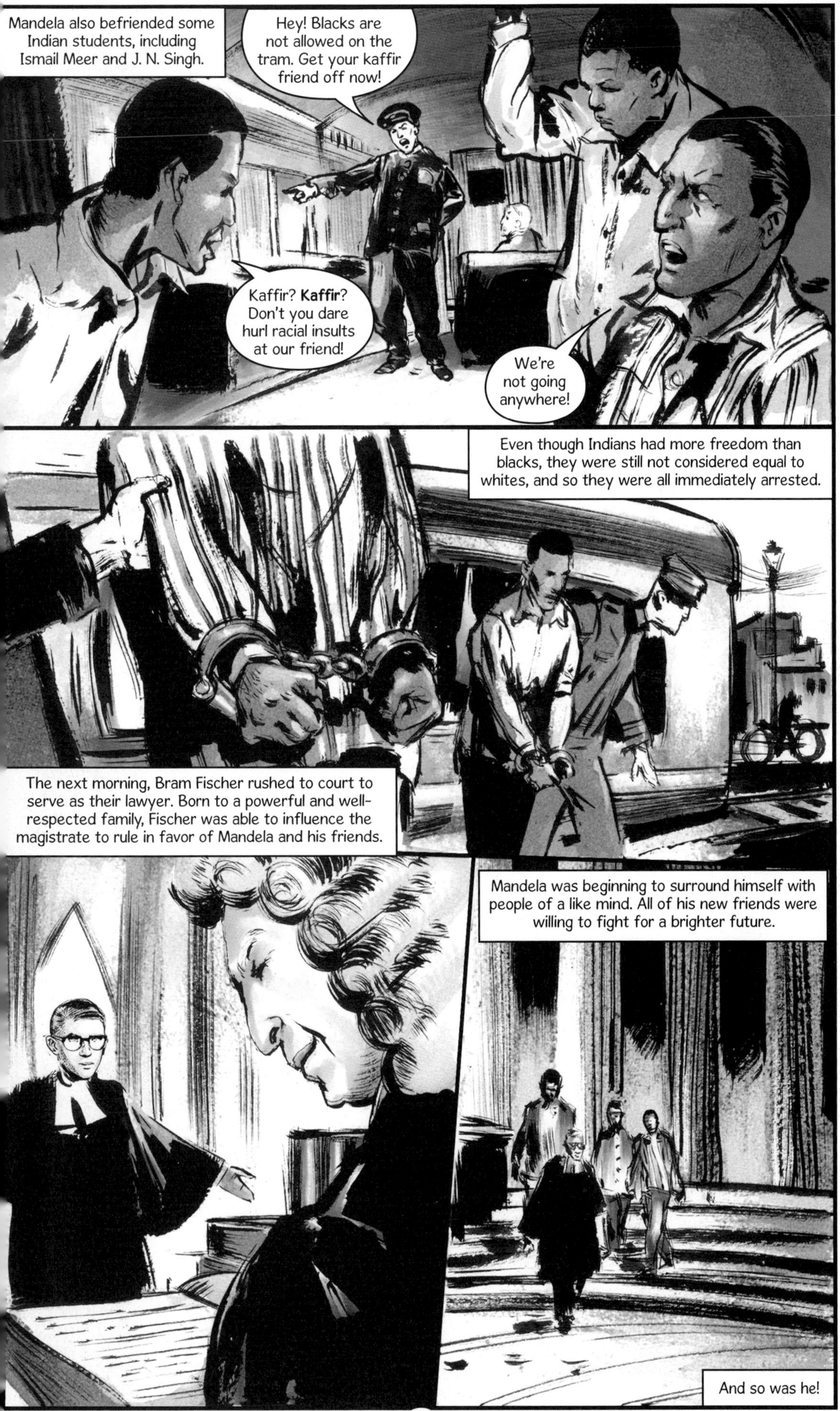

Mandela also befriended some Indian students, including Ismail Meer and J. N. Singh.
Hey! Blacks are not allowed on the tram. Get your kaffir friend off now!
Kaffir? **Kaffir**? Don't you dare hurl racial insults at our friend!
We're not going anywhere!
Even though Indians had more freedom than blacks, they were still not considered equal to whites, and so they were all immediately arrested.
The next morning, Bram Fischer rushed to court to serve as their lawyer. Born to a powerful and well-respected family, Fischer was able to influence the magistrate to rule in favor of Mandela and his friends.
Mandela was beginning to surround himself with people of a like mind. All of his new friends were willing to fight for a brighter future.
And so was he!

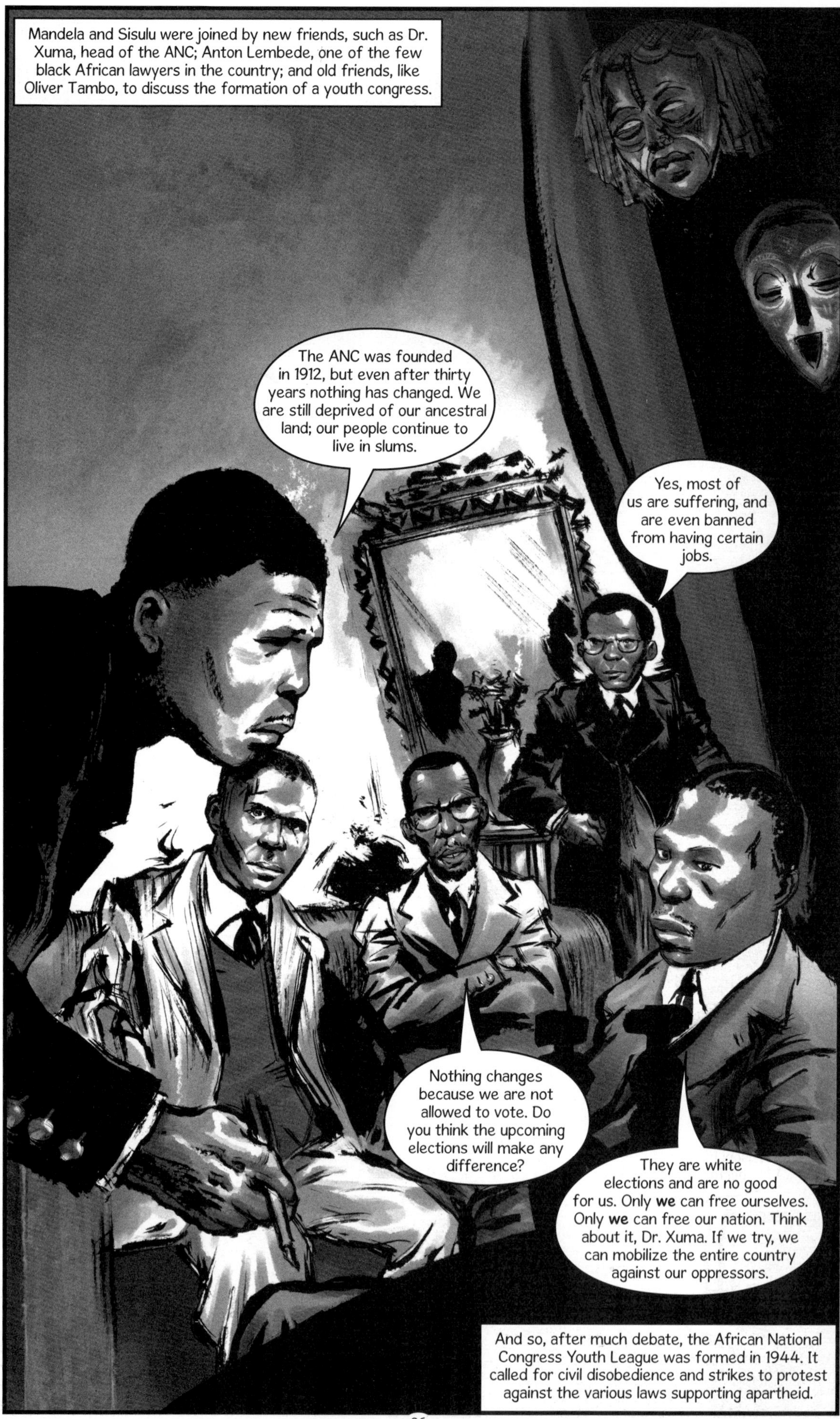
Mandela and Sisulu were joined by new friends, such as Dr. Xuma, head of the ANC; Anton Lembede, one of the few black African lawyers in the country; and old friends, like Oliver Tambo, to discuss the formation of a youth congress.
The ANC was founded in 1912, but even after thirty years nothing has changed. We are still deprived of our ancestral land; our people continue to live in slums.
Yes, most of us are suffering, and are even banned from having certain jobs.
Nothing changes because we are not allowed to vote. Do you think the upcoming elections will make any difference?
They are white elections and are no good for us. Only **we** can free ourselves. Only **we** can free our nation. Think about it, Dr. Xuma. If we try, we can mobilize the entire country against our oppressors.
And so, after much debate, the African National Congress Youth League was formed in 1944. It called for civil disobedience and strikes to protest against the various laws supporting apartheid.

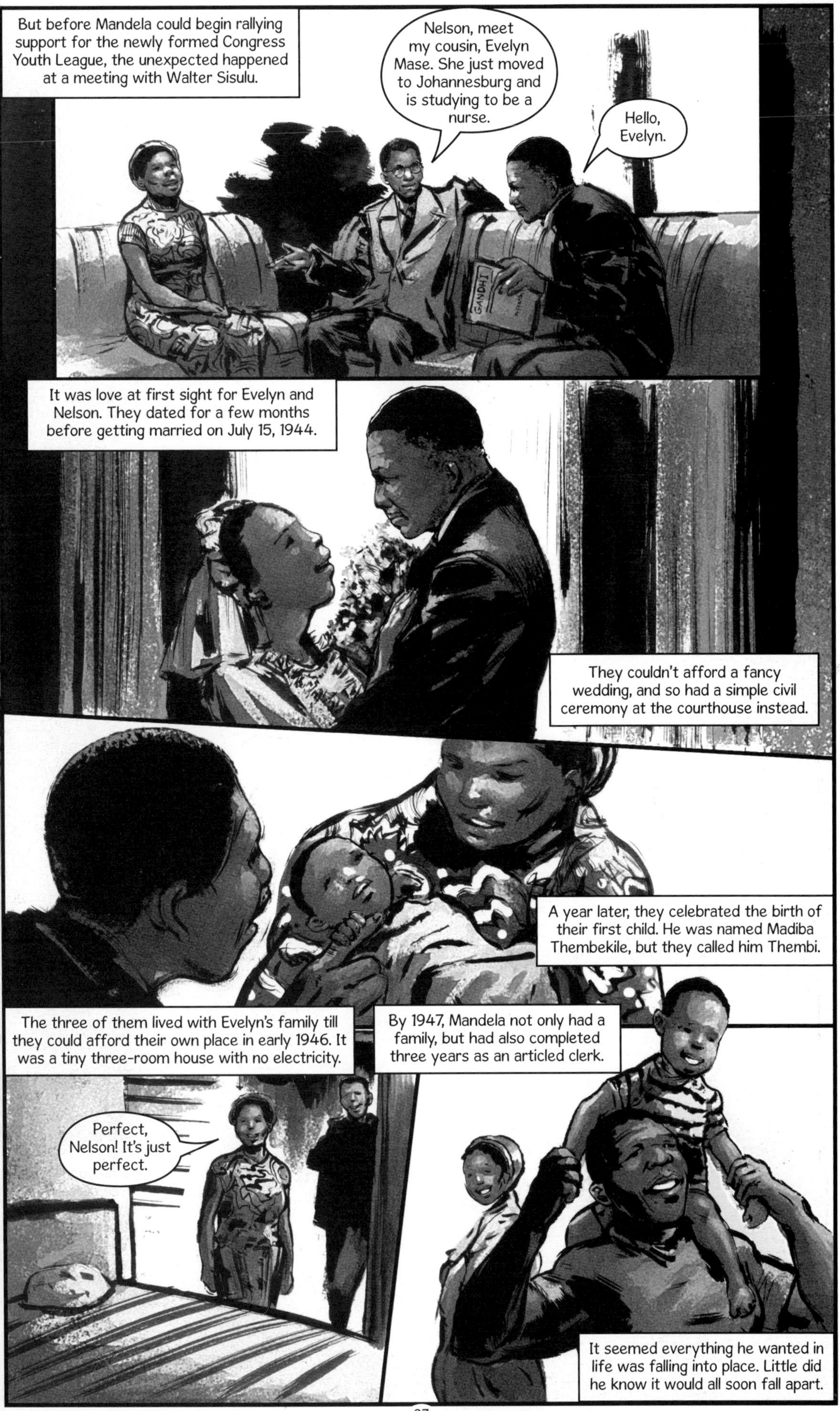

But before Mandela could begin rallying support for the newly formed Congress Youth League, the unexpected happened at a meeting with Walter Sisulu.
Nelson, meet my cousin, Evelyn Mase. She just moved to Johannesburg and is studying to be a nurse.
Hello, Evelyn.
GANDHI
It was love at first sight for Evelyn and Nelson. They dated for a few months before getting married on July 15, 1944.
They couldn't afford a fancy wedding, and so had a simple civil ceremony at the courthouse instead.
A year later, they celebrated the birth of their first child. He was named Madiba Thembekile, but they called him Thembi.
The three of them lived with Evelyn's family till they could afford their own place in early 1946. It was a tiny three-room house with no electricity.
Perfect, Nelson! It's just perfect.
By 1947, Mandela not only had a family, but had also completed three years as an articled clerk.
It seemed everything he wanted in life was falling into place. Little did he know it would all soon fall apart.

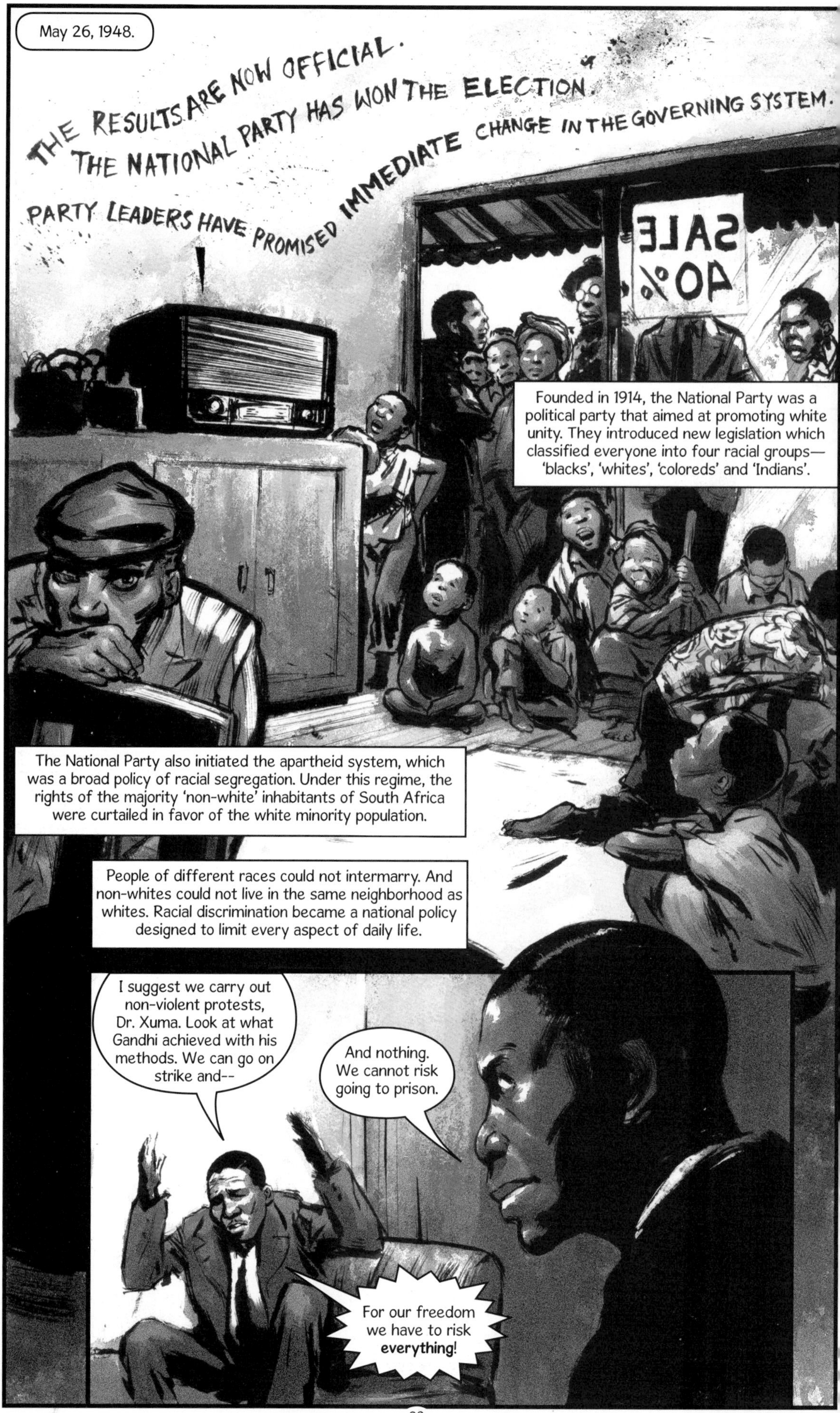

May 26, 1948.
THE RESULTS ARE NOW OFFICIAL.
THE NATIONAL PARTY HAS WON THE ELECTION.
PARTY LEADERS HAVE PROMISED IMMEDIATE CHANGE IN THE GOVERNING SYSTEM.
SALE 40%
Founded in 1914, the National Party was a political party that aimed at promoting white unity. They introduced new legislation which classified everyone into four racial groups—'blacks', 'whites', 'coloreds' and 'Indians'.
The National Party also initiated the apartheid system, which was a broad policy of racial segregation. Under this regime, the rights of the majority 'non-white' inhabitants of South Africa were curtailed in favor of the white minority population.
People of different races could not intermarry. And non-whites could not live in the same neighborhood as whites. Racial discrimination became a national policy designed to limit every aspect of daily life.
I suggest we carry out non-violent protests, Dr. Xuma. Look at what Gandhi achieved with his methods. We can go on strike and--
And nothing. We cannot risk going to prison.
For our freedom we have to risk **everything**!

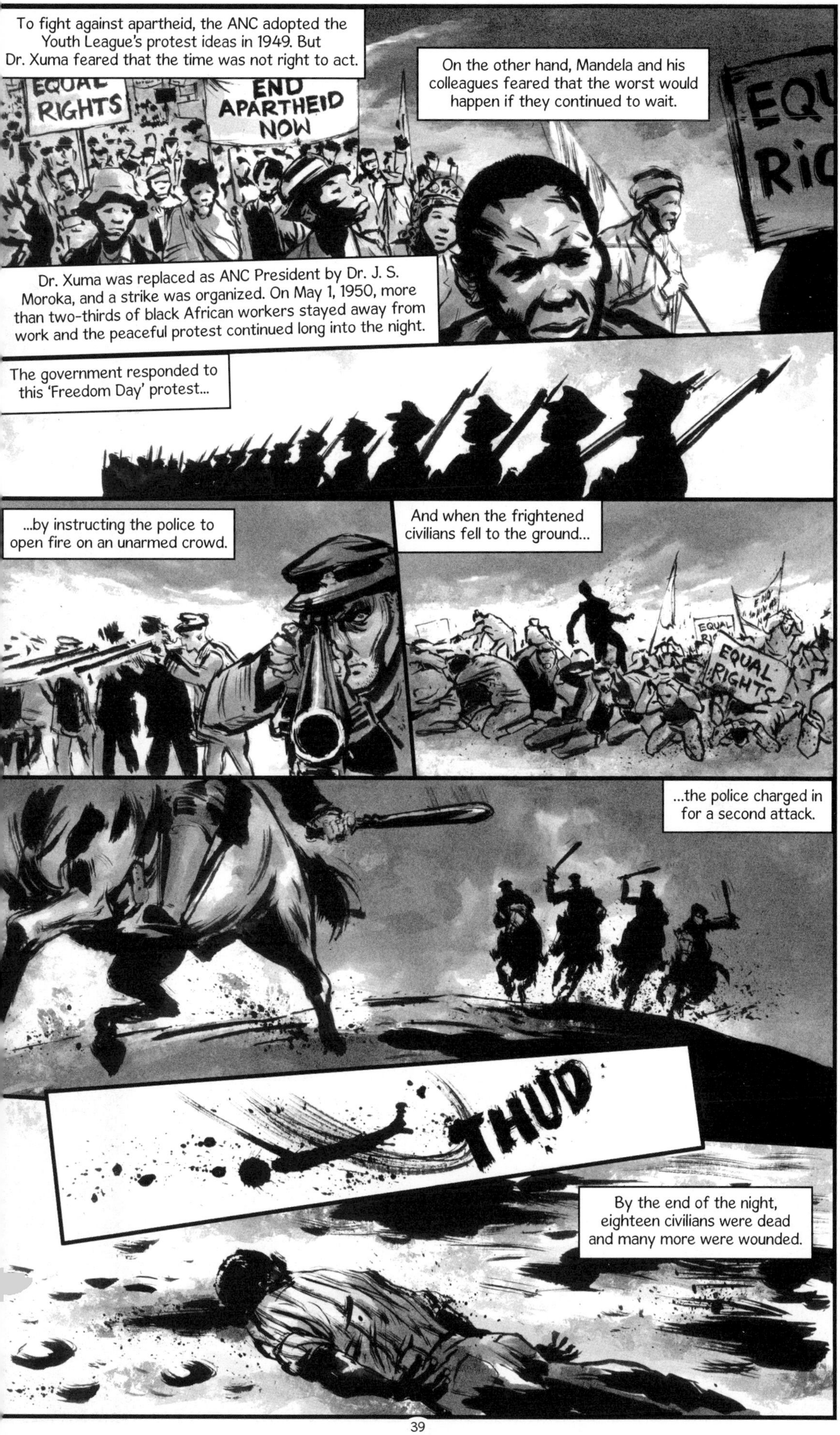
To fight against apartheid, the ANC adopted the Youth League's protest ideas in 1949. But Dr. Xuma feared that the time was not right to act.
EQUAL RIGHTS
END APARTHEID NOW
On the other hand, Mandela and his colleagues feared that the worst would happen if they continued to wait.
Dr. Xuma was replaced as ANC President by Dr. J. S. Moroka, and a strike was organized. On May 1, 1950, more than two-thirds of black African workers stayed away from work and the peaceful protest continued long into the night.
The government responded to this 'Freedom Day' protest...
...by instructing the police to open fire on an unarmed crowd.
And when the frightened civilians fell to the ground...
EQUAL RIGHTS
...the police charged in for a second attack.
THUD
By the end of the night, eighteen civilians were dead and many more were wounded.

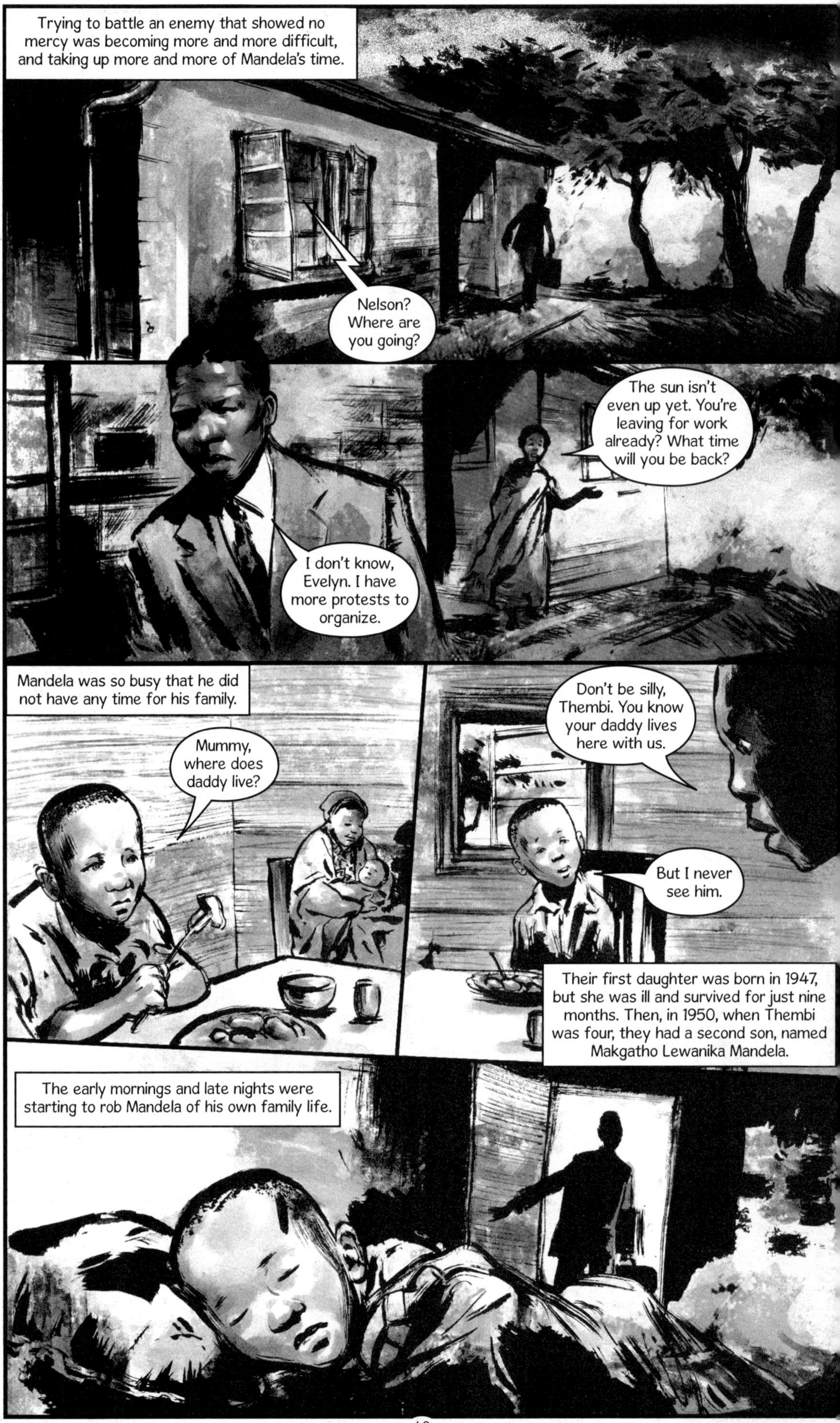

Trying to battle an enemy that showed no mercy was becoming more and more difficult, and taking up more and more of Mandela's time.
Nelson? Where are you going?
The sun isn't even up yet. You're leaving for work already? What time will you be back?
I don't know, Evelyn. I have more protests to organize.
Mandela was so busy that he did not have any time for his family.
Mummy, where does daddy live?
Don't be silly, Thembi. You know your daddy lives here with us.
But I never see him.
Their first daughter was born in 1947, but she was ill and survived for just nine months. Then, in 1950, when Thembi was four, they had a second son, named Makgatho Lewanika Mandela.
The early mornings and late nights were starting to rob Mandela of his own family life.

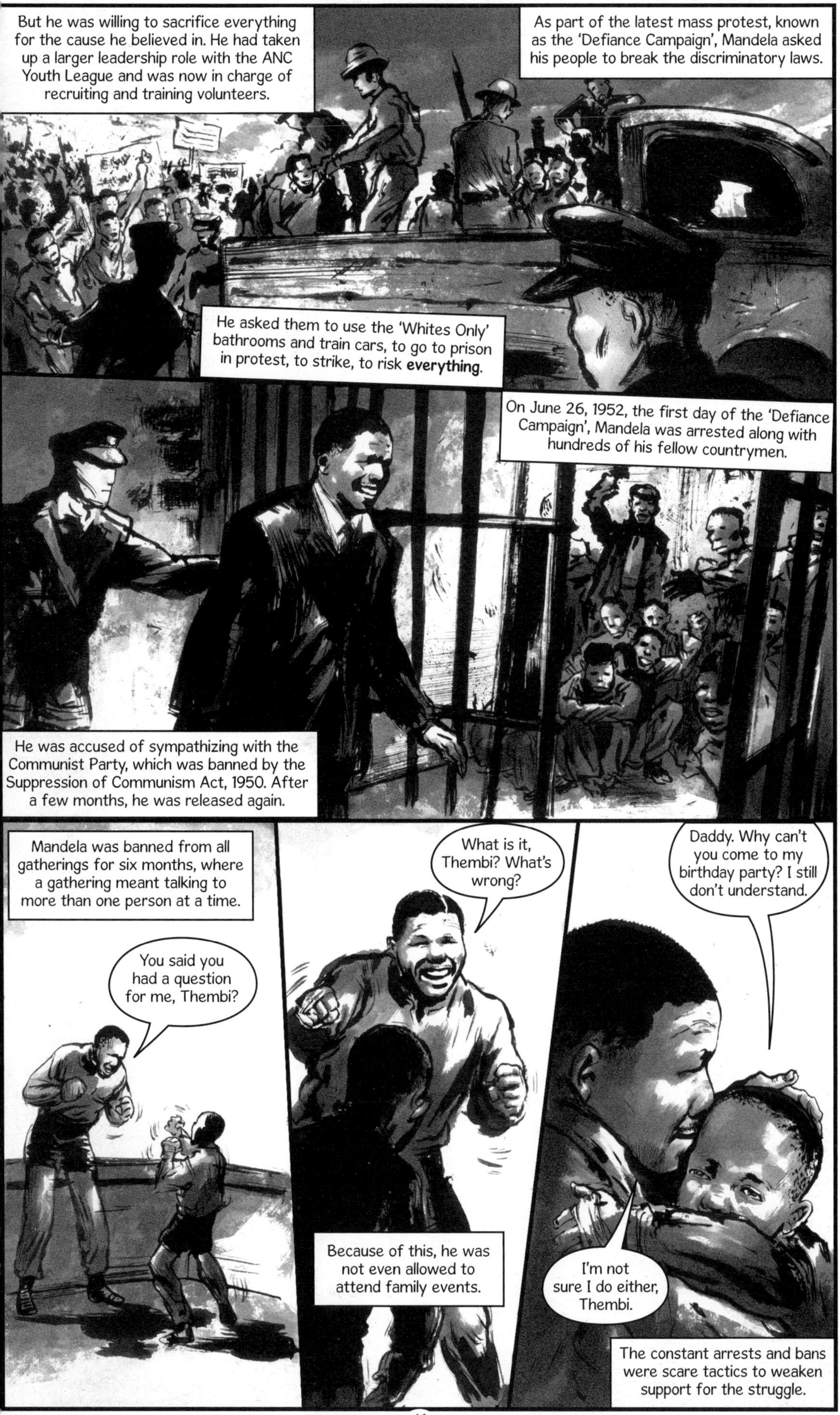
But he was willing to sacrifice everything for the cause he believed in. He had taken up a larger leadership role with the ANC Youth League and was now in charge of recruiting and training volunteers.
As part of the latest mass protest, known as the 'Defiance Campaign', Mandela asked his people to break the discriminatory laws.
He asked them to use the 'Whites Only' bathrooms and train cars, to go to prison in protest, to strike, to risk **everything**.
On June 26, 1952, the first day of the 'Defiance Campaign', Mandela was arrested along with hundreds of his fellow countrymen.
He was accused of sympathizing with the Communist Party, which was banned by the Suppression of Communism Act, 1950. After a few months, he was released again.
Mandela was banned from all gatherings for six months, where a gathering meant talking to more than one person at a time.
You said you had a question for me, Thembi?
What is it, Thembi? What's wrong?
Because of this, he was not even allowed to attend family events.
Daddy. Why can't you come to my birthday party? I still don't understand.
I'm not sure I do either, Thembi.
The constant arrests and bans were scare tactics to weaken support for the struggle.

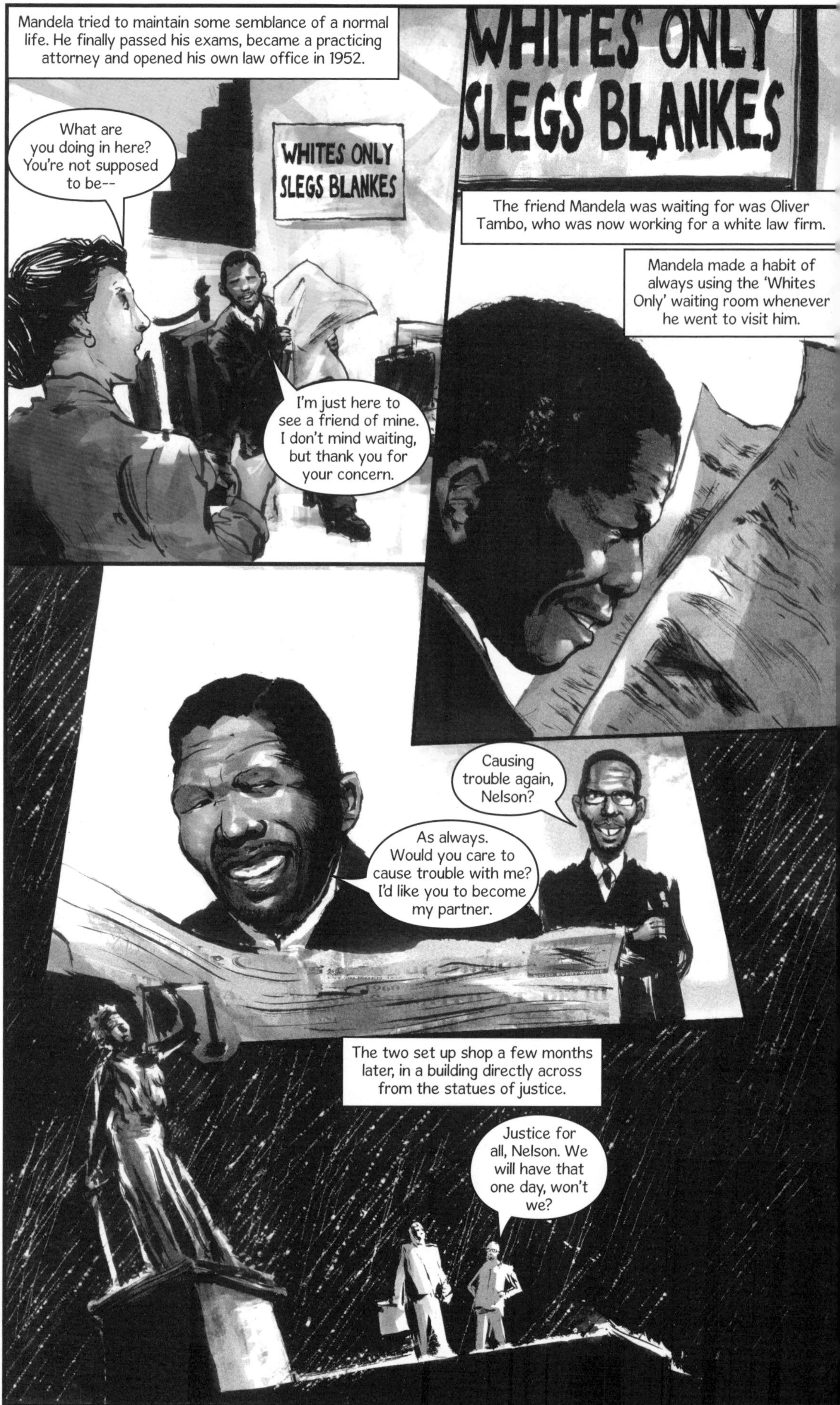
Mandela tried to maintain some semblance of a normal life. He finally passed his exams, became a practicing attorney and opened his own law office in 1952.
WHITES ONLY SLEGS BLANKES
What are you doing in here? You're not supposed to be--
WHITES ONLY SLEGS BLANKES
I'm just here to see a friend of mine. I don't mind waiting, but thank you for your concern.
The friend Mandela was waiting for was Oliver Tambo, who was now working for a white law firm.
Mandela made a habit of always using the 'Whites Only' waiting room whenever he went to visit him.
Causing trouble again, Nelson?
As always. Would you care to cause trouble with me? I'd like you to become my partner.
The two set up shop a few months later, in a building directly across from the statues of justice.
Justice for all, Nelson. We will have that one day, won't we?

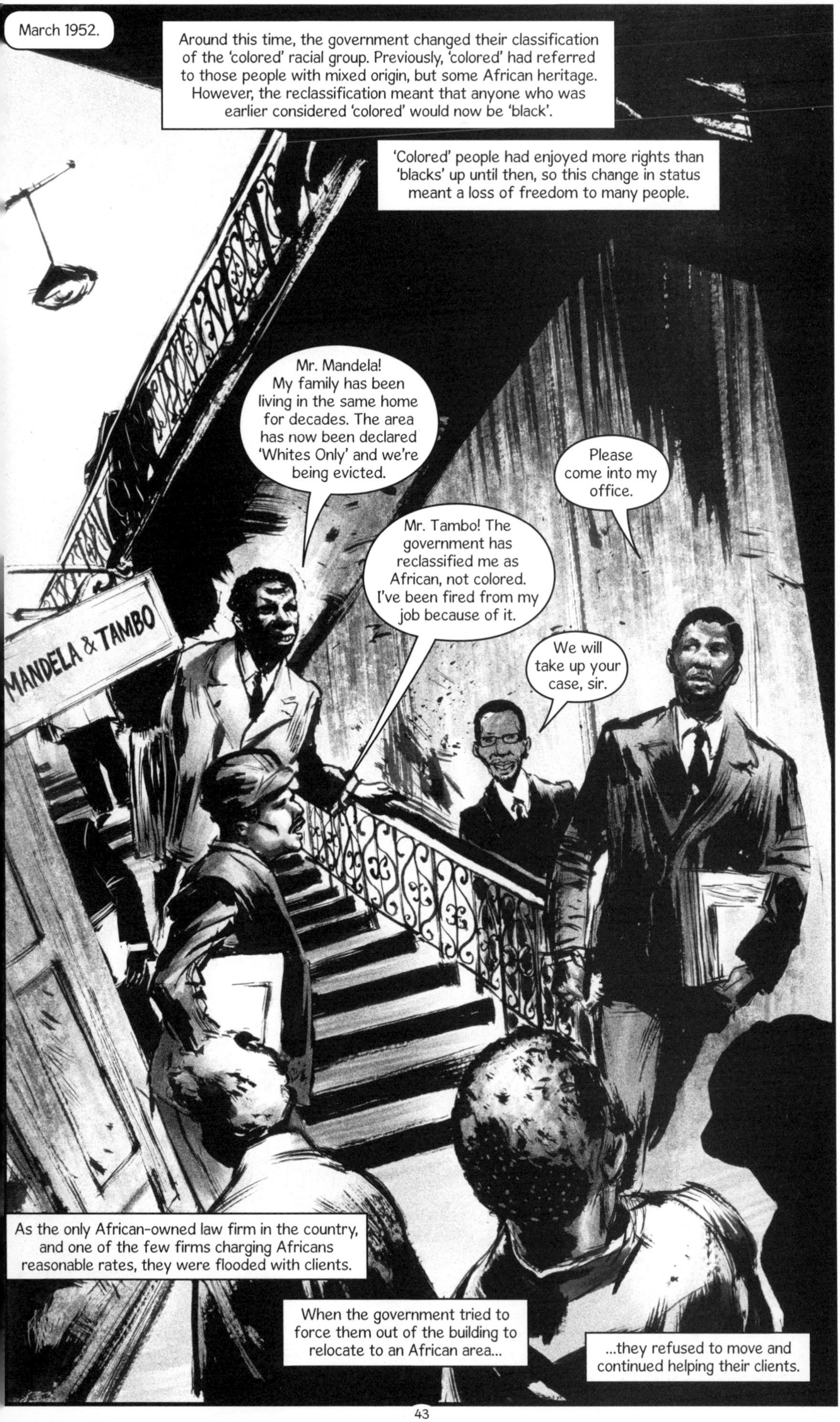
March 1952.
Around this time, the government changed their classification of the 'colored' racial group. Previously, 'colored' had referred to those people with mixed origin, but some African heritage. However, the reclassification meant that anyone who was earlier considered 'colored' would now be 'black'.
'Colored' people had enjoyed more rights than 'blacks' up until then, so this change in status meant a loss of freedom to many people.
MANDELA & TAMBO
Mr. Mandela! My family has been living in the same home for decades. The area has now been declared 'Whites Only' and we're being evicted.
Please come into my office.
Mr. Tambo! The government has reclassified me as African, not colored. I've been fired from my job because of it.
We will take up your case, sir.
As the only African-owned law firm in the country, and one of the few firms charging Africans reasonable rates, they were flooded with clients.
When the government tried to force them out of the building to relocate to an African area...
...they refused to move and continued helping their clients.

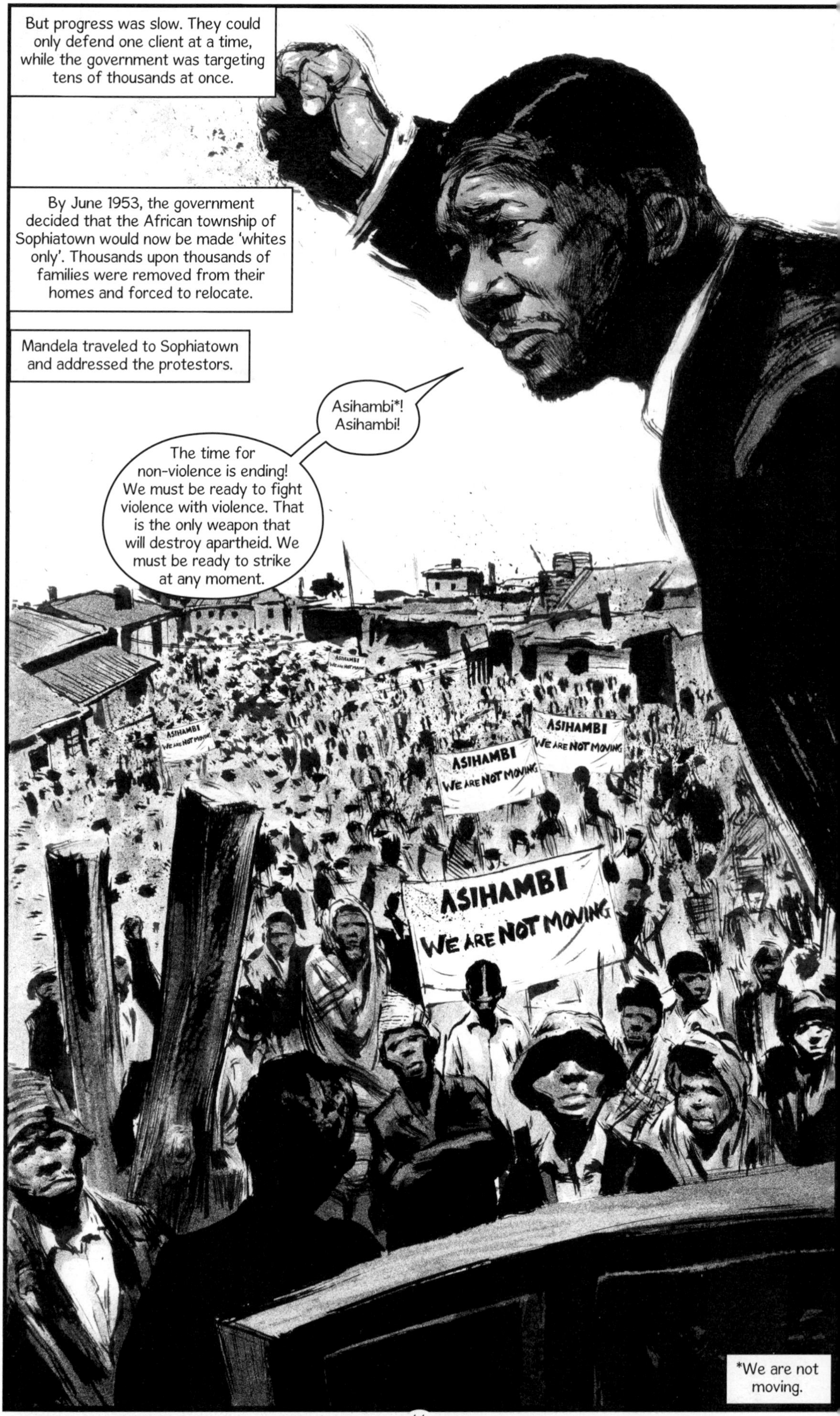
But progress was slow. They could only defend one client at a time, while the government was targeting tens of thousands at once.
By June 1953, the government decided that the African township of Sophiatown would now be made 'whites only'. Thousands upon thousands of families were removed from their homes and forced to relocate.
Mandela traveled to Sophiatown and addressed the protestors.
Asihambi*! Asihambi!
The time for non-violence is ending! We must be ready to fight violence with violence. That is the only weapon that will destroy apartheid. We must be ready to strike at any moment.
ASIHAMBI WE ARE NOT MOVING
ASIHAMBI WE ARE NOT MOVING
ASIHAMBI WE ARE NOT MOVING
ASIHAMBI WE ARE NOT MOVING
*We are not moving.

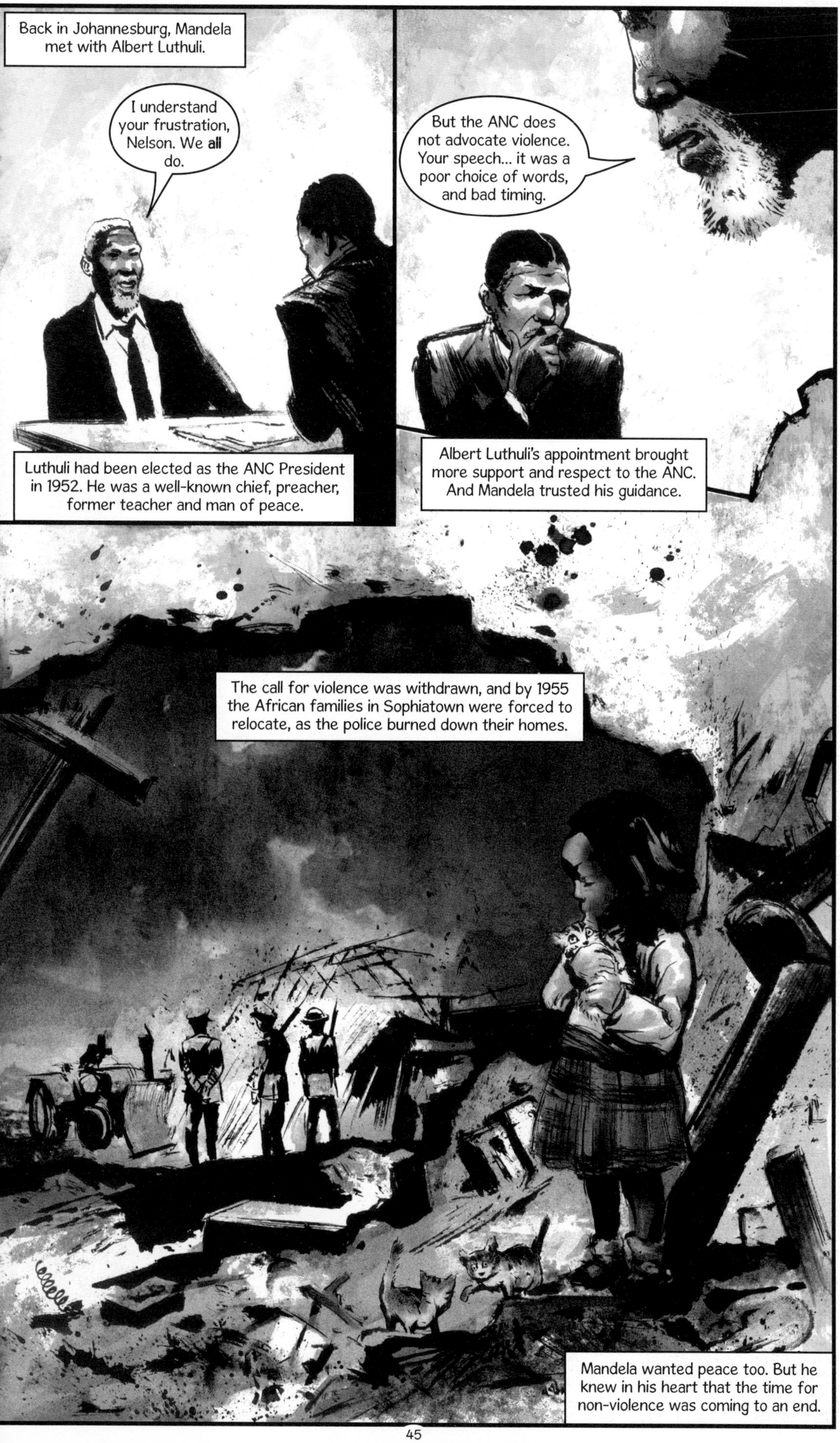
Back in Johannesburg, Mandela met with Albert Luthuli.
I understand your frustration, Nelson. We **all** do.
Luthuli had been elected as the ANC President in 1952. He was a well-known chief, preacher, former teacher and man of peace.
But the ANC does not advocate violence. Your speech... it was a poor choice of words, and bad timing.
Albert Luthuli's appointment brought more support and respect to the ANC. And Mandela trusted his guidance.
The call for violence was withdrawn, and by 1955 the African families in Sophiatown were forced to relocate, as the police burned down their homes.
Mandela wanted peace too. But he knew in his heart that the time for non-violence was coming to an end.

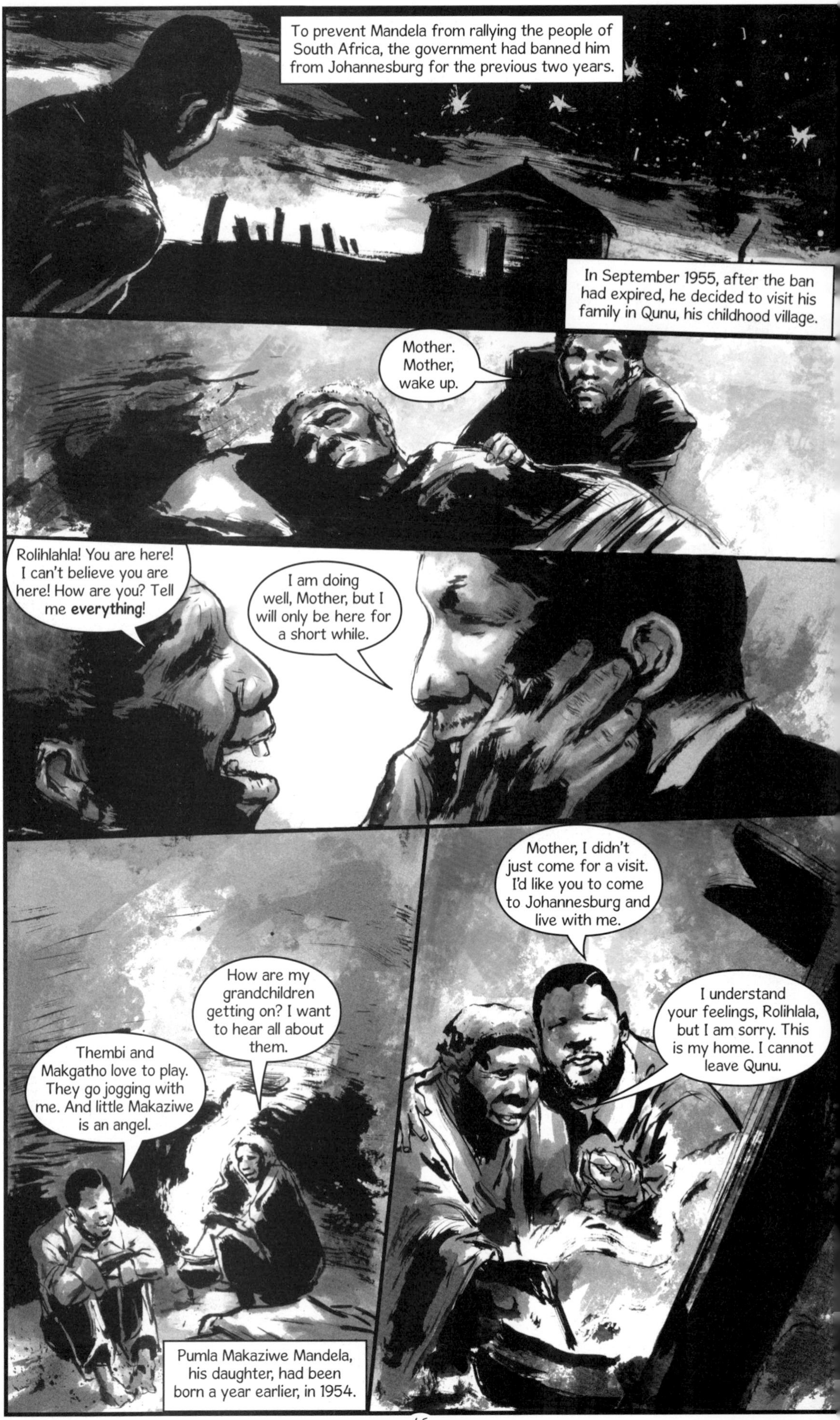
To prevent Mandela from rallying the people of South Africa, the government had banned him from Johannesburg for the previous two years.
In September 1955, after the ban had expired, he decided to visit his family in Qunu, his childhood village.
Mother. Mother, wake up.
Rolihlahla! You are here! I can't believe you are here! How are you? Tell me **everything**!
I am doing well, Mother, but I will only be here for a short while.
How are my grandchildren getting on? I want to hear all about them.
Thembi and Makgatho love to play. They go jogging with me. And little Makaziwe is an angel.
Pumla Makaziwe Mandela, his daughter, had been born a year earlier, in 1954.
Mother, I didn't just come for a visit. I'd like you to come to Johannesburg and live with me.
I understand your feelings, Rolihlala, but I am sorry. This is my home. I cannot leave Qunu.

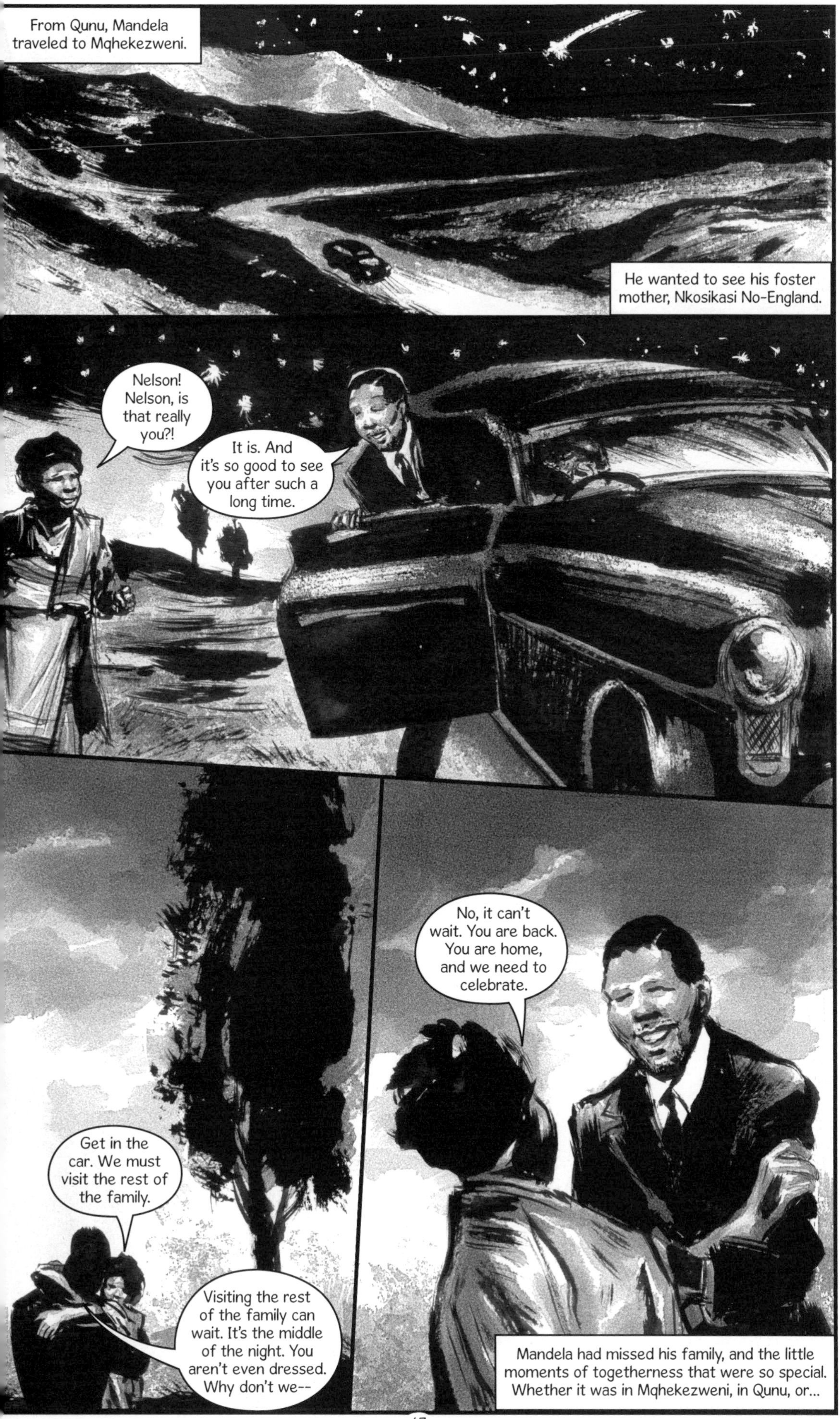
From Qunu, Mandela traveled to Mqhekezweni.
He wanted to see his foster mother, Nkosikasi No-England.
Nelson! Nelson, is that really you?!
It is. And it's so good to see you after such a long time.
Get in the car. We must visit the rest of the family.
Visiting the rest of the family can wait. It's the middle of the night. You aren't even dressed. Why don't we--
No, it can't wait. You are back. You are home, and we need to celebrate.
Mandela had missed his family, and the little moments of togetherness that were so special. Whether it was in Mqhekezweni, in Qunu, or...

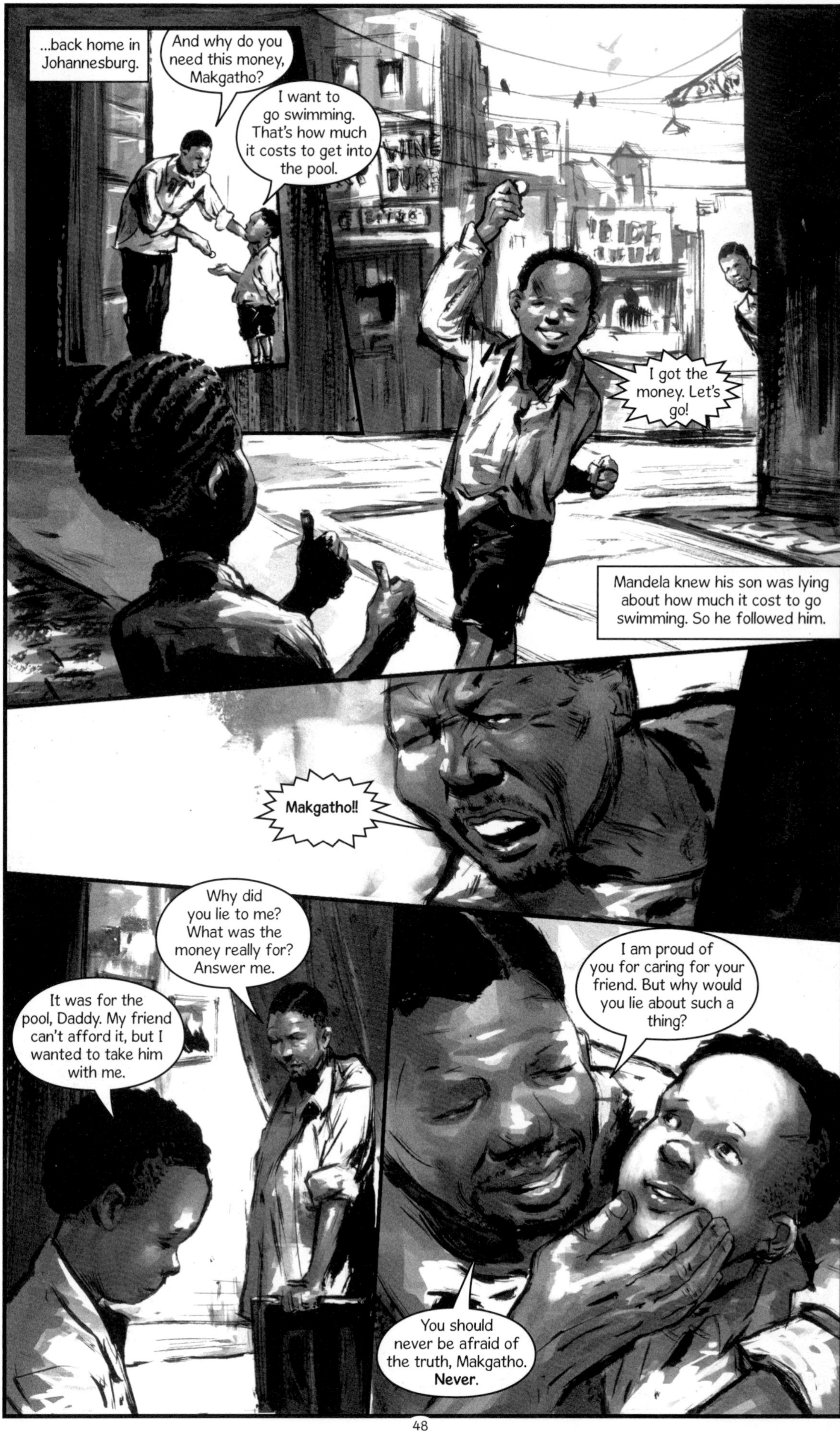
...back home in Johannesburg.
And why do you need this money, Makgatho?
I want to go swimming. That's how much it costs to get into the pool.
I got the money. Let's go!
Mandela knew his son was lying about how much it cost to go swimming. So he followed him.
Makgatho!!
Why did you lie to me? What was the money really for? Answer me.
It was for the pool, Daddy. My friend can't afford it, but I wanted to take him with me.
I am proud of you for caring for your friend. But why would you lie about such a thing?
You should never be afraid of the truth, Makgatho. **Never**.

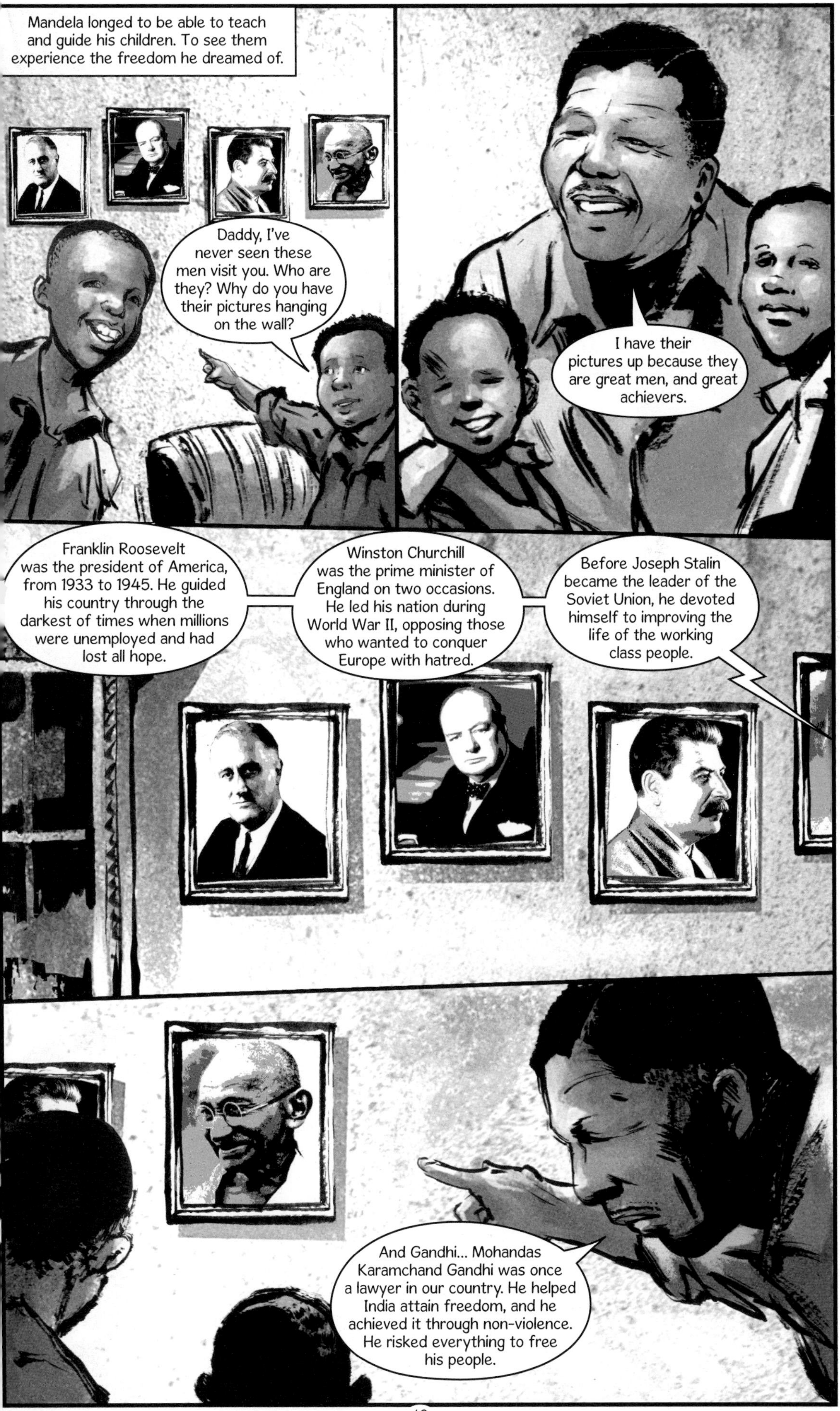
Mandela longed to be able to teach and guide his children. To see them experience the freedom he dreamed of.
Daddy, I've never seen these men visit you. Who are they? Why do you have their pictures hanging on the wall?
I have their pictures up because they are great men, and great achievers.
Franklin Roosevelt was the president of America, from 1933 to 1945. He guided his country through the darkest of times when millions were unemployed and had lost all hope.
Winston Churchill was the prime minister of England on two occasions. He led his nation during World War II, opposing those who wanted to conquer Europe with hatred.
Before Joseph Stalin became the leader of the Soviet Union, he devoted himself to improving the life of the working class people.
And Gandhi... Mohandas Karamchand Gandhi was once a lawyer in our country. He helped India attain freedom, and he achieved it through non-violence. He risked everything to free his people.

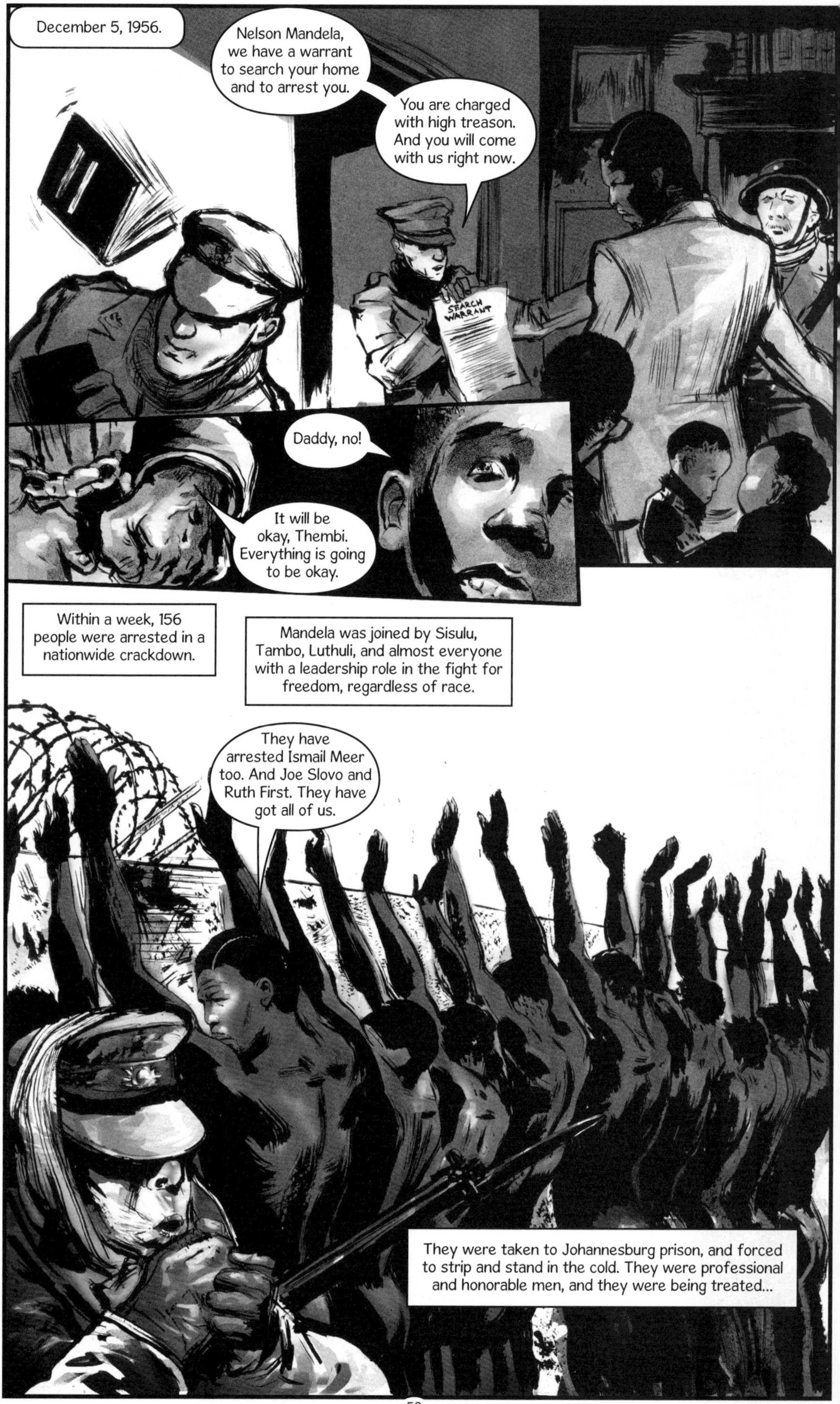

December 5, 1956.
Nelson Mandela, we have a warrant to search your home and to arrest you.
You are charged with high treason. And you will come with us right now.
SEARCH WARRANT
Daddy, no!
It will be okay, Thembi. Everything is going to be okay.
Within a week, 156 people were arrested in a nationwide crackdown.
Mandela was joined by Sisulu, Tambo, Luthuli, and almost everyone with a leadership role in the fight for freedom, regardless of race.
They have arrested Ismail Meer too. And Joe Slovo and Ruth First. They have got all of us.
They were taken to Johannesburg prison, and forced to strip and stand in the cold. They were professional and honorable men, and they were being treated...

December 19, 1956.

...like animals! These men are human beings, who deserve to be treated as such. This is a disgrace!

Bram Fischer, Mandela's university friend, once again rushed to his side in defense; along with a team of dedicated lawyers.

A cage had been constructed to keep the defendants apart from everyone else. The cage even ensured they were separated from Fischer and the rest of their defense team.

DANGEROUS PLEASE DO NOT FEED

This cage has to be taken down now or we will all walk out in protest. I have never seen anything like this in a court of law.

This trial was to be a preparatory examination. If there was enough evidence against them, the case would then go to the Supreme Court and they could possibly face the ultimate penalty... death!

Please maintain order in the court! We will have the cage taken down. We need to continue with the proceedings.

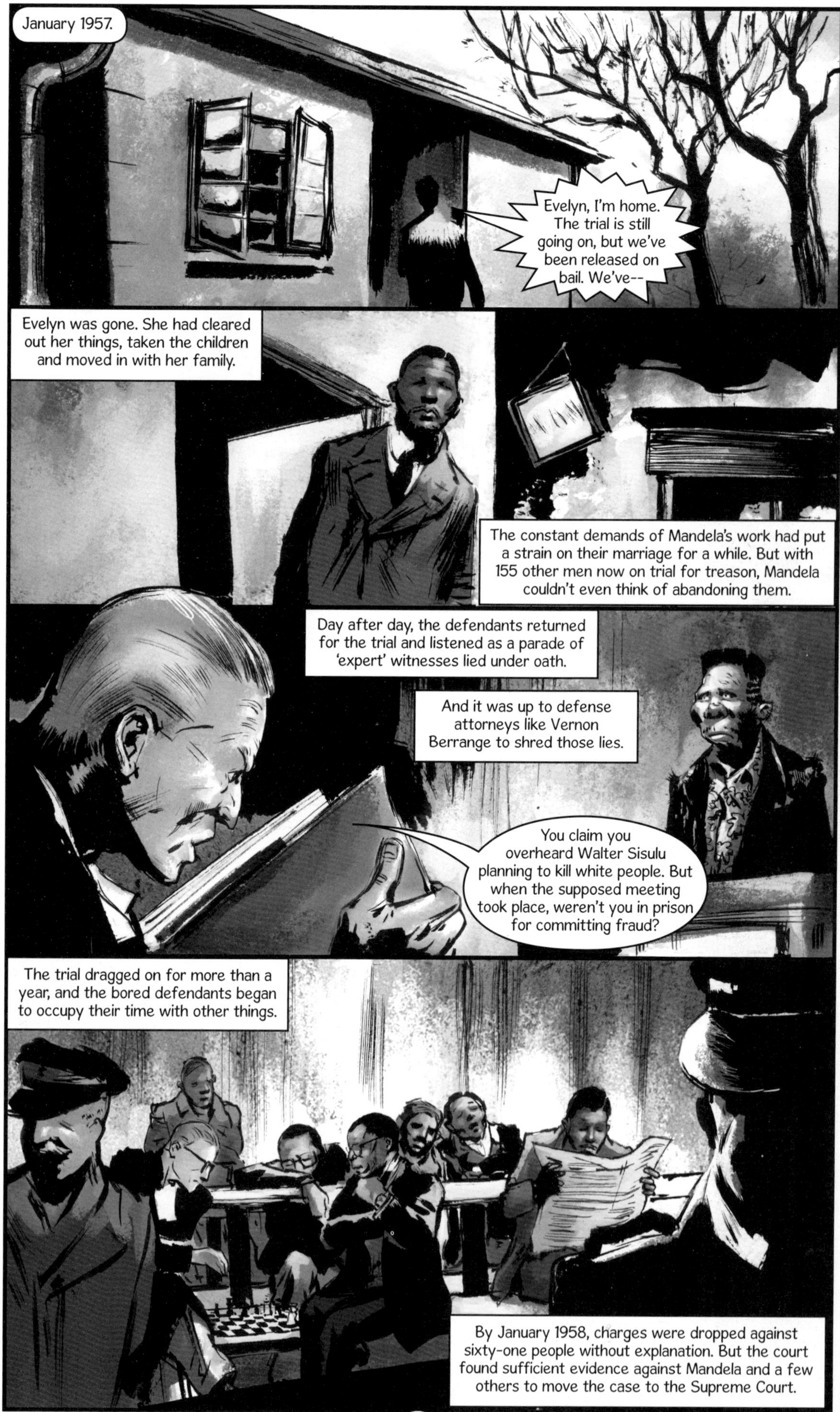
January 1957.
Evelyn, I'm home. The trial is still going on, but we've been released on bail. We've--
Evelyn was gone. She had cleared out her things, taken the children and moved in with her family.
The constant demands of Mandela's work had put a strain on their marriage for a while. But with 155 other men now on trial for treason, Mandela couldn't even think of abandoning them.
Day after day, the defendants returned for the trial and listened as a parade of 'expert' witnesses lied under oath.
And it was up to defense attorneys like Vernon Berrange to shred those lies.
You claim you overheard Walter Sisulu planning to kill white people. But when the supposed meeting took place, weren't you in prison for committing fraud?
The trial dragged on for more than a year, and the bored defendants began to occupy their time with other things.
By January 1958, charges were dropped against sixty-one people without explanation. But the court found sufficient evidence against Mandela and a few others to move the case to the Supreme Court.

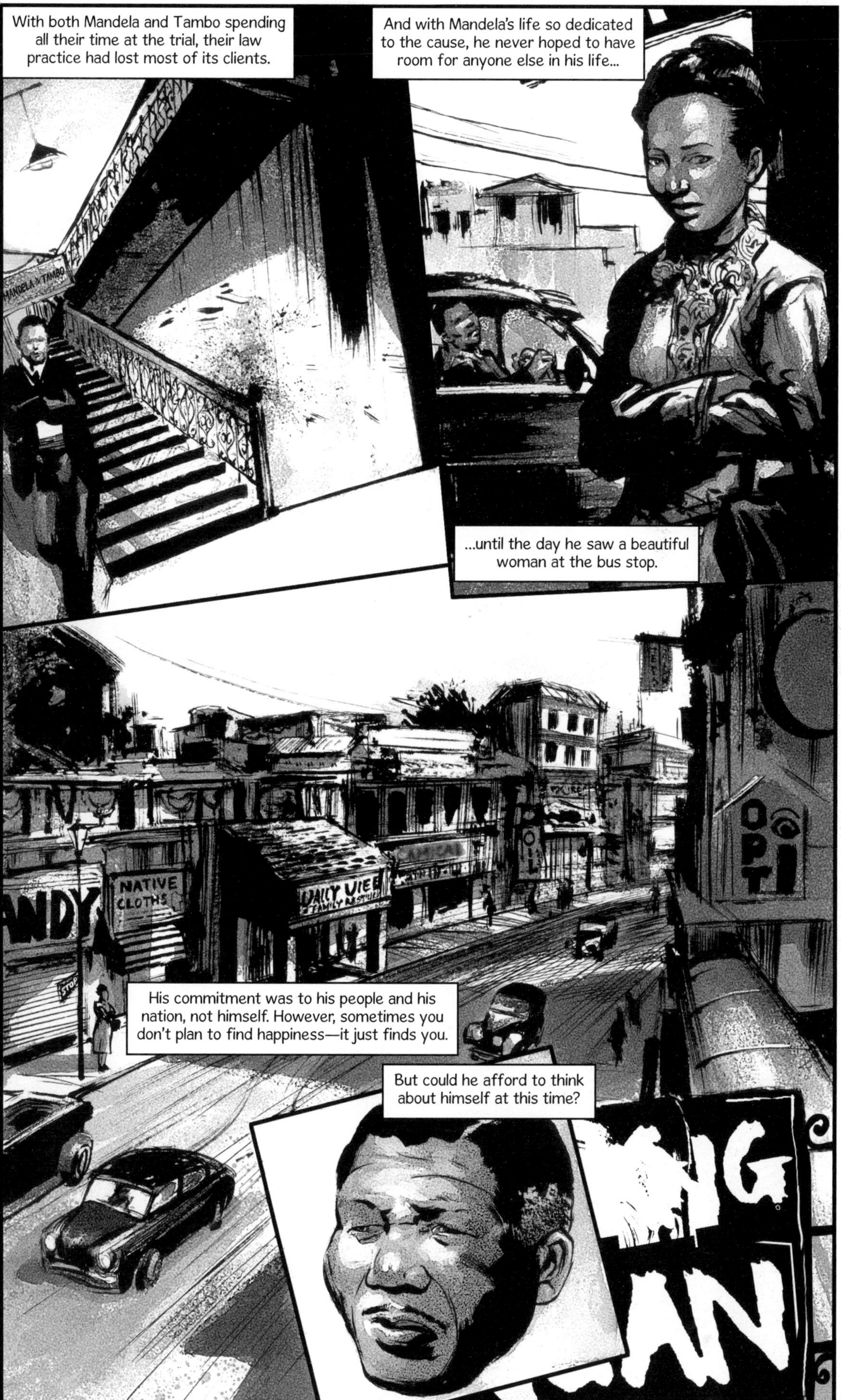
With both Mandela and Tambo spending all their time at the trial, their law practice had lost most of its clients.
MANDELA & TAMBO
And with Mandela's life so dedicated to the cause, he never hoped to have room for anyone else in his life...
...until the day he saw a beautiful woman at the bus stop.
NATIVE CLOTHS
ANDY
DAILY VIEW
OPTI
STOP
His commitment was to his people and his nation, not himself. However, sometimes you don't plan to find happiness—it just finds you.
But could he afford to think about himself at this time?

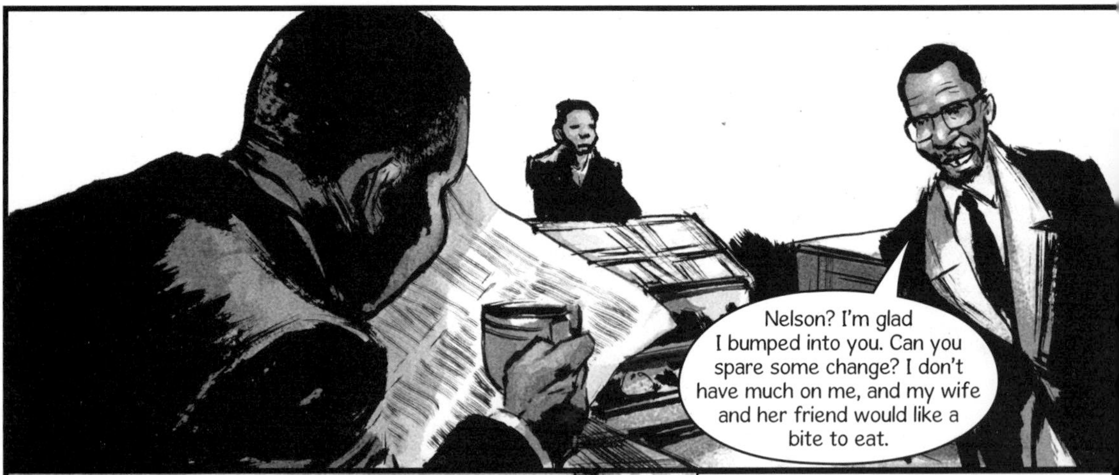
Nelson? I'm glad I bumped into you. Can you spare some change? I don't have much on me, and my wife and her friend would like a bite to eat.

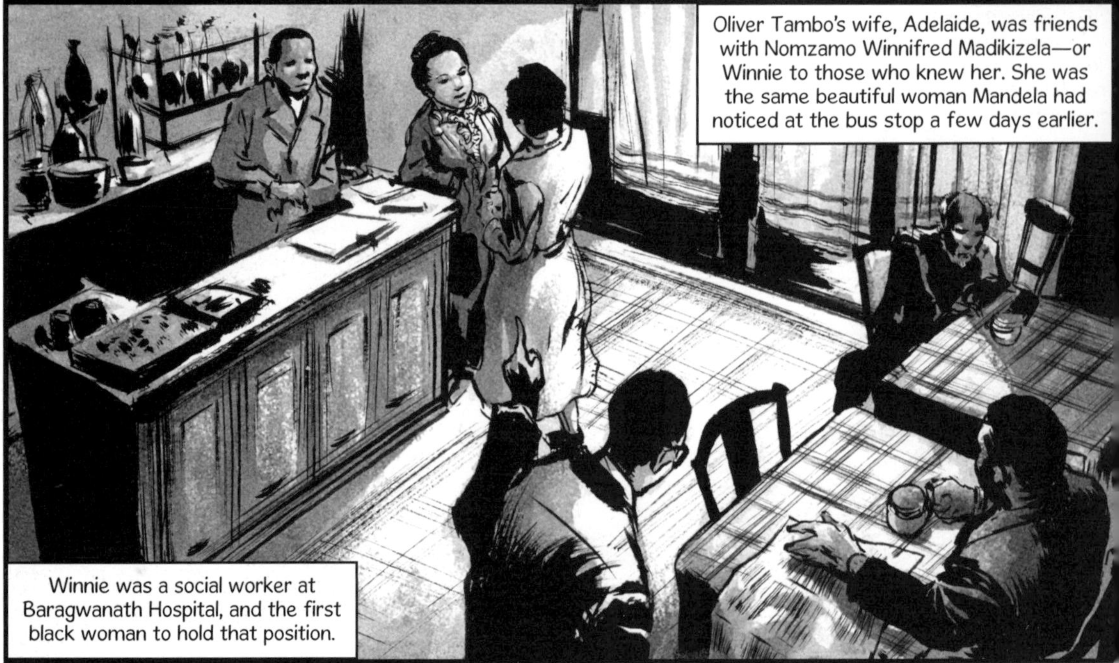
Oliver Tambo's wife, Adelaide, was friends with Nomzamo Winnifred Madikizela—or Winnie to those who knew her. She was the same beautiful woman Mandela had noticed at the bus stop a few days earlier.
Winnie was a social worker at Baragwanath Hospital, and the first black woman to hold that position.

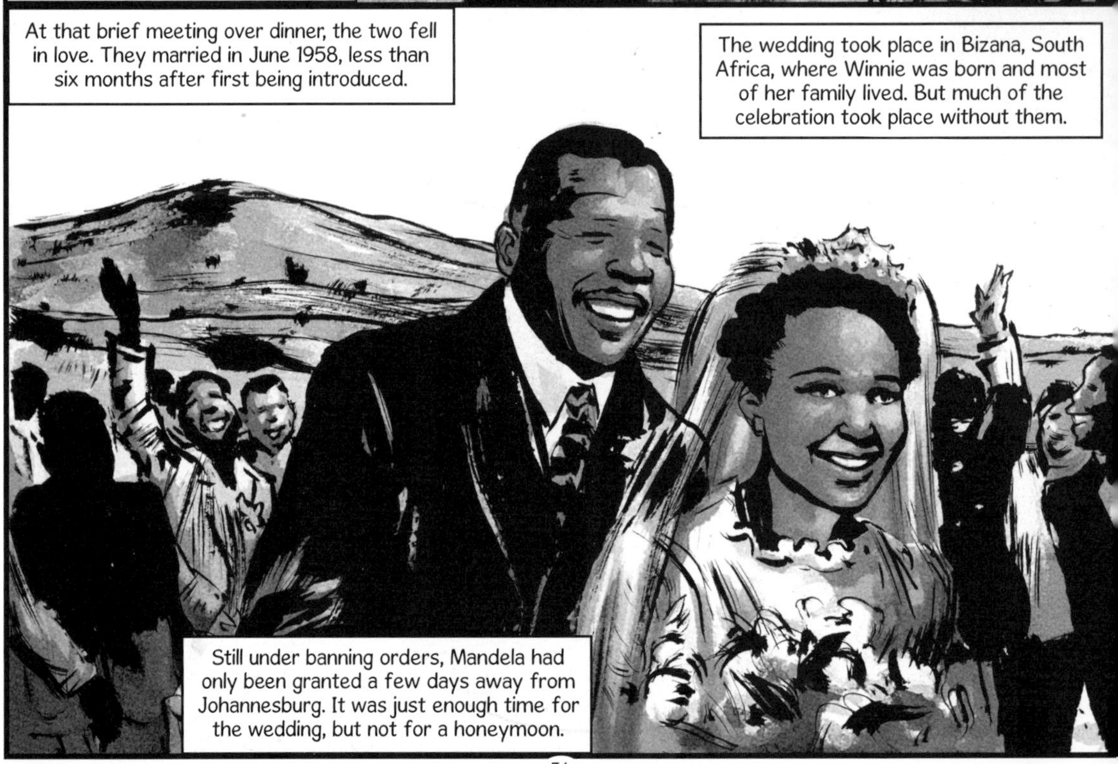
At that brief meeting over dinner, the two fell in love. They married in June 1958, less than six months after first being introduced.
The wedding took place in Bizana, South Africa, where Winnie was born and most of her family lived. But much of the celebration took place without them.
Still under banning orders, Mandela had only been granted a few days away from Johannesburg. It was just enough time for the wedding, but not for a honeymoon.

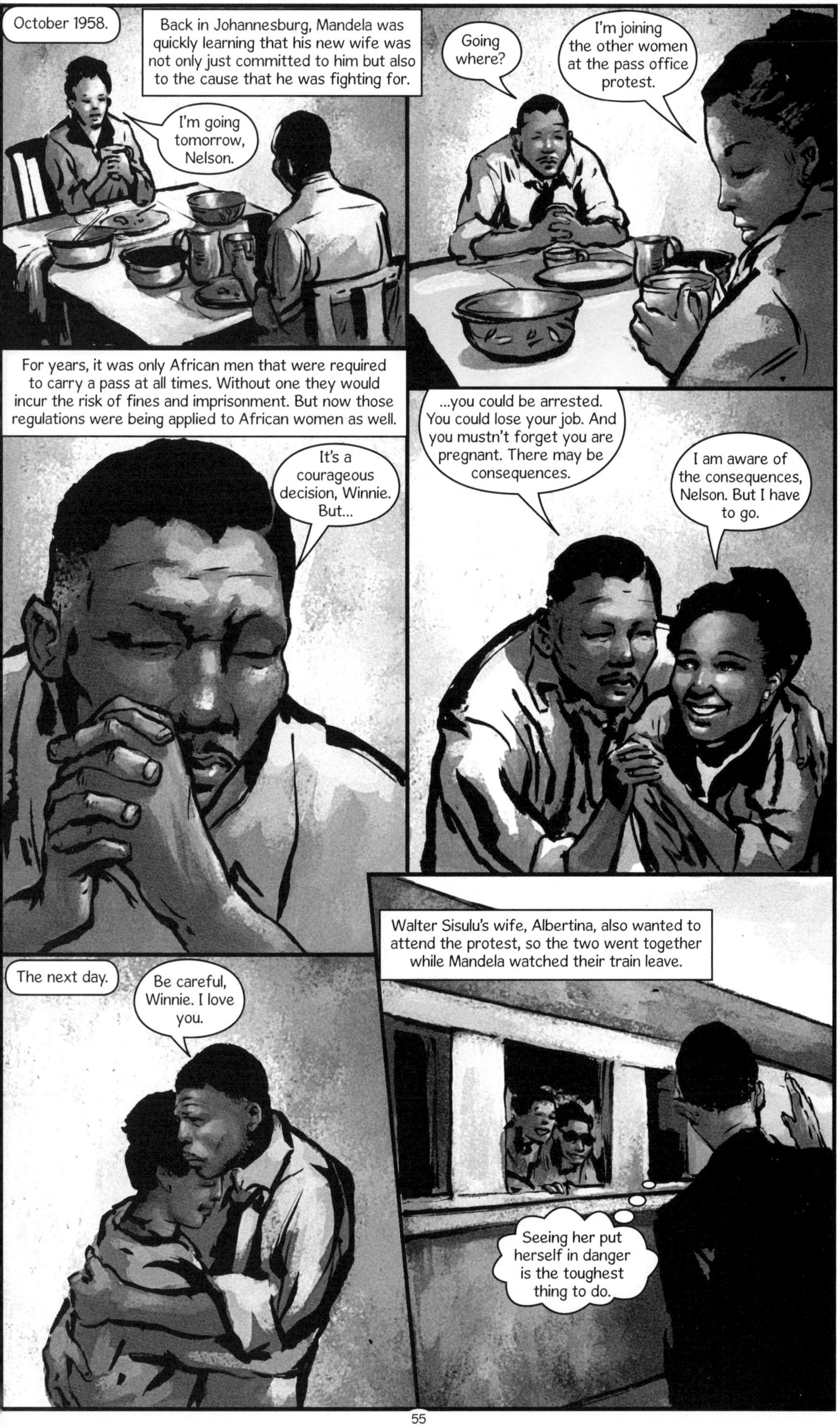
October 1958.
Back in Johannesburg, Mandela was quickly learning that his new wife was not only just committed to him but also to the cause that he was fighting for.
I'm going tomorrow, Nelson.
Going where?
I'm joining the other women at the pass office protest.
For years, it was only African men that were required to carry a pass at all times. Without one they would incur the risk of fines and imprisonment. But now those regulations were being applied to African women as well.
It's a courageous decision, Winnie. But...
...you could be arrested. You could lose your job. And you mustn't forget you are pregnant. There may be consequences.
I am aware of the consequences, Nelson. But I have to go.
The next day.
Be careful, Winnie. I love you.
Walter Sisulu's wife, Albertina, also wanted to attend the protest, so the two went together while Mandela watched their train leave.
Seeing her put herself in danger is the toughest thing to do.

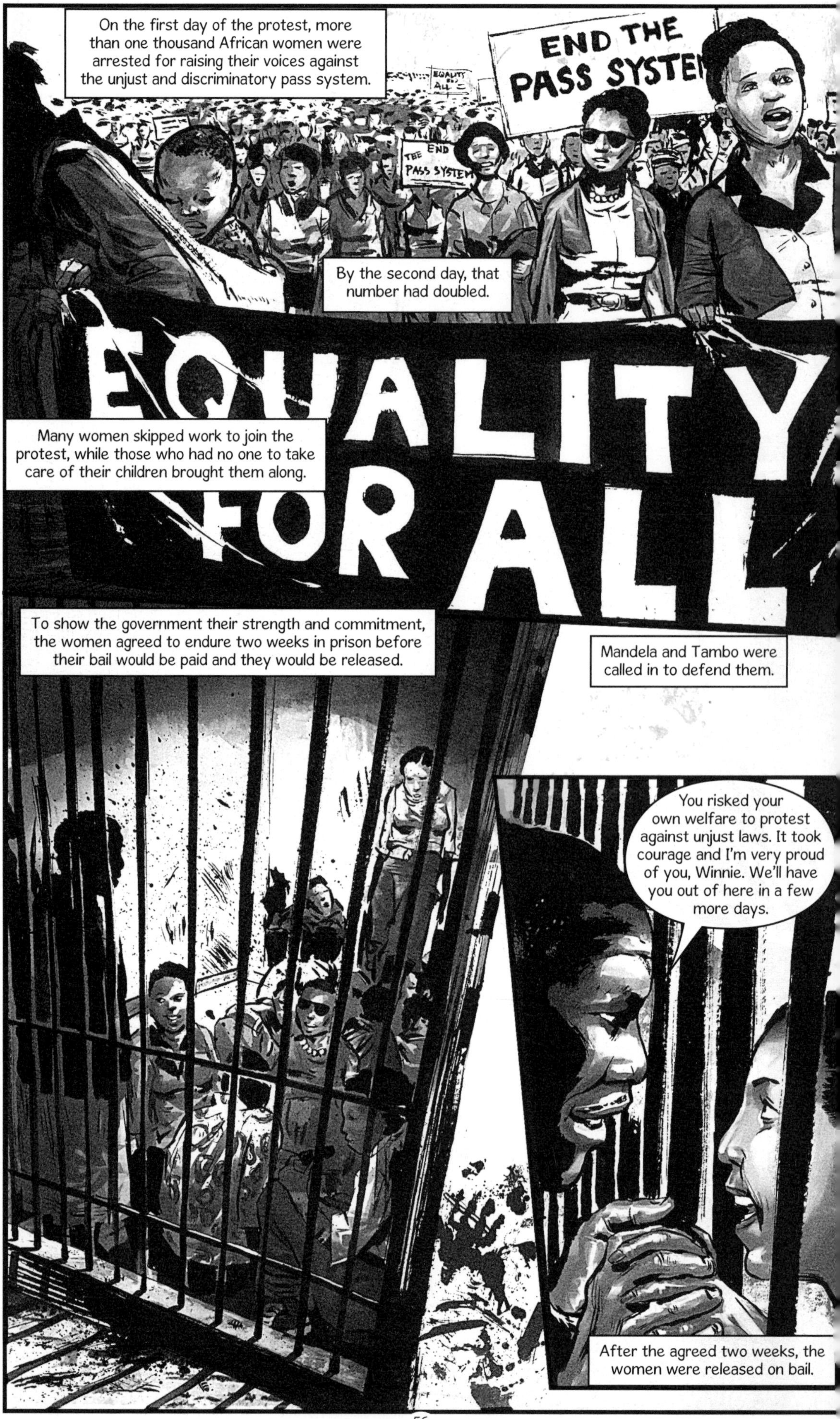
On the first day of the protest, more than one thousand African women were arrested for raising their voices against the unjust and discriminatory pass system.
END THE PASS SYSTEM
END THE PASS SYSTEM
By the second day, that number had doubled.
EQUALITY FOR ALL
Many women skipped work to join the protest, while those who had no one to take care of their children brought them along.
To show the government their strength and commitment, the women agreed to endure two weeks in prison before their bail would be paid and they would be released.
Mandela and Tambo were called in to defend them.
You risked your own welfare to protest against unjust laws. It took courage and I'm very proud of you, Winnie. We'll have you out of here in a few more days.
After the agreed two weeks, the women were released on bail.

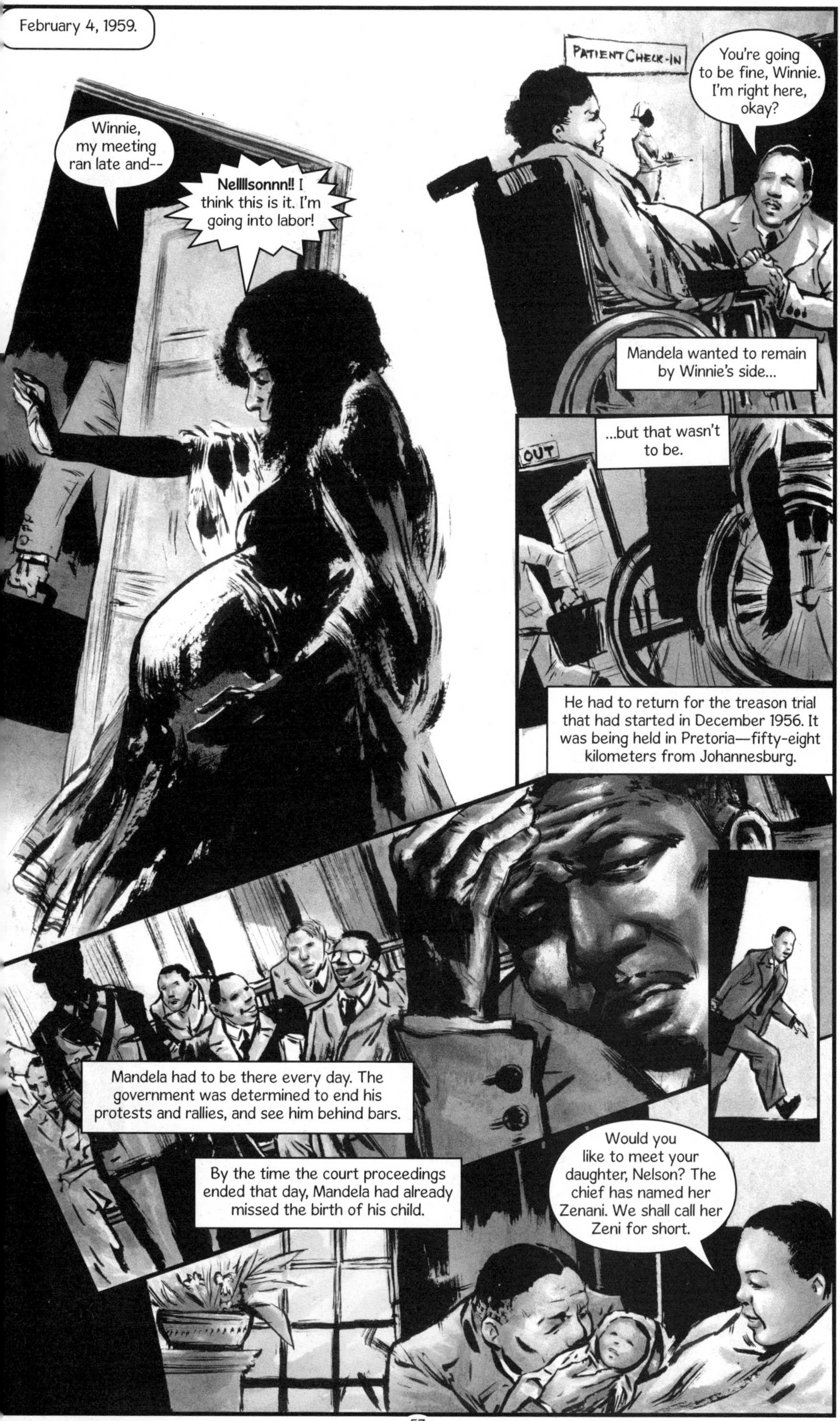

February 4, 1959.
Winnie, my meeting ran late and--
Nellllsonnn!! I think this is it. I'm going into labor!
PATIENT CHECK-IN
You're going to be fine, Winnie. I'm right here, okay?
Mandela wanted to remain by Winnie's side...
OUT
...but that wasn't to be.
He had to return for the treason trial that had started in December 1956. It was being held in Pretoria—fifty-eight kilometers from Johannesburg.
Mandela had to be there every day. The government was determined to end his protests and rallies, and see him behind bars.
By the time the court proceedings ended that day, Mandela had already missed the birth of his child.
Would you like to meet your daughter, Nelson? The chief has named her Zenani. We shall call her Zeni for short.

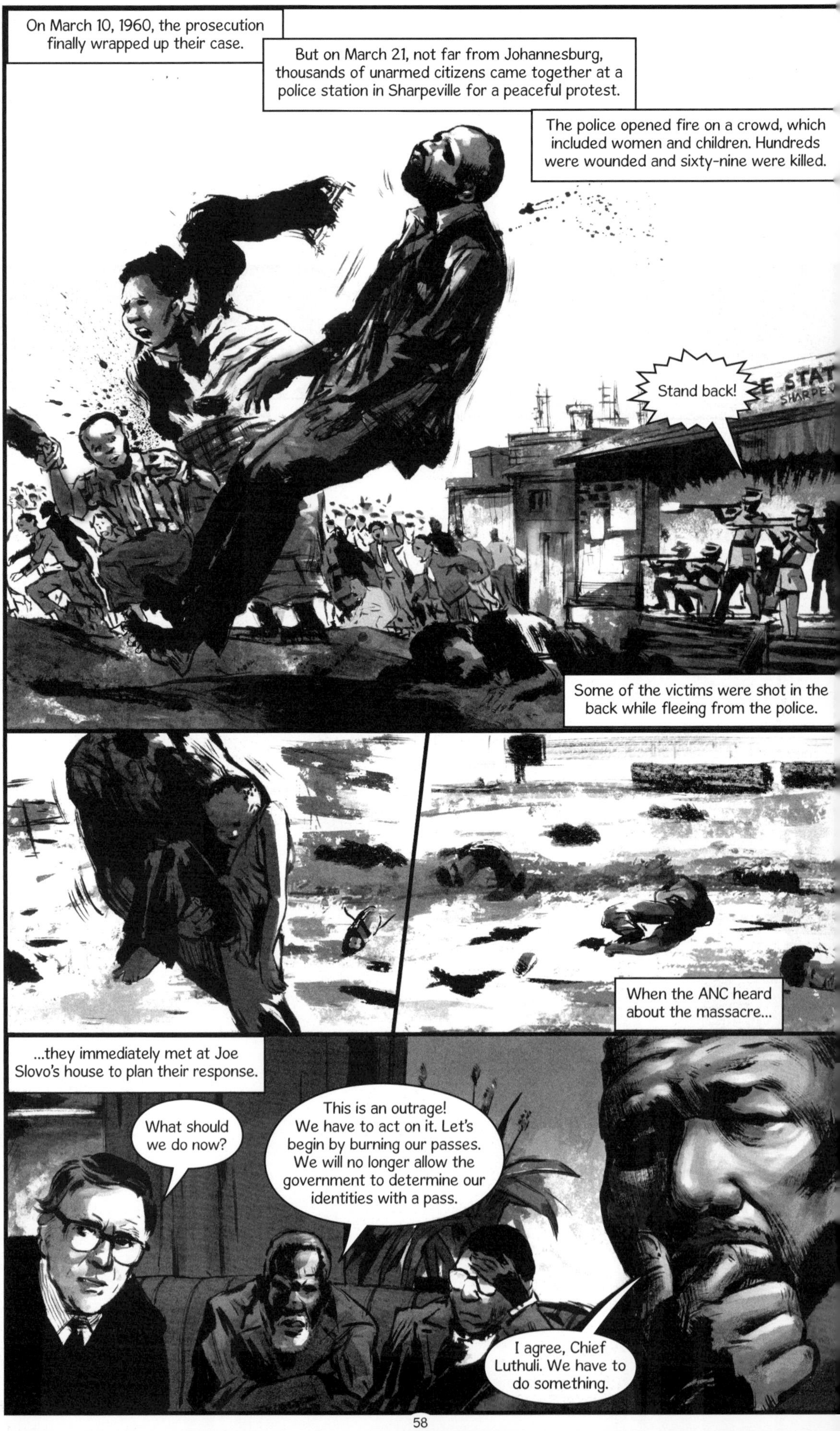
On March 10, 1960, the prosecution finally wrapped up their case.
But on March 21, not far from Johannesburg, thousands of unarmed citizens came together at a police station in Sharpeville for a peaceful protest.
The police opened fire on a crowd, which included women and children. Hundreds were wounded and sixty-nine were killed.
Stand back!
Some of the victims were shot in the back while fleeing from the police.
When the ANC heard about the massacre...
...they immediately met at Joe Slovo's house to plan their response.
What should we do now?
This is an outrage! We have to act on it. Let's begin by burning our passes. We will no longer allow the government to determine our identities with a pass.
I agree, Chief Luthuli. We have to do something.

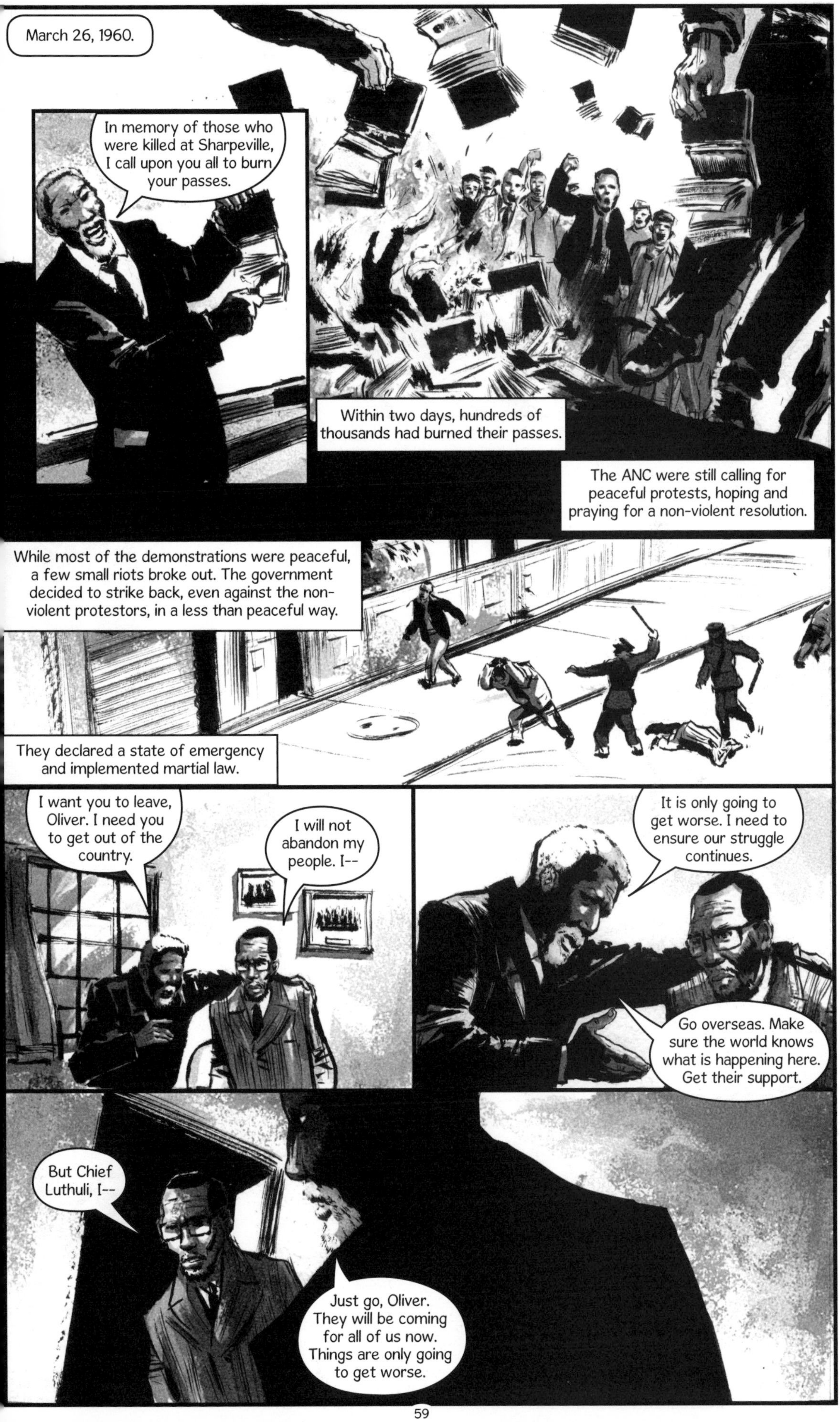

March 26, 1960.
In memory of those who were killed at Sharpeville, I call upon you all to burn your passes.
Within two days, hundreds of thousands had burned their passes.
The ANC were still calling for peaceful protests, hoping and praying for a non-violent resolution.
While most of the demonstrations were peaceful, a few small riots broke out. The government decided to strike back, even against the non-violent protestors, in a less than peaceful way.
They declared a state of emergency and implemented martial law.
I want you to leave, Oliver. I need you to get out of the country.
I will not abandon my people. I--
It is only going to get worse. I need to ensure our struggle continues.
Go overseas. Make sure the world knows what is happening here. Get their support.
But Chief Luthuli, I--
Just go, Oliver. They will be coming for all of us now. Things are only going to get worse.

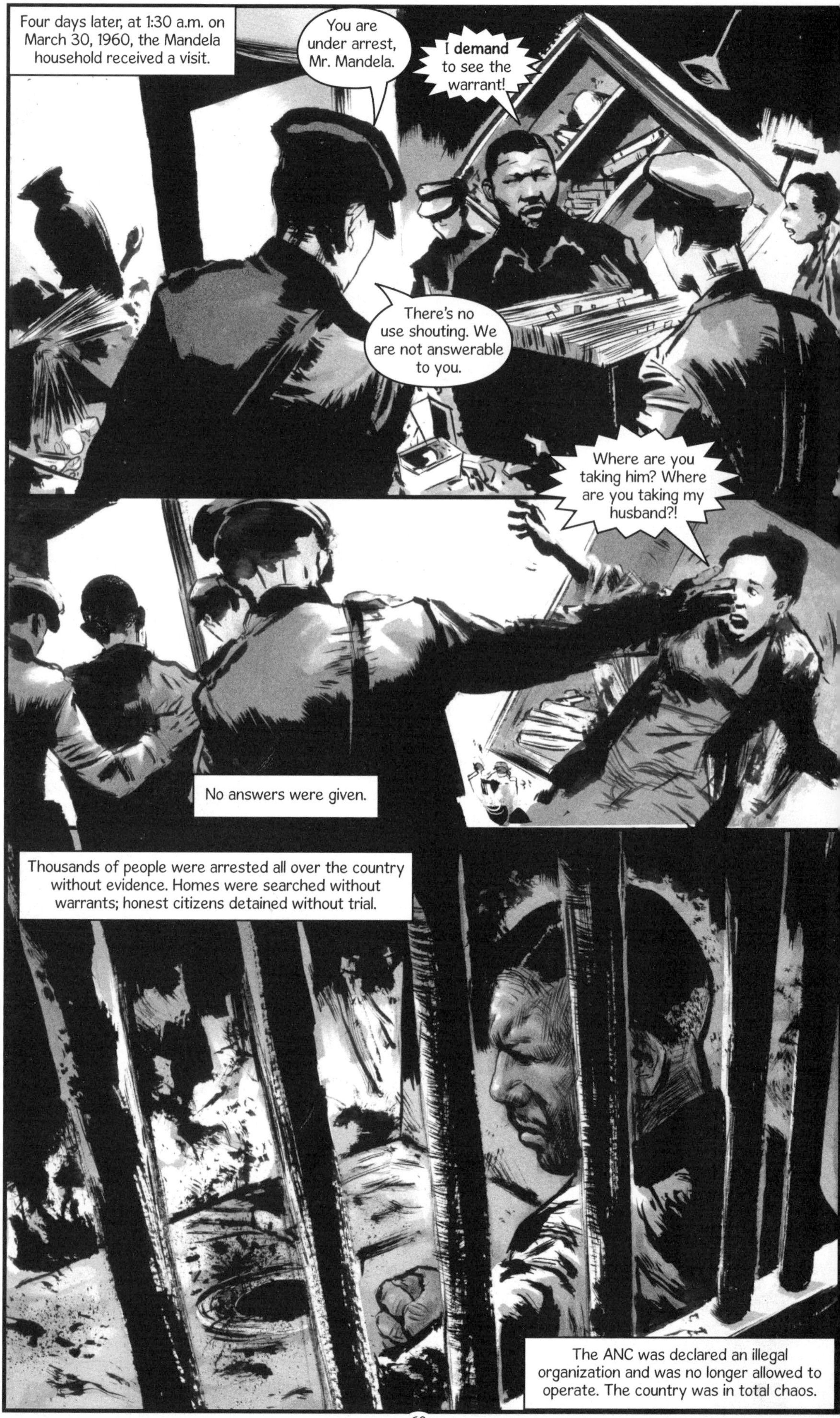
Four days later, at 1:30 a.m. on March 30, 1960, the Mandela household received a visit.
You are under arrest, Mr. Mandela.
I **demand** to see the warrant!
There's no use shouting. We are not answerable to you.
Where are you taking him? Where are you taking my husband?!
No answers were given.
Thousands of people were arrested all over the country without evidence. Homes were searched without warrants; honest citizens detained without trial.
The ANC was declared an illegal organization and was no longer allowed to operate. The country was in total chaos.

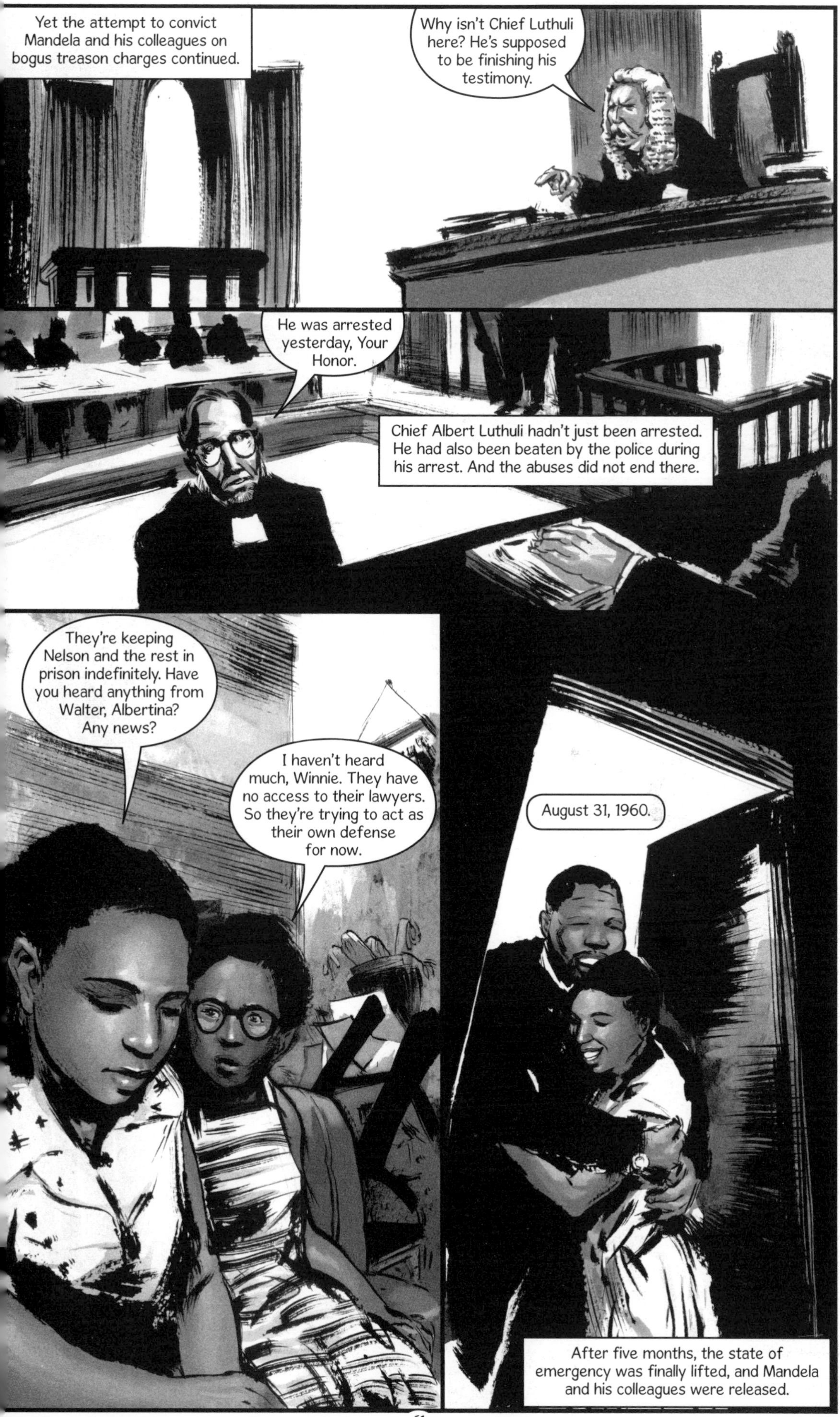

Yet the attempt to convict Mandela and his colleagues on bogus treason charges continued.
Why isn't Chief Luthuli here? He's supposed to be finishing his testimony.
He was arrested yesterday, Your Honor.
Chief Albert Luthuli hadn't just been arrested. He had also been beaten by the police during his arrest. And the abuses did not end there.
They're keeping Nelson and the rest in prison indefinitely. Have you heard anything from Walter, Albertina? Any news?
I haven't heard much, Winnie. They have no access to their lawyers. So they're trying to act as their own defense for now.
August 31, 1960.
After five months, the state of emergency was finally lifted, and Mandela and his colleagues were released.

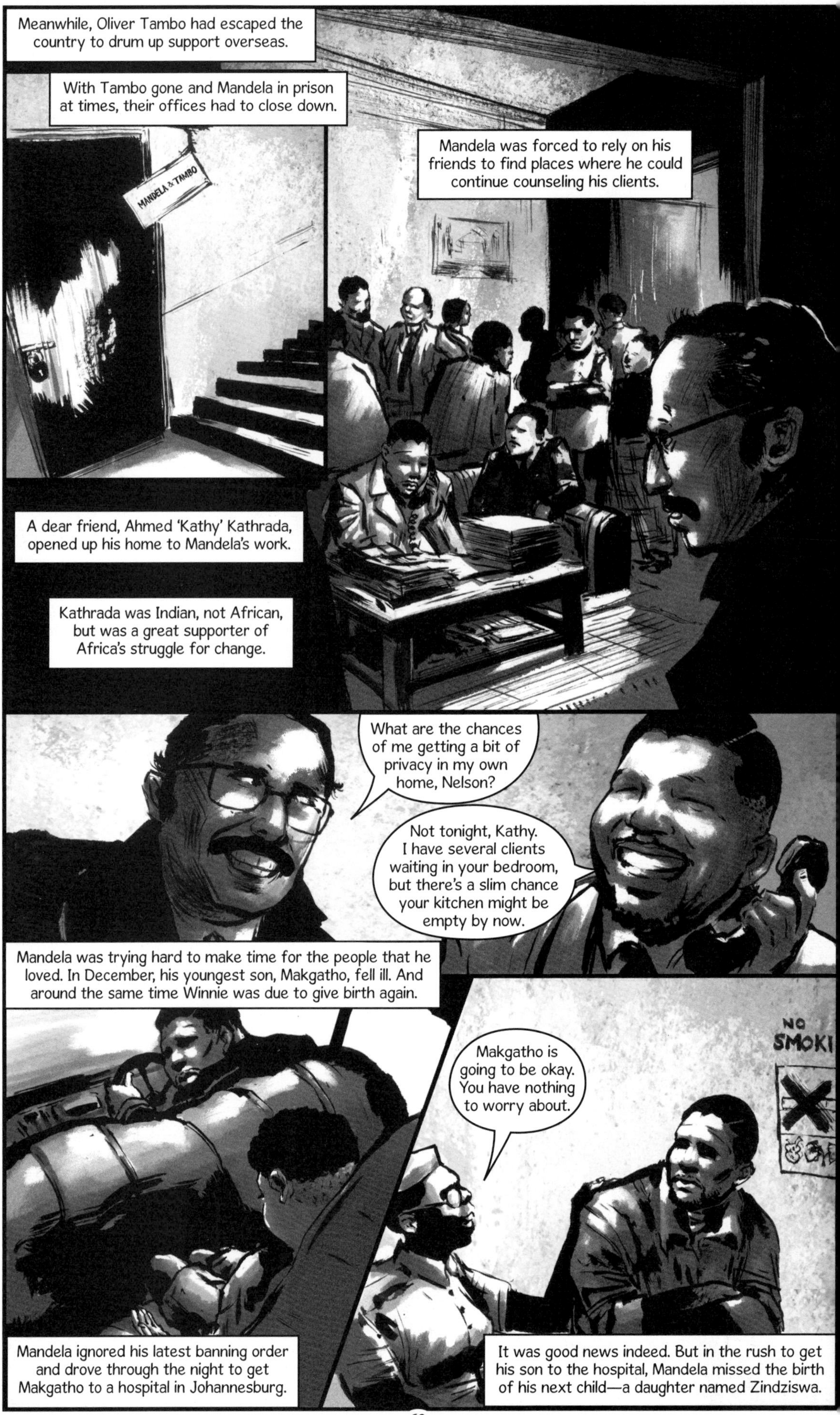
Meanwhile, Oliver Tambo had escaped the country to drum up support overseas.
With Tambo gone and Mandela in prison at times, their offices had to close down.
MANDELA & TAMBO
Mandela was forced to rely on his friends to find places where he could continue counseling his clients.
A dear friend, Ahmed 'Kathy' Kathrada, opened up his home to Mandela's work.
Kathrada was Indian, not African, but was a great supporter of Africa's struggle for change.
What are the chances of me getting a bit of privacy in my own home, Nelson?
Not tonight, Kathy. I have several clients waiting in your bedroom, but there's a slim chance your kitchen might be empty by now.
Mandela was trying hard to make time for the people that he loved. In December, his youngest son, Makgatho, fell ill. And around the same time Winnie was due to give birth again.
Makgatho is going to be okay. You have nothing to worry about.
NO SMOKI
Mandela ignored his latest banning order and drove through the night to get Makgatho to a hospital in Johannesburg.
It was good news indeed. But in the rush to get his son to the hospital, Mandela missed the birth of his next child—a daughter named Zindziswa.

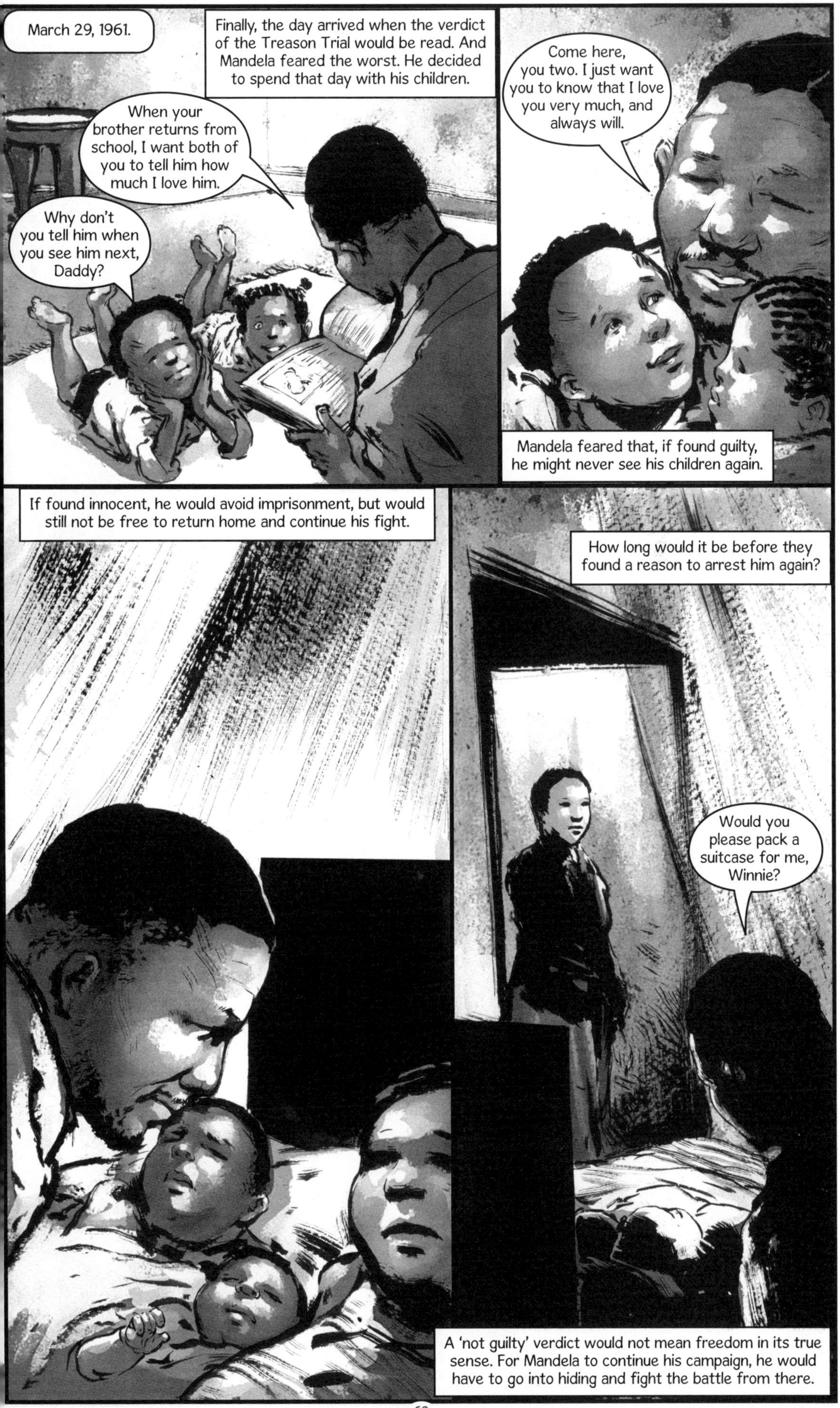
March 29, 1961.
Finally, the day arrived when the verdict of the Treason Trial would be read. And Mandela feared the worst. He decided to spend that day with his children.
When your brother returns from school, I want both of you to tell him how much I love him.
Why don't you tell him when you see him next, Daddy?
Come here, you two. I just want you to know that I love you very much, and always will.
Mandela feared that, if found guilty, he might never see his children again.
If found innocent, he would avoid imprisonment, but would still not be free to return home and continue his fight.
How long would it be before they found a reason to arrest him again?
Would you please pack a suitcase for me, Winnie?
A 'not guilty' verdict would not mean freedom in its true sense. For Mandela to continue his campaign, he would have to go into hiding and fight the battle from there.

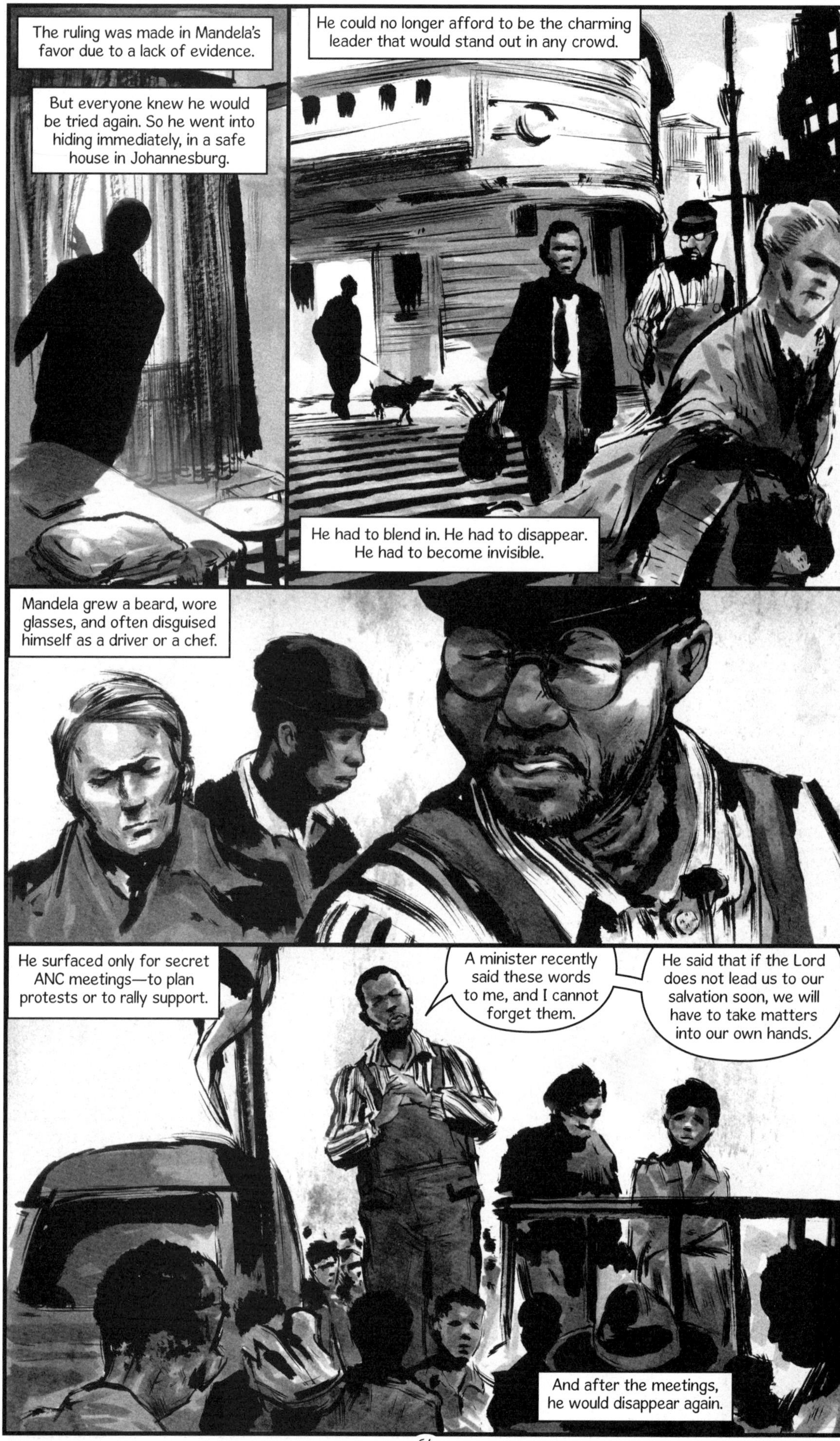
The ruling was made in Mandela's favor due to a lack of evidence.
But everyone knew he would be tried again. So he went into hiding immediately, in a safe house in Johannesburg.
He could no longer afford to be the charming leader that would stand out in any crowd.
He had to blend in. He had to disappear. He had to become invisible.
Mandela grew a beard, wore glasses, and often disguised himself as a driver or a chef.
He surfaced only for secret ANC meetings—to plan protests or to rally support.
A minister recently said these words to me, and I cannot forget them.
He said that if the Lord does not lead us to our salvation soon, we will have to take matters into our own hands.
And after the meetings, he would disappear again.

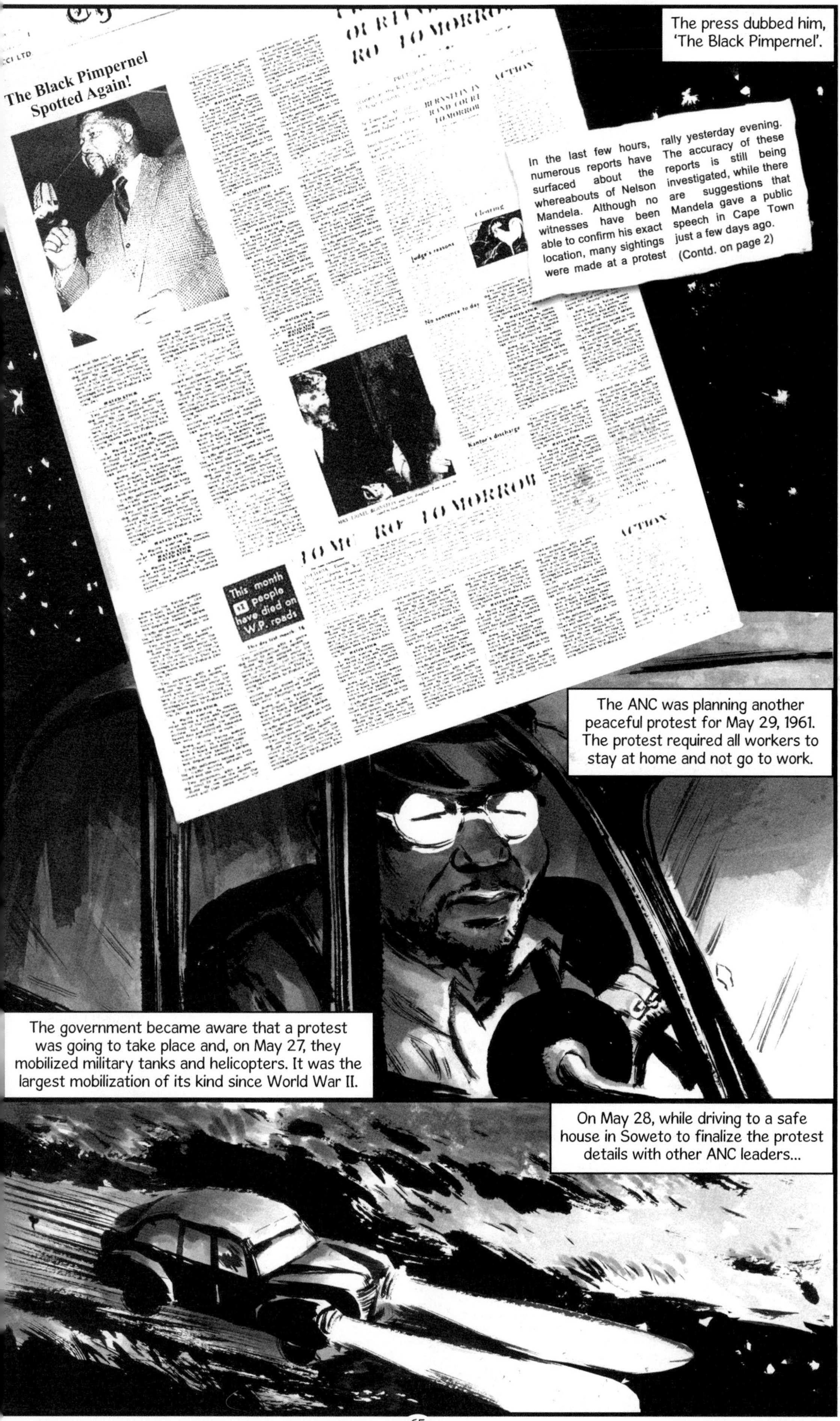
The press dubbed him, 'The Black Pimpernel'.
The Black Pimpernel Spotted Again!
In the last few hours, numerous reports have surfaced about the whereabouts of Nelson Mandela. Although no witnesses have been able to confirm his exact location, many sightings were made at a protest rally yesterday evening. The accuracy of these reports is still being investigated, while there are suggestions that Mandela gave a public speech in Cape Town just a few days ago. (Contd. on page 2)
This month 11 people have died on W.P. roads
The ANC was planning another peaceful protest for May 29, 1961. The protest required all workers to stay at home and not go to work.
The government became aware that a protest was going to take place and, on May 27, they mobilized military tanks and helicopters. It was the largest mobilization of its kind since World War II.
On May 28, while driving to a safe house in Soweto to finalize the protest details with other ANC leaders...

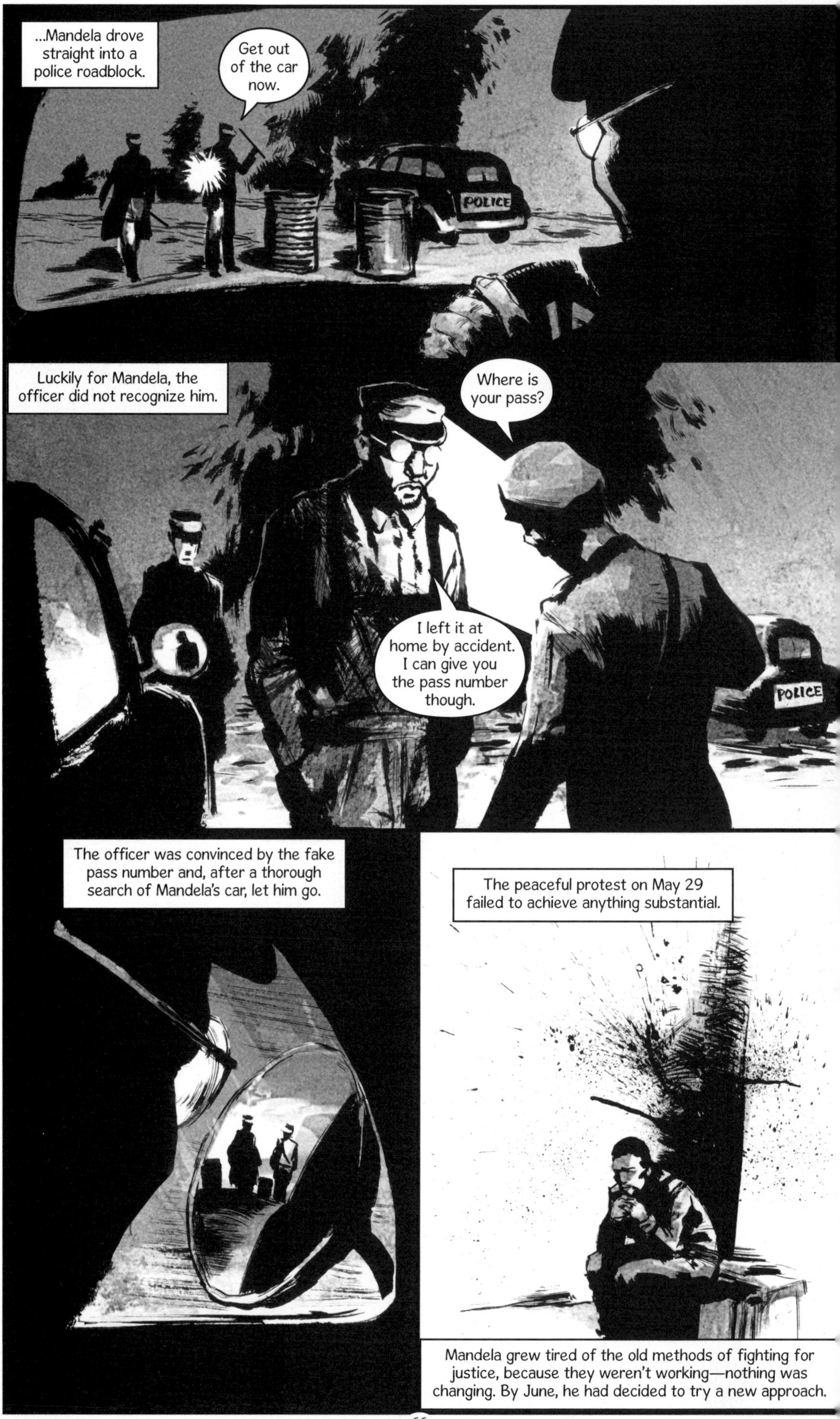

...Mandela drove straight into a police roadblock.
Get out of the car now.
POLICE
Luckily for Mandela, the officer did not recognize him.
Where is your pass?
I left it at home by accident. I can give you the pass number though.
POLICE
The officer was convinced by the fake pass number and, after a thorough search of Mandela's car, let him go.
The peaceful protest on May 29 failed to achieve anything substantial.
Mandela grew tired of the old methods of fighting for justice, because they weren't working—nothing was changing. By June, he had decided to try a new approach.

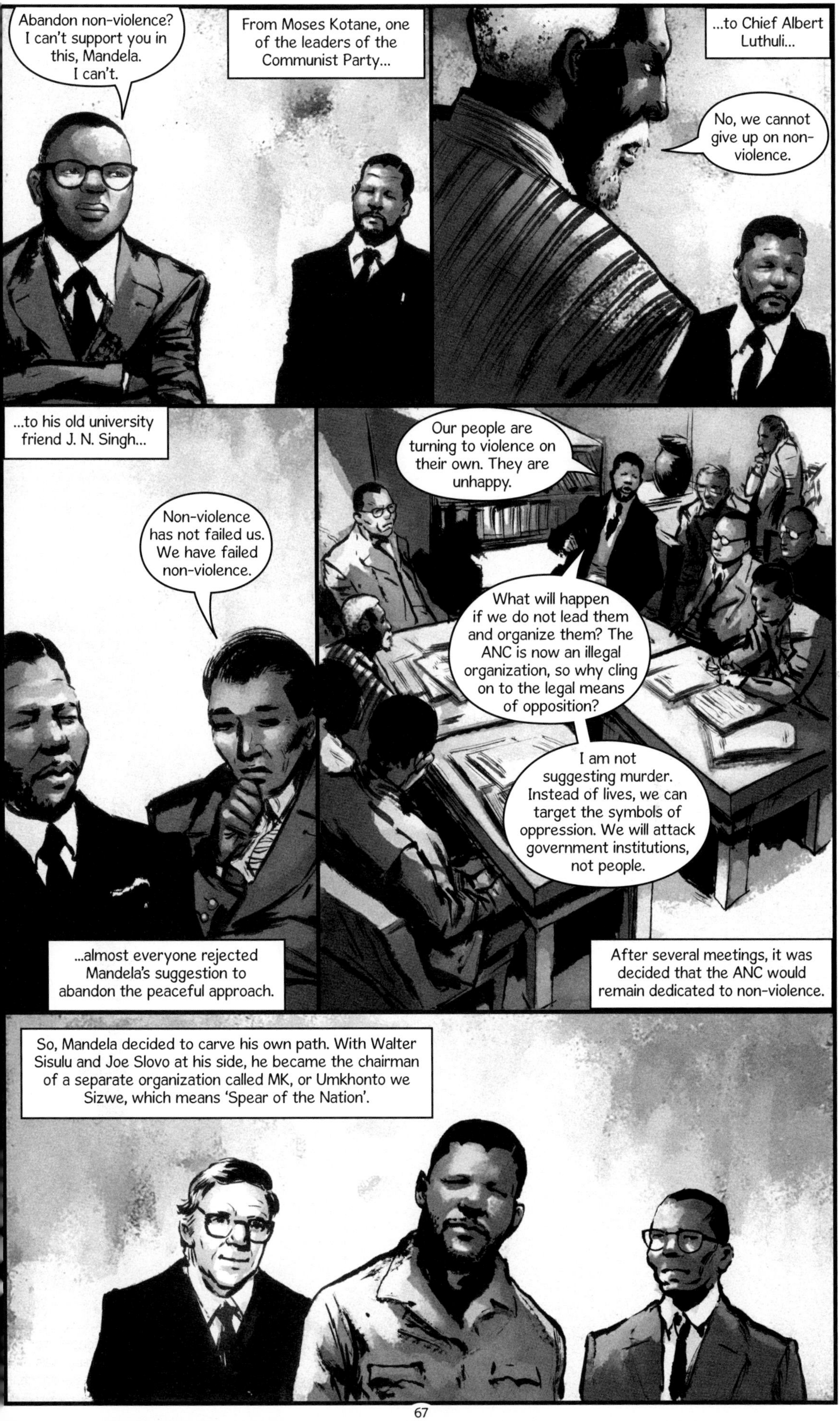

Abandon non-violence? I can't support you in this, Mandela. I can't.
From Moses Kotane, one of the leaders of the Communist Party...
...to Chief Albert Luthuli...
No, we cannot give up on non-violence.
...to his old university friend J. N. Singh...
Non-violence has not failed us. We have failed non-violence.
...almost everyone rejected Mandela's suggestion to abandon the peaceful approach.
Our people are turning to violence on their own. They are unhappy.
What will happen if we do not lead them and organize them? The ANC is now an illegal organization, so why cling on to the legal means of opposition?
I am not suggesting murder. Instead of lives, we can target the symbols of oppression. We will attack government institutions, not people.
After several meetings, it was decided that the ANC would remain dedicated to non-violence.
So, Mandela decided to carve his own path. With Walter Sisulu and Joe Slovo at his side, he became the chairman of a separate organization called MK, or Umkhonto we Sizwe, which means 'Spear of the Nation'.

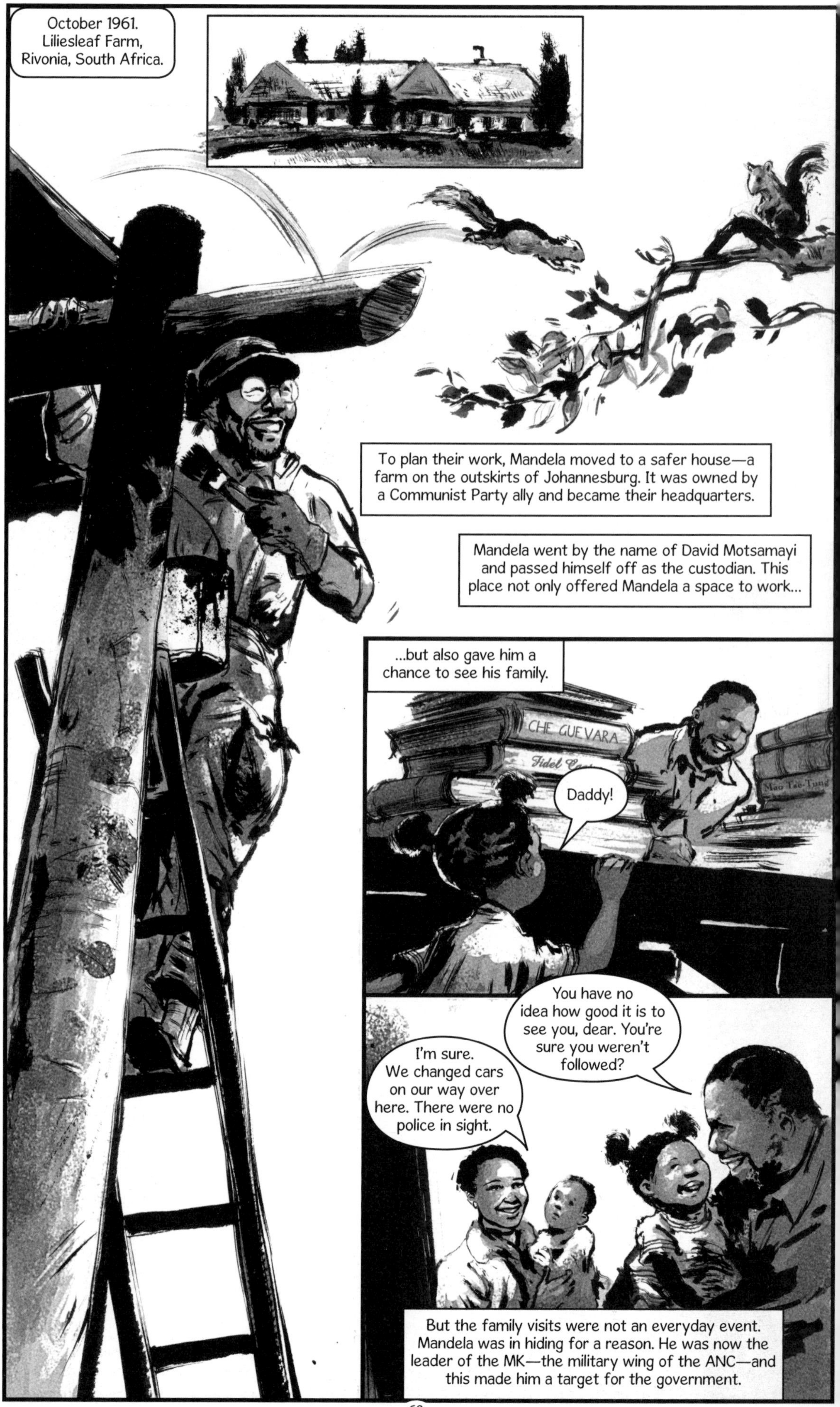
October 1961.
Liliesleaf Farm,
Rivonia, South Africa.
To plan their work, Mandela moved to a safer house—a farm on the outskirts of Johannesburg. It was owned by a Communist Party ally and became their headquarters.
Mandela went by the name of David Motsamayi and passed himself off as the custodian. This place not only offered Mandela a space to work...
...but also gave him a chance to see his family.
CHE GUEVARA
Mao Tse-Tung
Daddy!
You have no idea how good it is to see you, dear. You're sure you weren't followed?
I'm sure. We changed cars on our way over here. There were no police in sight.
But the family visits were not an everyday event. Mandela was in hiding for a reason. He was now the leader of the MK—the military wing of the ANC—and this made him a target for the government.

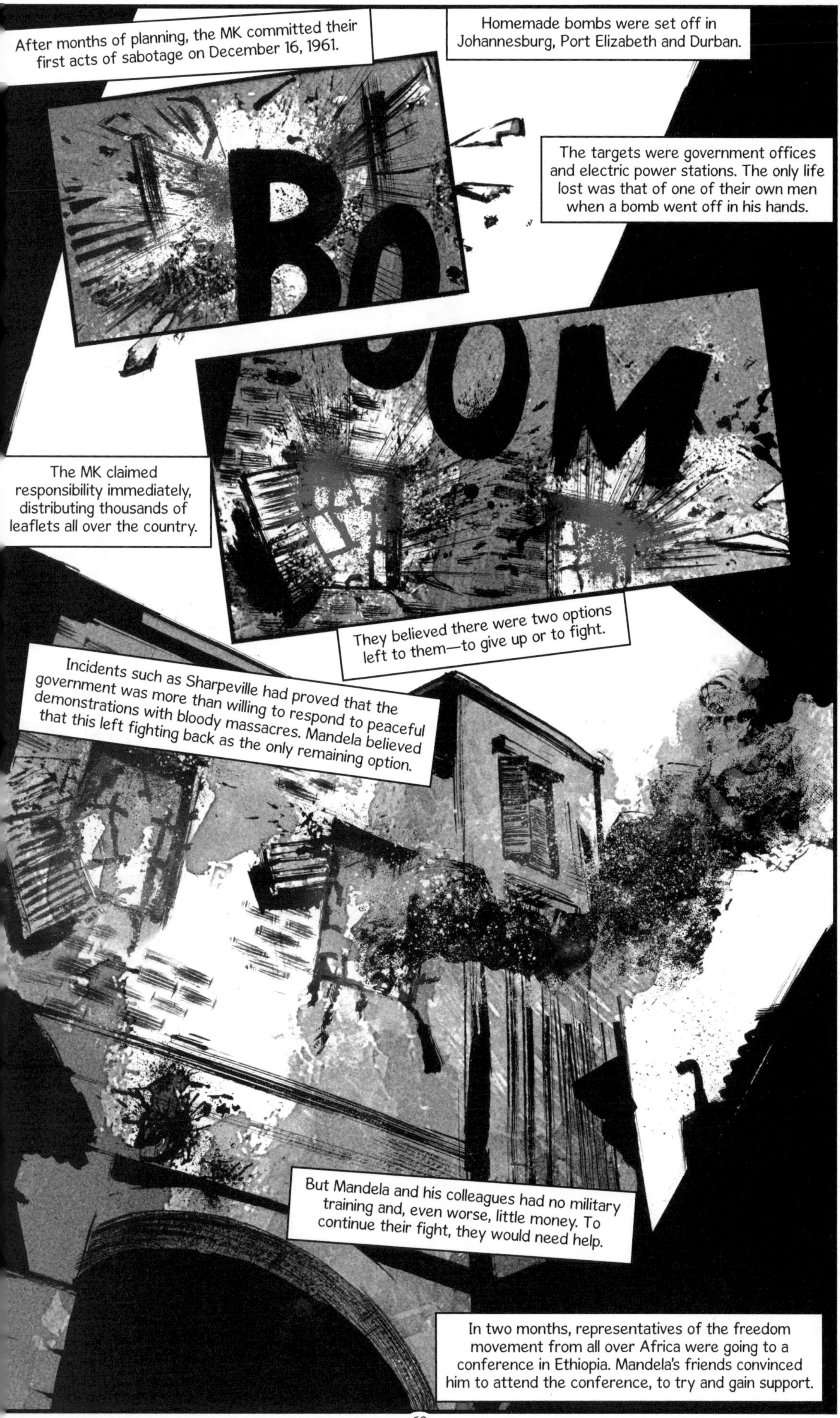
After months of planning, the MK committed their first acts of sabotage on December 16, 1961.
Homemade bombs were set off in Johannesburg, Port Elizabeth and Durban.
BOOM
The targets were government offices and electric power stations. The only life lost was that of one of their own men when a bomb went off in his hands.
The MK claimed responsibility immediately, distributing thousands of leaflets all over the country.
They believed there were two options left to them—to give up or to fight.
Incidents such as Sharpeville had proved that the government was more than willing to respond to peaceful demonstrations with bloody massacres. Mandela believed that this left fighting back as the only remaining option.
But Mandela and his colleagues had no military training and, even worse, little money. To continue their fight, they would need help.
In two months, representatives of the freedom movement from all over Africa were going to a conference in Ethiopia. Mandela's friends convinced him to attend the conference, to try and gain support.

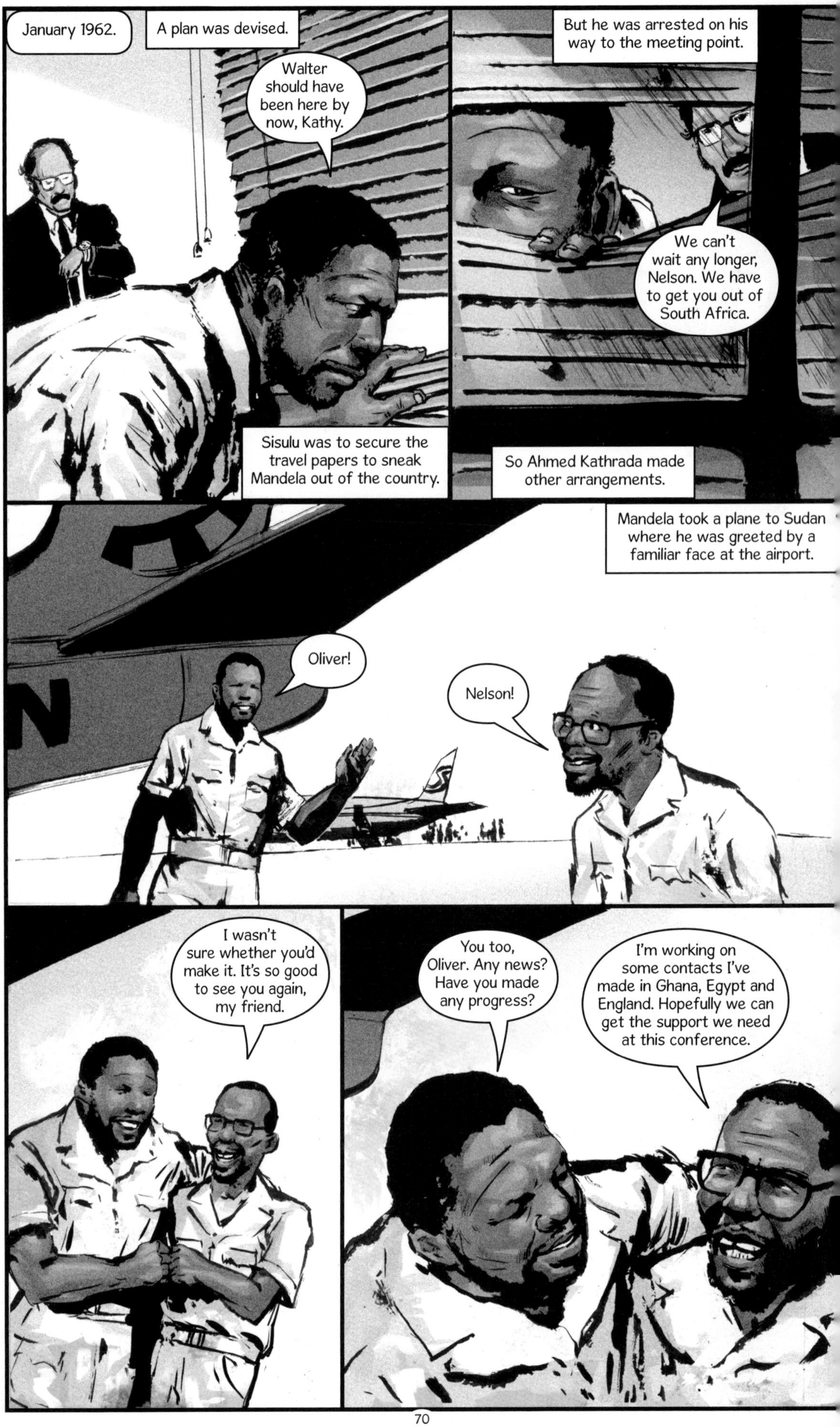

January 1962.
A plan was devised.
Walter should have been here by now, Kathy.
Sisulu was to secure the travel papers to sneak Mandela out of the country.
But he was arrested on his way to the meeting point.
We can't wait any longer, Nelson. We have to get you out of South Africa.
So Ahmed Kathrada made other arrangements.
Mandela took a plane to Sudan where he was greeted by a familiar face at the airport.
Oliver!
Nelson!
I wasn't sure whether you'd make it. It's so good to see you again, my friend.
You too, Oliver. Any news? Have you made any progress?
I'm working on some contacts I've made in Ghana, Egypt and England. Hopefully we can get the support we need at this conference.

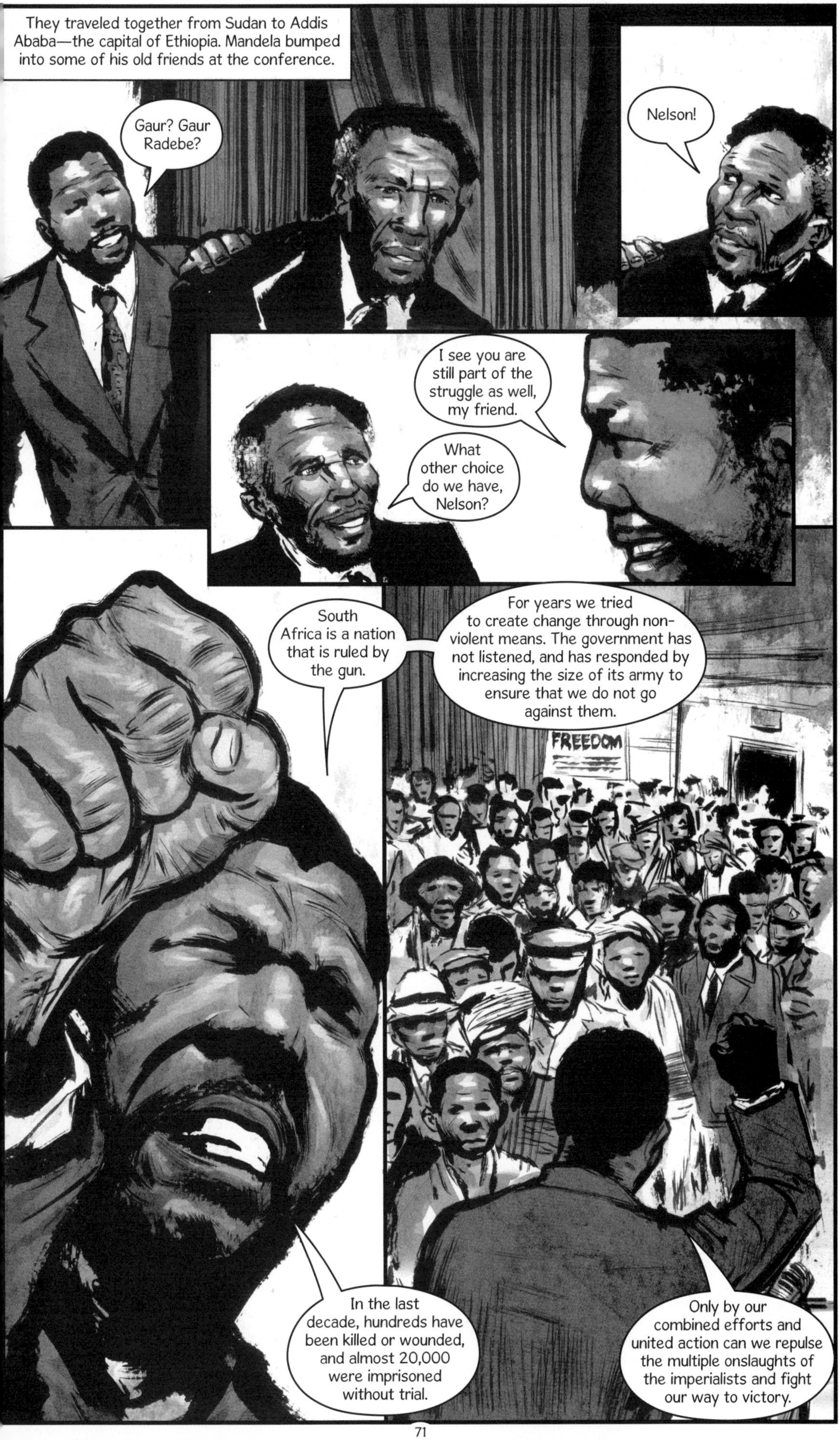
They traveled together from Sudan to Addis Ababa—the capital of Ethiopia. Mandela bumped into some of his old friends at the conference.
Gaur? Gaur Radebe?
Nelson!
I see you are still part of the struggle as well, my friend.
What other choice do we have, Nelson?
South Africa is a nation that is ruled by the gun.
For years we tried to create change through non-violent means. The government has not listened, and has responded by increasing the size of its army to ensure that we do not go against them.
FREEDOM
In the last decade, hundreds have been killed or wounded, and almost 20,000 were imprisoned without trial.
Only by our combined efforts and united action can we repulse the multiple onslaughts of the imperialists and fight our way to victory.

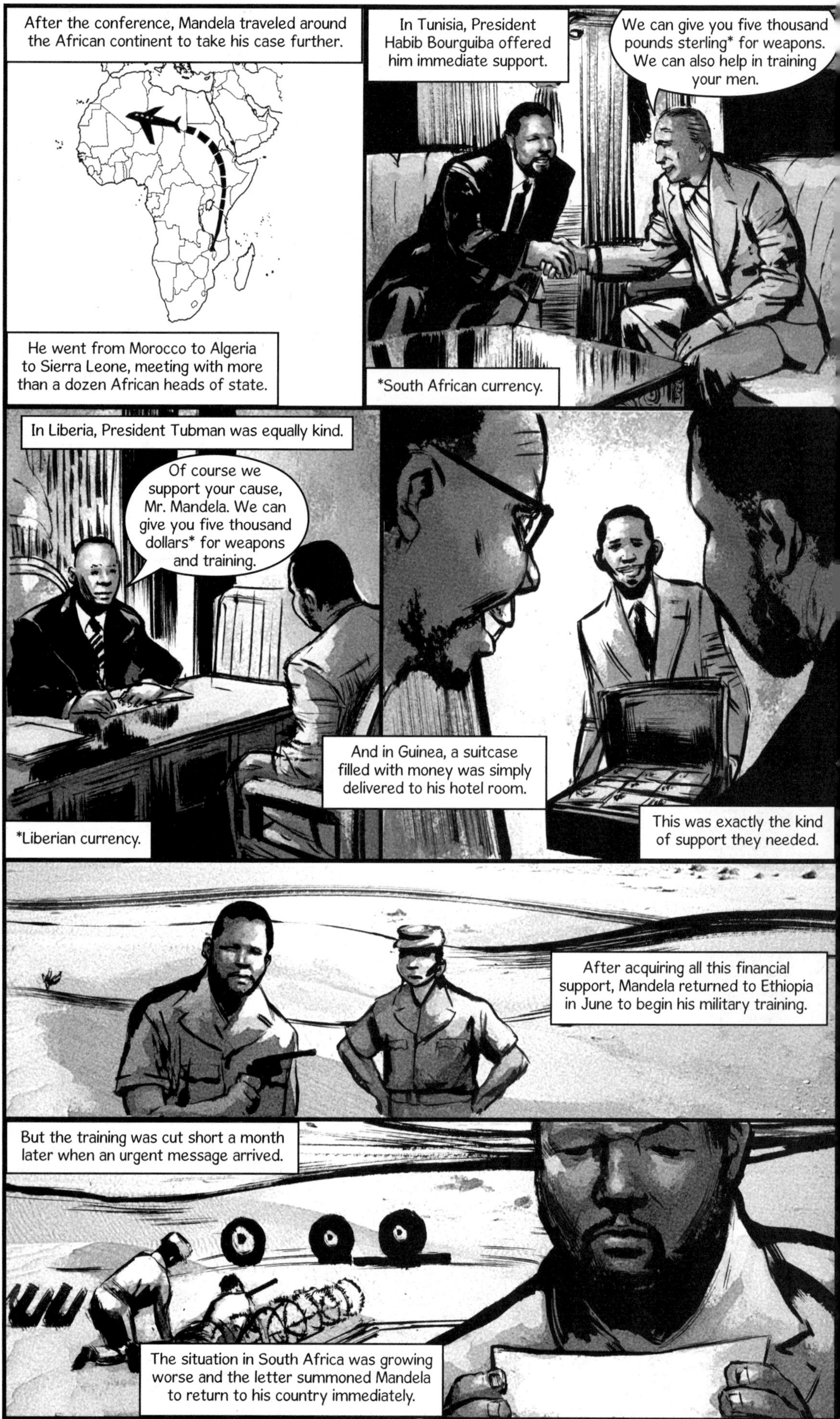
After the conference, Mandela traveled around the African continent to take his case further.
He went from Morocco to Algeria to Sierra Leone, meeting with more than a dozen African heads of state.
In Tunisia, President Habib Bourguiba offered him immediate support.
We can give you five thousand pounds sterling* for weapons. We can also help in training your men.
*South African currency.
In Liberia, President Tubman was equally kind.
Of course we support your cause, Mr. Mandela. We can give you five thousand dollars* for weapons and training.
*Liberian currency.
And in Guinea, a suitcase filled with money was simply delivered to his hotel room.
This was exactly the kind of support they needed.
After acquiring all this financial support, Mandela returned to Ethiopia in June to begin his military training.
But the training was cut short a month later when an urgent message arrived.
The situation in South Africa was growing worse and the letter summoned Mandela to return to his country immediately.

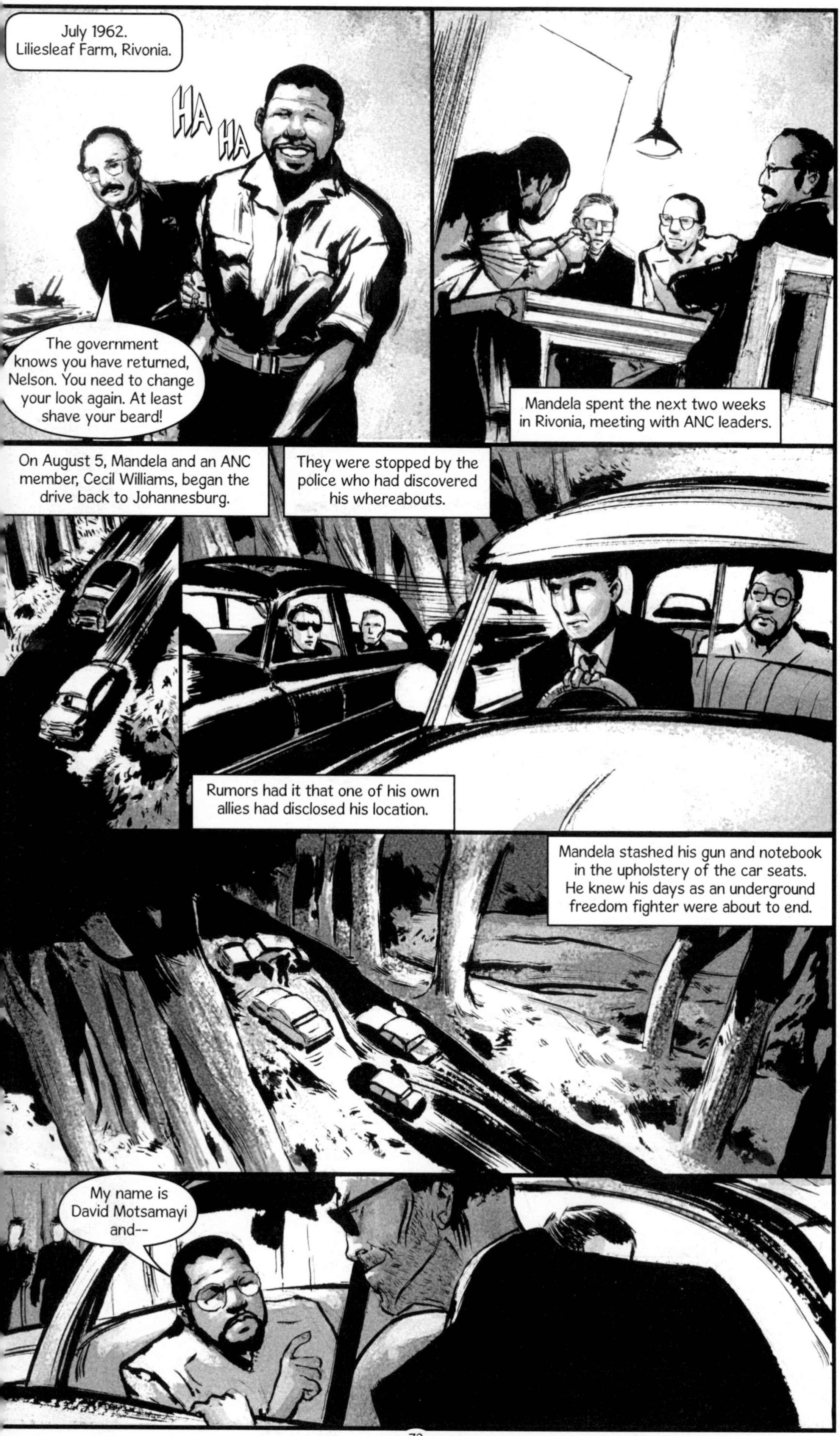
July 1962.
Liliesleaf Farm, Rivonia.
HA HA
The government knows you have returned, Nelson. You need to change your look again. At least shave your beard!
Mandela spent the next two weeks in Rivonia, meeting with ANC leaders.
On August 5, Mandela and an ANC member, Cecil Williams, began the drive back to Johannesburg.
They were stopped by the police who had discovered his whereabouts.
Rumors had it that one of his own allies had disclosed his location.
Mandela stashed his gun and notebook in the upholstery of the car seats. He knew his days as an underground freedom fighter were about to end.
My name is David Motsamayi and--

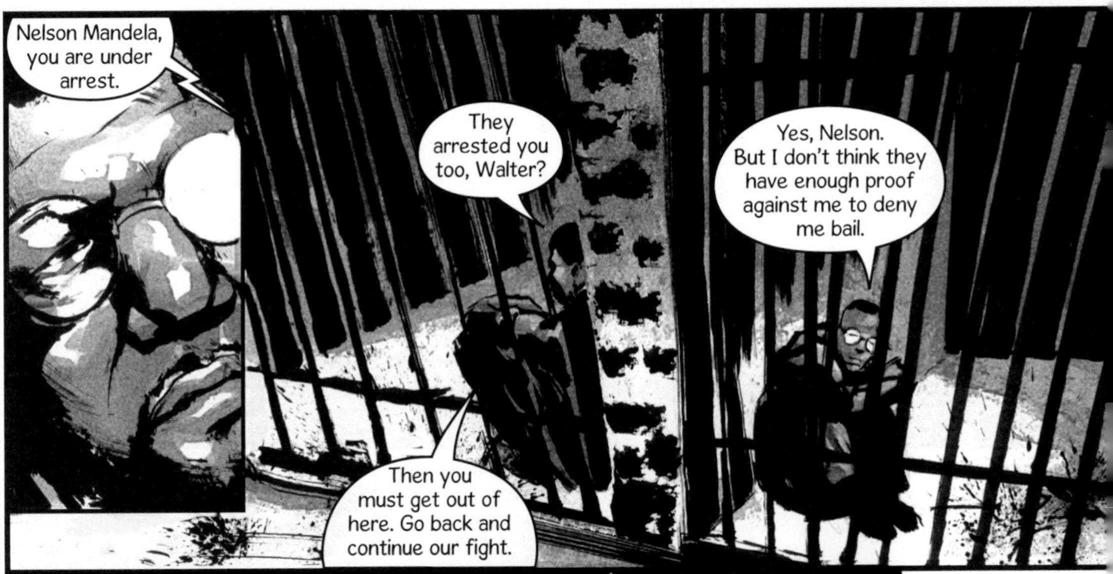
Nelson Mandela, you are under arrest.
They arrested you too, Walter?
Yes, Nelson. But I don't think they have enough proof against me to deny me bail.
Then you must get out of here. Go back and continue our fight.

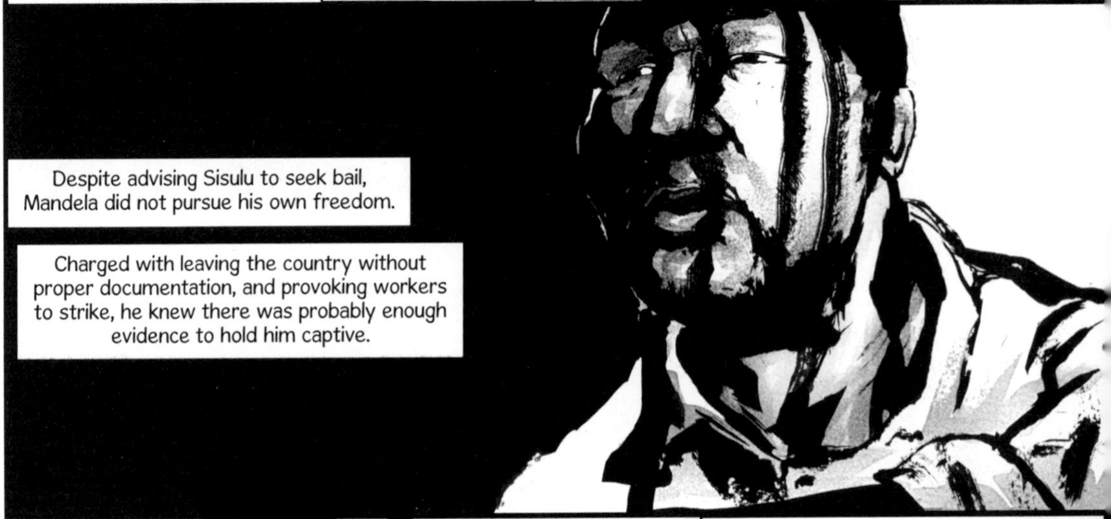
Despite advising Sisulu to seek bail, Mandela did not pursue his own freedom.
Charged with leaving the country without proper documentation, and provoking workers to strike, he knew there was probably enough evidence to hold him captive.

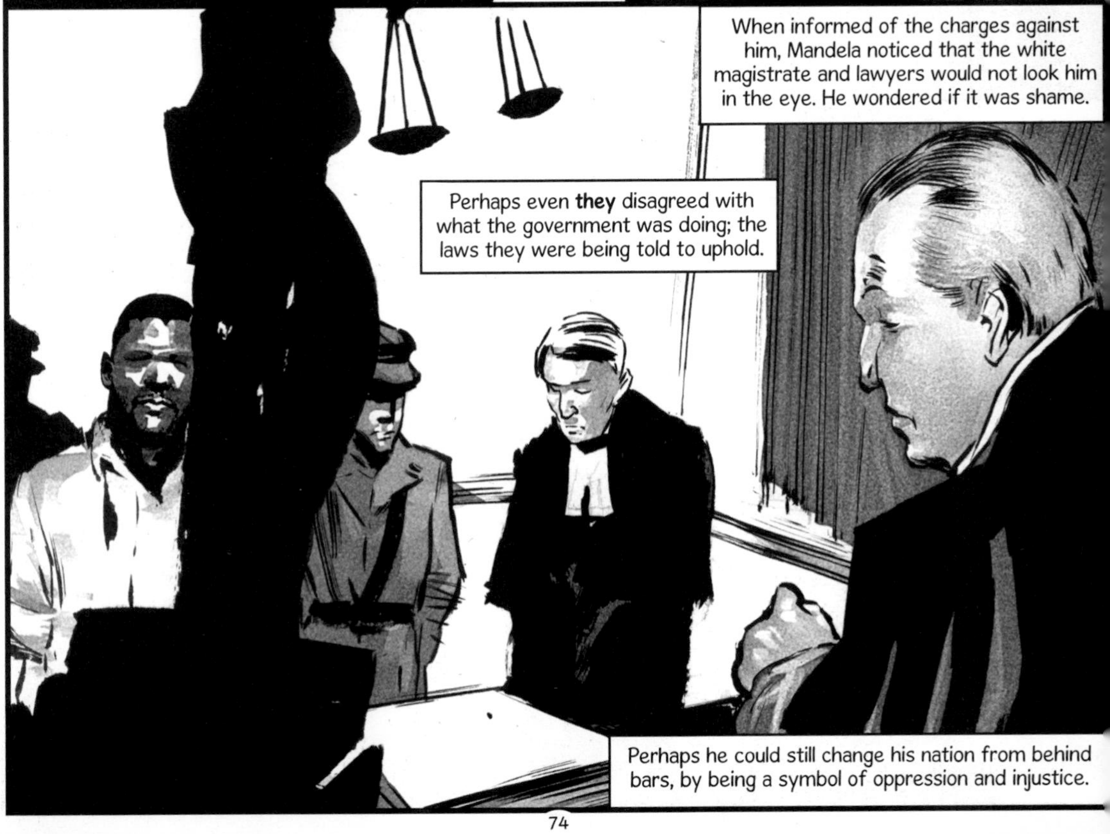
When informed of the charges against him, Mandela noticed that the white magistrate and lawyers would not look him in the eye. He wondered if it was shame.
Perhaps even **they** disagreed with what the government was doing; the laws they were being told to uphold.
Perhaps he could still change his nation from behind bars, by being a symbol of oppression and injustice.

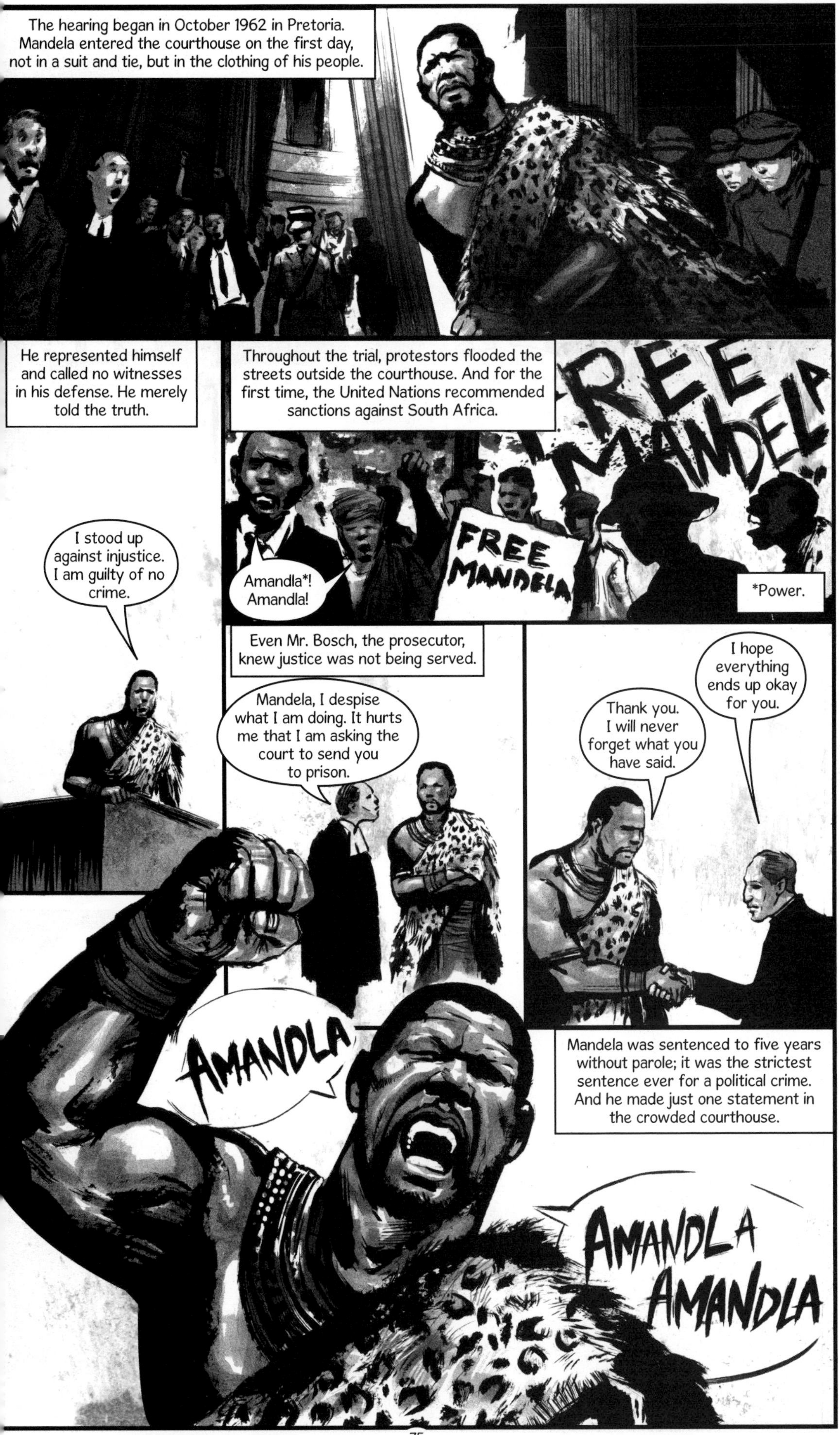
The hearing began in October 1962 in Pretoria. Mandela entered the courthouse on the first day, not in a suit and tie, but in the clothing of his people.
He represented himself and called no witnesses in his defense. He merely told the truth.
Throughout the trial, protestors flooded the streets outside the courthouse. And for the first time, the United Nations recommended sanctions against South Africa.
FREE MANDELA
Amandla*! Amandla!
FREE MANDELA
*Power.
I stood up against injustice. I am guilty of no crime.
Even Mr. Bosch, the prosecutor, knew justice was not being served.
Mandela, I despise what I am doing. It hurts me that I am asking the court to send you to prison.
I hope everything ends up okay for you.
Thank you. I will never forget what you have said.
Mandela was sentenced to five years without parole; it was the strictest sentence ever for a political crime. And he made just one statement in the crowded courthouse.
AMANDLA
AMANDLA
AMANDLA

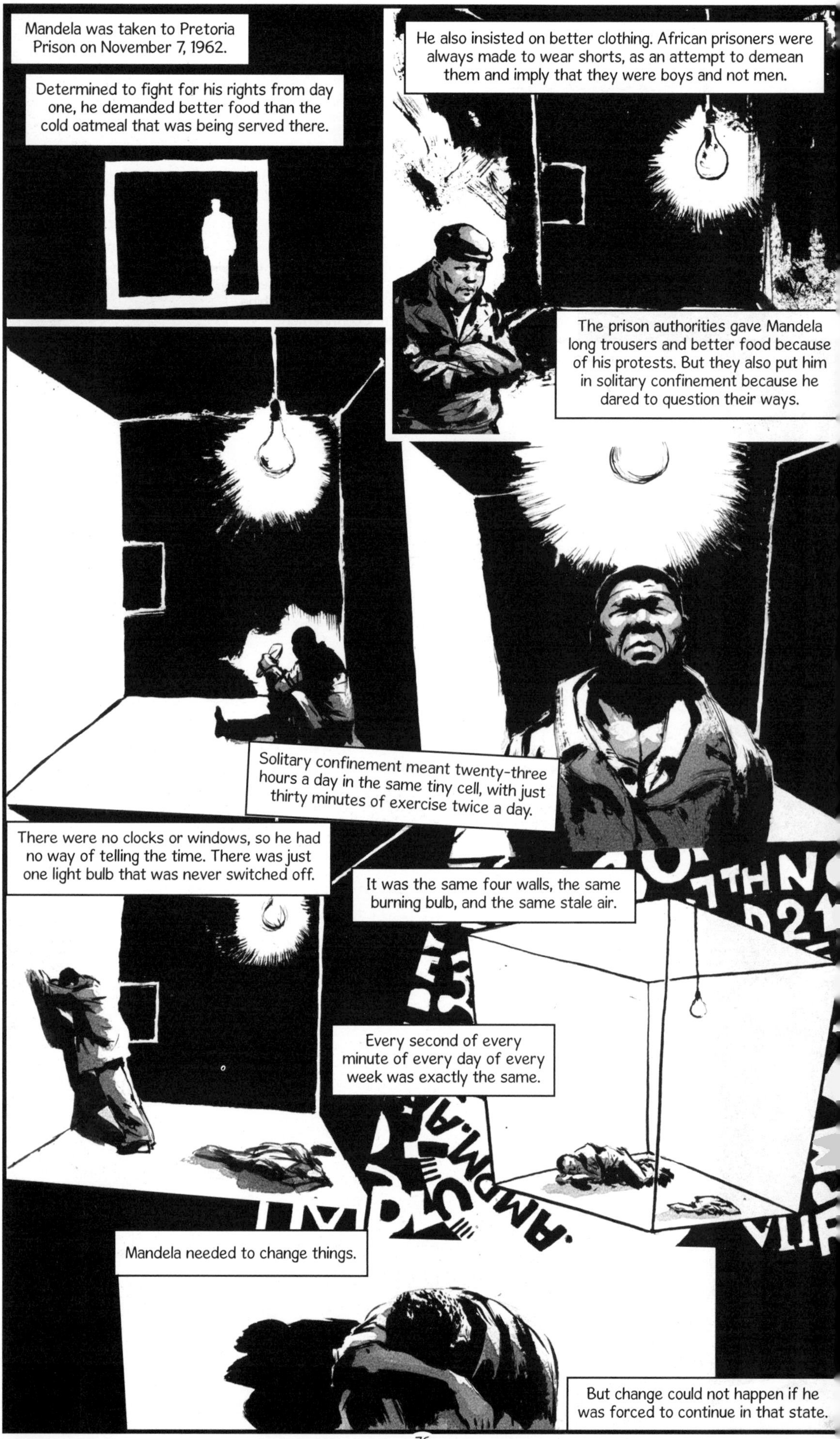
Mandela was taken to Pretoria Prison on November 7, 1962.
Determined to fight for his rights from day one, he demanded better food than the cold oatmeal that was being served there.
He also insisted on better clothing. African prisoners were always made to wear shorts, as an attempt to demean them and imply that they were boys and not men.
The prison authorities gave Mandela long trousers and better food because of his protests. But they also put him in solitary confinement because he dared to question their ways.
Solitary confinement meant twenty-three hours a day in the same tiny cell, with just thirty minutes of exercise twice a day.
There were no clocks or windows, so he had no way of telling the time. There was just one light bulb that was never switched off.
It was the same four walls, the same burning bulb, and the same stale air.
Every second of every minute of every day of every week was exactly the same.
Mandela needed to change things.
But change could not happen if he was forced to continue in that state.

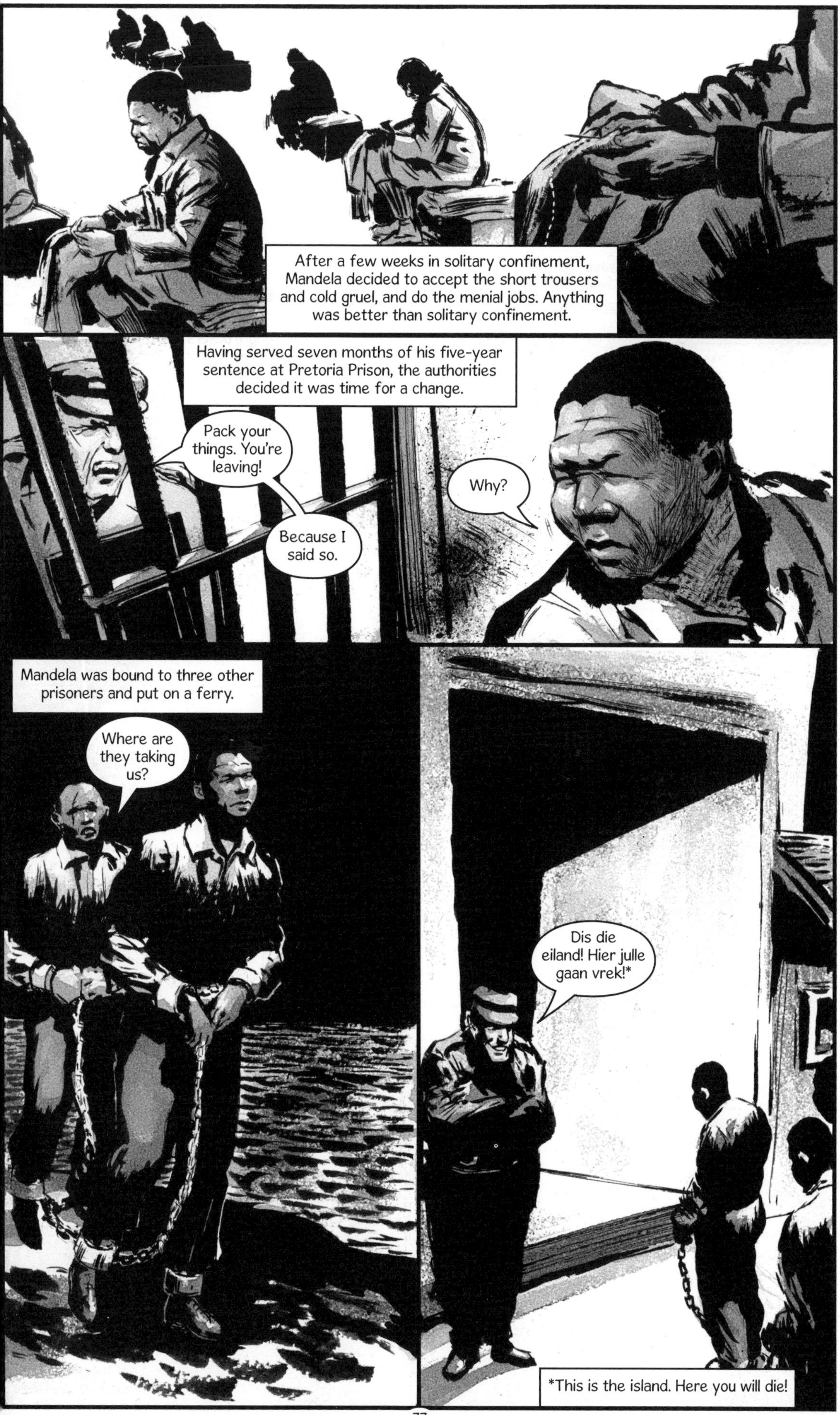
After a few weeks in solitary confinement, Mandela decided to accept the short trousers and cold gruel, and do the menial jobs. Anything was better than solitary confinement.
Having served seven months of his five-year sentence at Pretoria Prison, the authorities decided it was time for a change.
Pack your things. You're leaving!
Why?
Because I said so.
Mandela was bound to three other prisoners and put on a ferry.
Where are they taking us?
Dis die eiland! Hier julle gaan vrek!*
*This is the island. Here you will die!

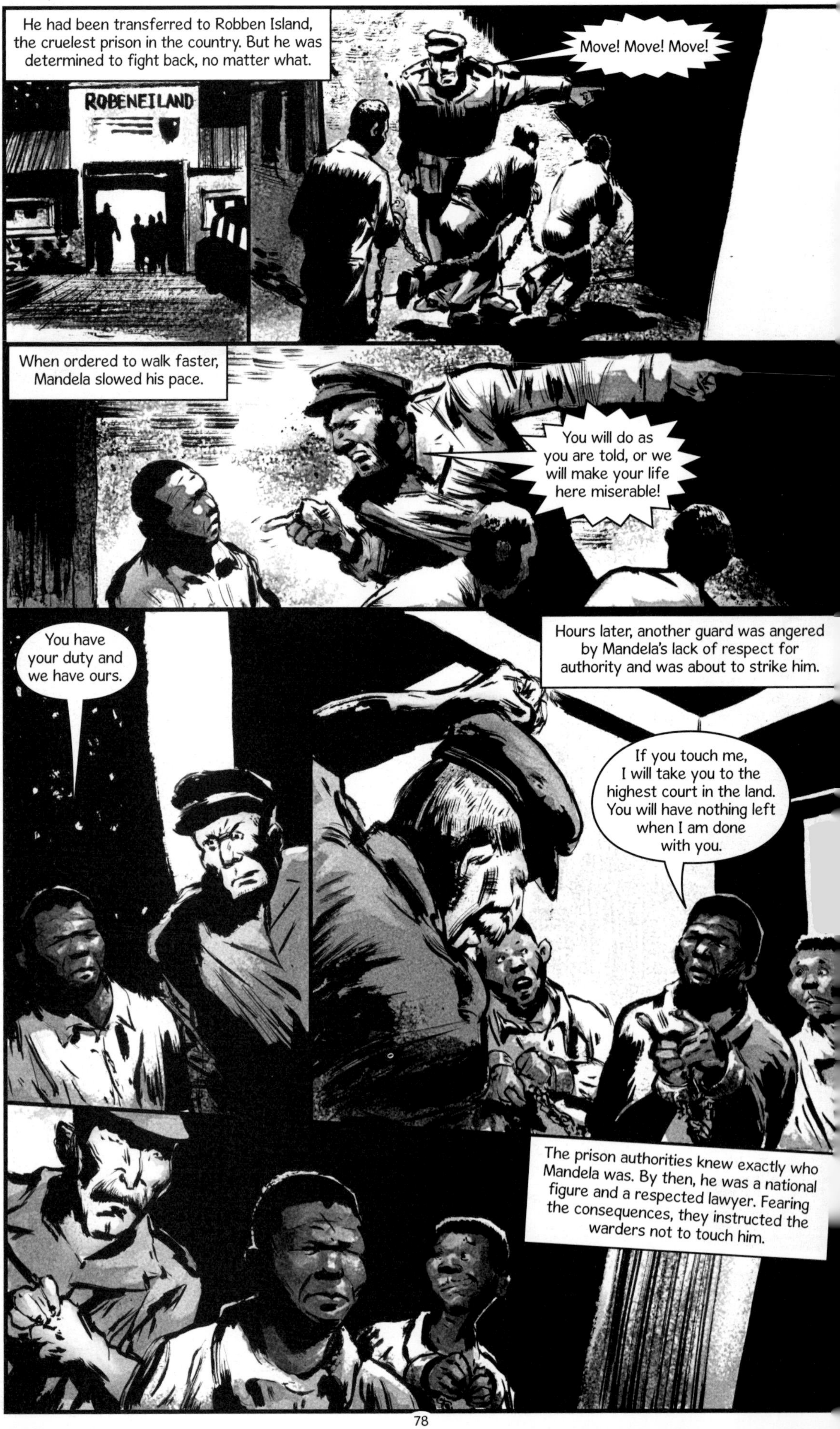
He had been transferred to Robben Island, the cruelest prison in the country. But he was determined to fight back, no matter what.
ROBENEILAND
Move! Move! Move!
When ordered to walk faster, Mandela slowed his pace.
You will do as you are told, or we will make your life here miserable!
You have your duty and we have ours.
Hours later, another guard was angered by Mandela's lack of respect for authority and was about to strike him.
If you touch me, I will take you to the highest court in the land. You will have nothing left when I am done with you.
The prison authorities knew exactly who Mandela was. By then, he was a national figure and a respected lawyer. Fearing the consequences, they instructed the warders not to touch him.

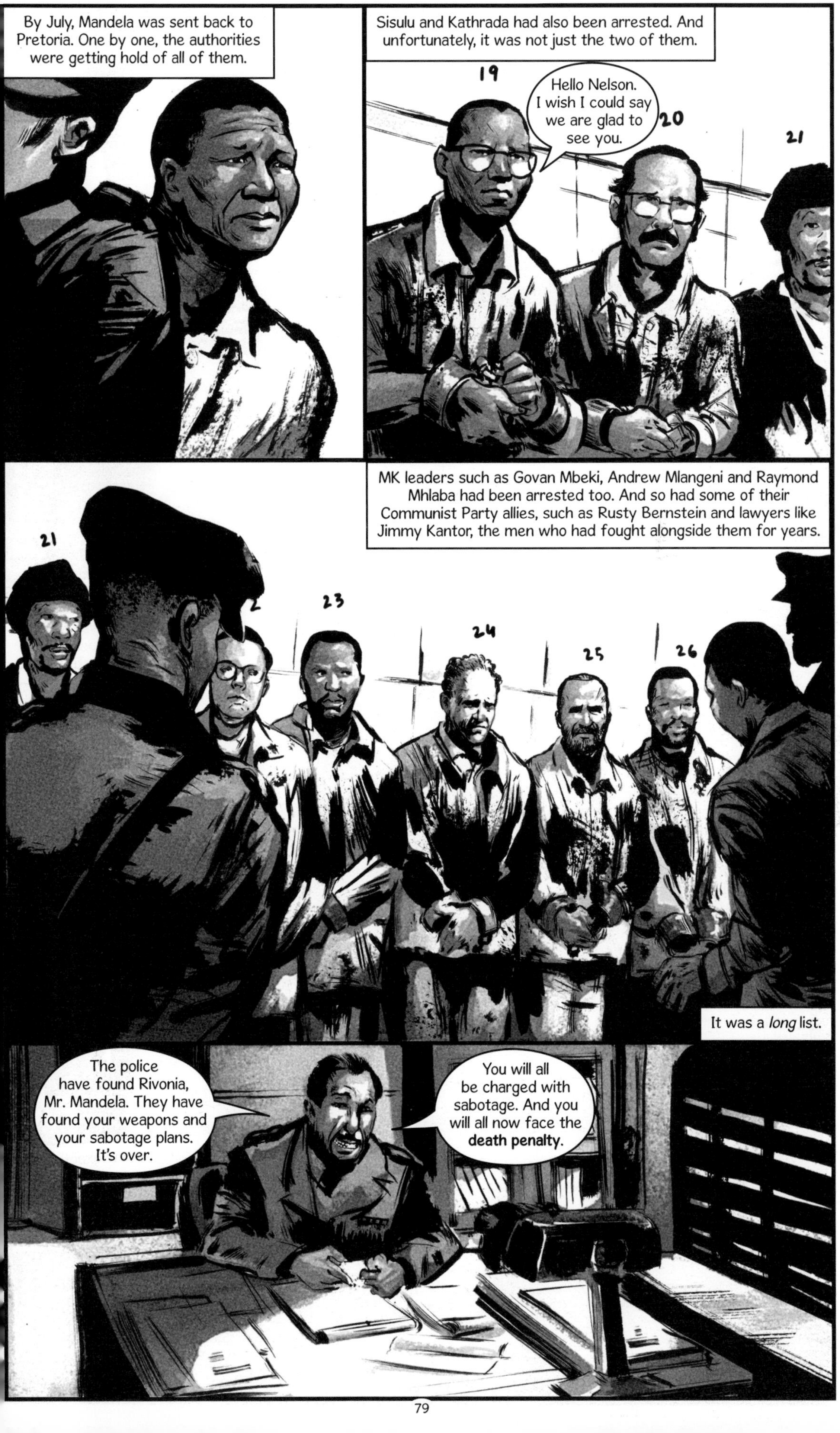
By July, Mandela was sent back to Pretoria. One by one, the authorities were getting hold of all of them.
Sisulu and Kathrada had also been arrested. And unfortunately, it was not just the two of them.
Hello Nelson. I wish I could say we are glad to see you.
MK leaders such as Govan Mbeki, Andrew Mlangeni and Raymond Mhlaba had been arrested too. And so had some of their Communist Party allies, such as Rusty Bernstein and lawyers like Jimmy Kantor, the men who had fought alongside them for years.
It was a *long* list.
The police have found Rivonia, Mr. Mandela. They have found your weapons and your sabotage plans. It's over.
You will all be charged with sabotage. And you will all now face the **death penalty**.

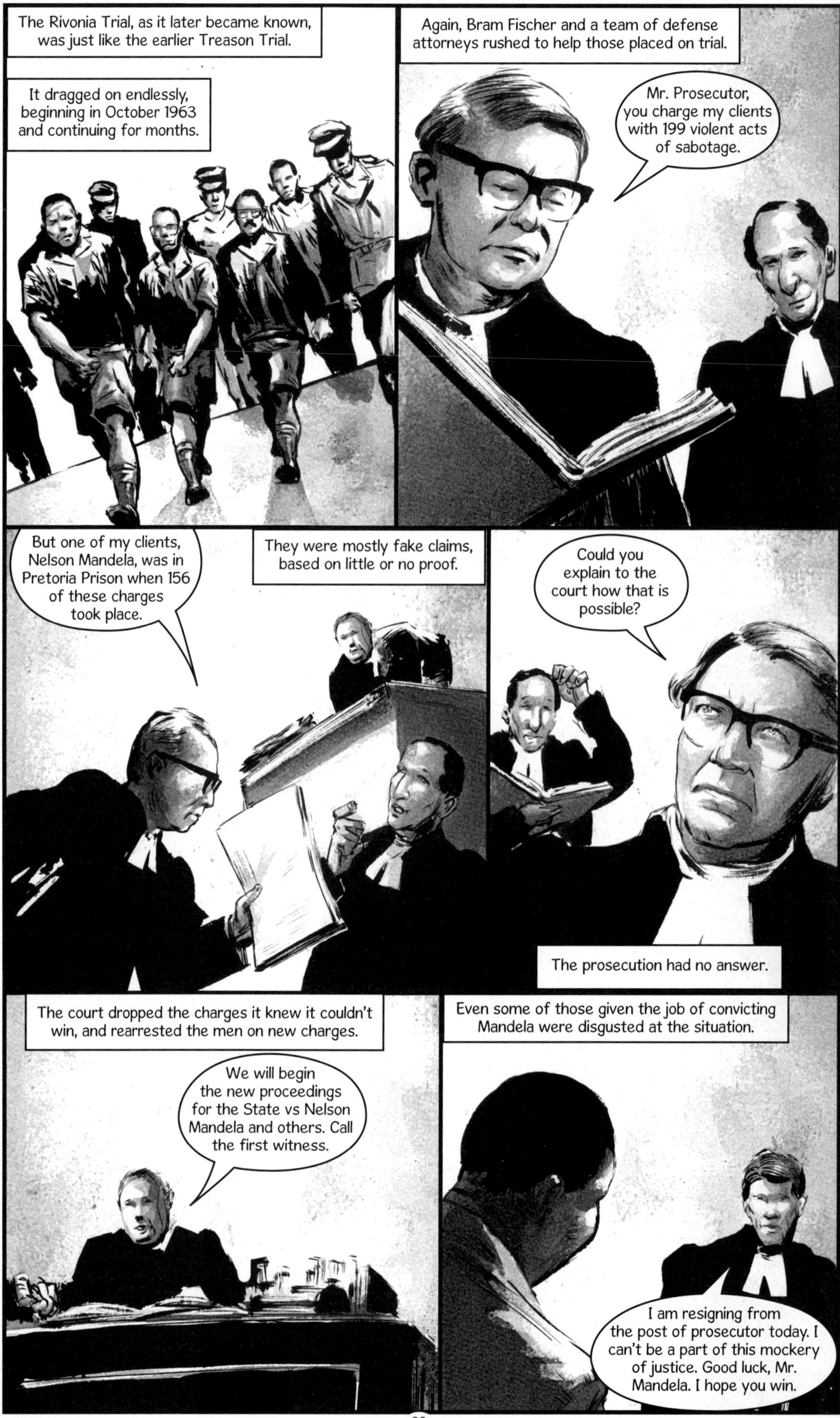

The Rivonia Trial, as it later became known, was just like the earlier Treason Trial.
It dragged on endlessly, beginning in October 1963 and continuing for months.
Again, Bram Fischer and a team of defense attorneys rushed to help those placed on trial.
Mr. Prosecutor, you charge my clients with 199 violent acts of sabotage.
But one of my clients, Nelson Mandela, was in Pretoria Prison when 156 of these charges took place.
They were mostly fake claims, based on little or no proof.
Could you explain to the court how that is possible?
The prosecution had no answer.
The court dropped the charges it knew it couldn't win, and rearrested the men on new charges.
We will begin the new proceedings for the State vs Nelson Mandela and others. Call the first witness.
Even some of those given the job of convicting Mandela were disgusted at the situation.
I am resigning from the post of prosecutor today. I can't be a part of this mockery of justice. Good luck, Mr. Mandela. I hope you win.

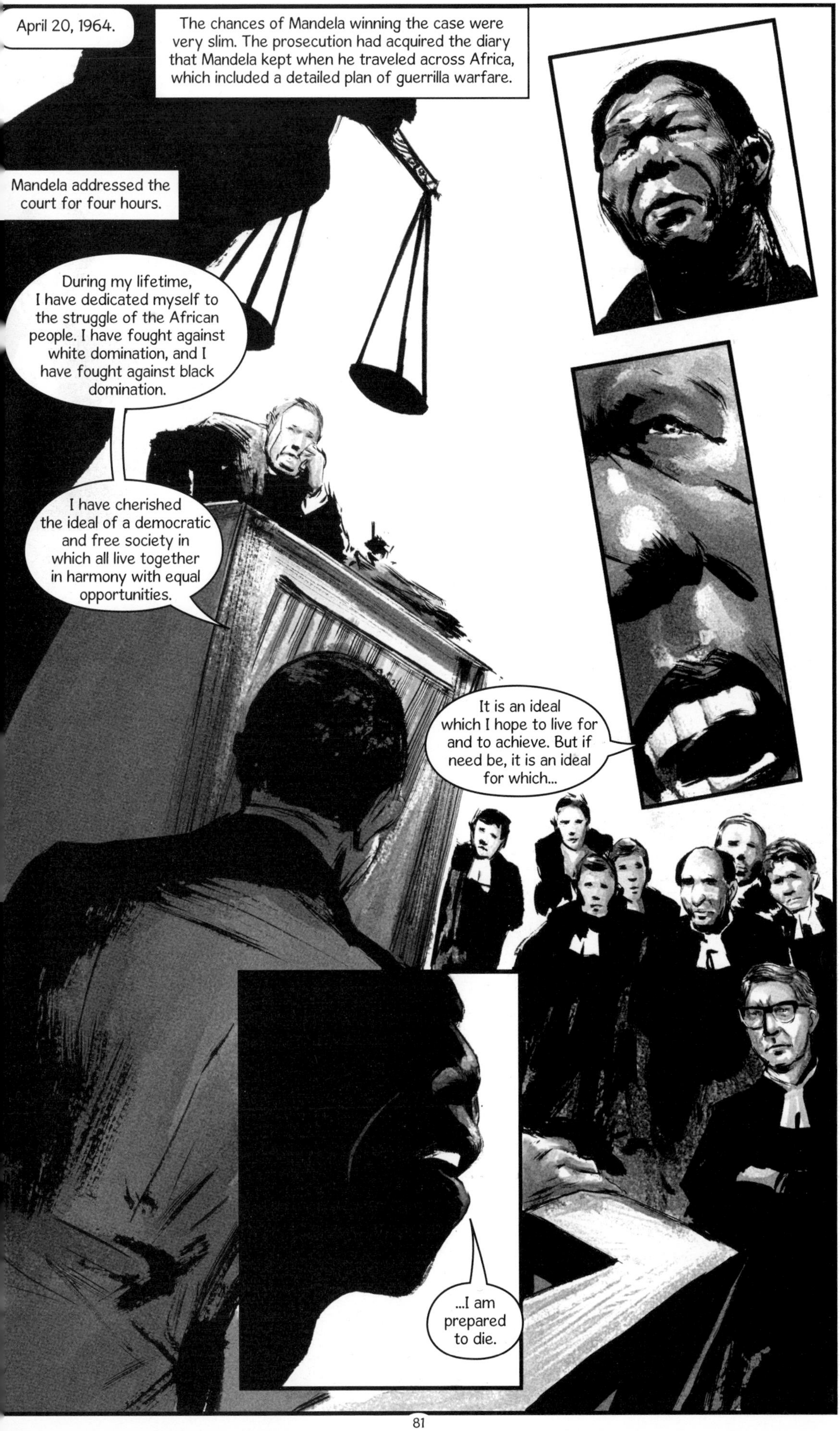
April 20, 1964.
The chances of Mandela winning the case were very slim. The prosecution had acquired the diary that Mandela kept when he traveled across Africa, which included a detailed plan of guerrilla warfare.
Mandela addressed the court for four hours.
During my lifetime, I have dedicated myself to the struggle of the African people. I have fought against white domination, and I have fought against black domination.
I have cherished the ideal of a democratic and free society in which all live together in harmony with equal opportunities.
It is an ideal which I hope to live for and to achieve. But if need be, it is an ideal for which...
...I am prepared to die.

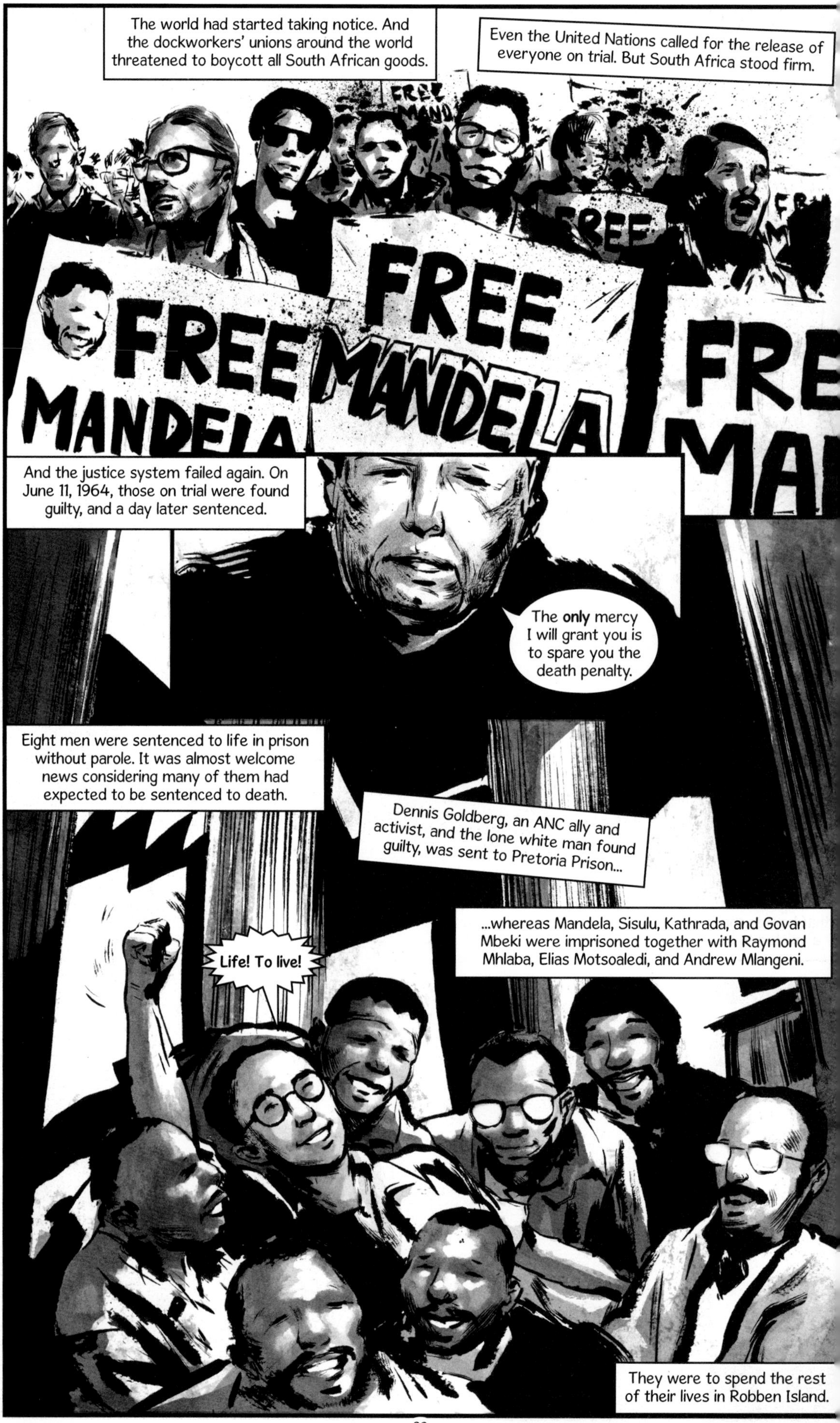

The world had started taking notice. And the dockworkers' unions around the world threatened to boycott all South African goods.
Even the United Nations called for the release of everyone on trial. But South Africa stood firm.
FREE MANDELA
FREE MANDELA
FRE MA
And the justice system failed again. On June 11, 1964, those on trial were found guilty, and a day later sentenced.
The **only** mercy I will grant you is to spare you the death penalty.
Eight men were sentenced to life in prison without parole. It was almost welcome news considering many of them had expected to be sentenced to death.
Dennis Goldberg, an ANC ally and activist, and the lone white man found guilty, was sent to Pretoria Prison...
...whereas Mandela, Sisulu, Kathrada, and Govan Mbeki were imprisoned together with Raymond Mhlaba, Elias Motsoaledi, and Andrew Mlangeni.
Life! To live!
They were to spend the rest of their lives in Robben Island.

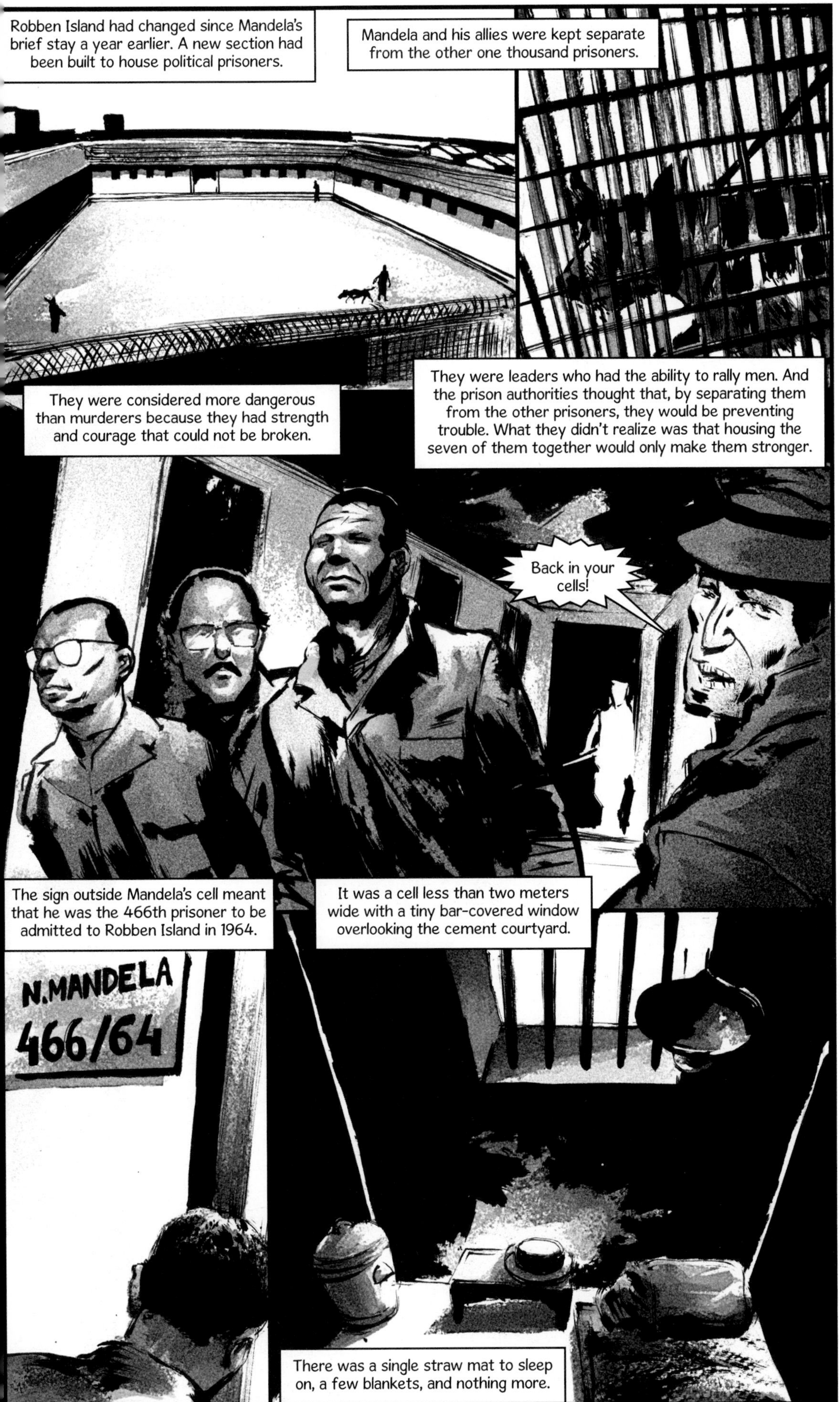
Robben Island had changed since Mandela's brief stay a year earlier. A new section had been built to house political prisoners.
Mandela and his allies were kept separate from the other one thousand prisoners.
They were considered more dangerous than murderers because they had strength and courage that could not be broken.
They were leaders who had the ability to rally men. And the prison authorities thought that, by separating them from the other prisoners, they would be preventing trouble. What they didn't realize was that housing the seven of them together would only make them stronger.
Back in your cells!
The sign outside Mandela's cell meant that he was the 466th prisoner to be admitted to Robben Island in 1964.
It was a cell less than two meters wide with a tiny bar-covered window overlooking the cement courtyard.
N.MANDELA
466/64
There was a single straw mat to sleep on, a few blankets, and nothing more.

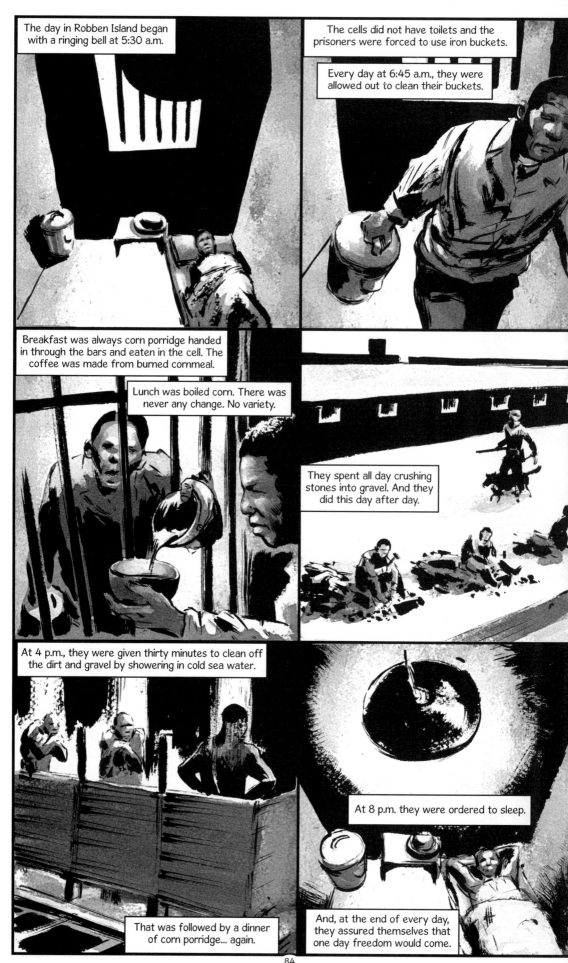

The day in Robben Island began with a ringing bell at 5:30 a.m.

The cells did not have toilets and the prisoners were forced to use iron buckets.

Every day at 6:45 a.m., they were allowed out to clean their buckets.

Breakfast was always corn porridge handed in through the bars and eaten in the cell. The coffee was made from burned cornmeal.

Lunch was boiled corn. There was never any change. No variety.

They spent all day crushing stones into gravel. And they did this day after day.

At 4 p.m., they were given thirty minutes to clean off the dirt and gravel by showering in cold sea water.

At 8 p.m. they were ordered to sleep.

That was followed by a dinner of corn porridge... again.

And, at the end of every day, they assured themselves that one day freedom would come.

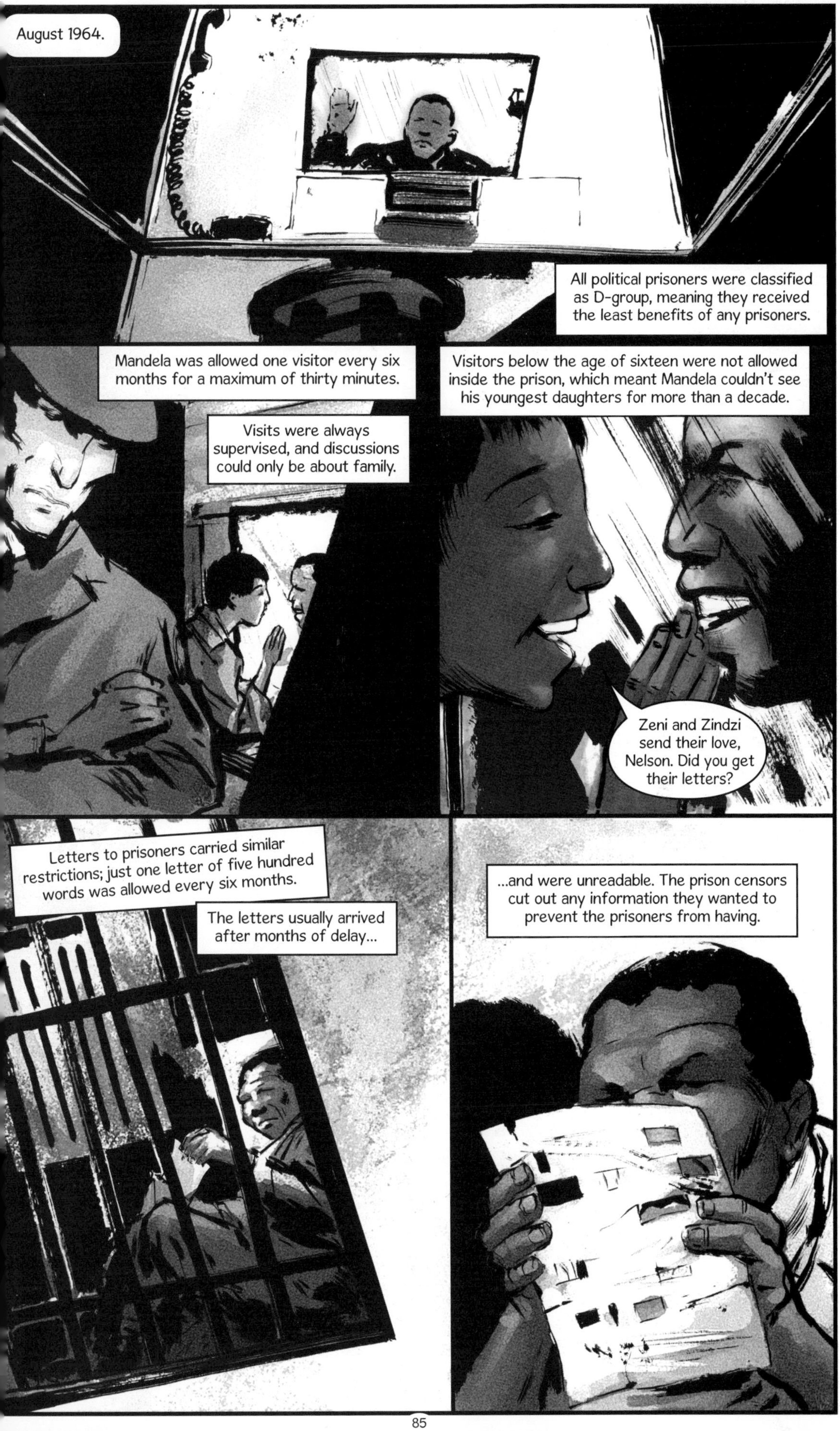
August 1964.
All political prisoners were classified as D-group, meaning they received the least benefits of any prisoners.
Mandela was allowed one visitor every six months for a maximum of thirty minutes.
Visits were always supervised, and discussions could only be about family.
Visitors below the age of sixteen were not allowed inside the prison, which meant Mandela couldn't see his youngest daughters for more than a decade.
Zeni and Zindzi send their love, Nelson. Did you get their letters?
Letters to prisoners carried similar restrictions; just one letter of five hundred words was allowed every six months.
The letters usually arrived after months of delay...
...and were unreadable. The prison censors cut out any information they wanted to prevent the prisoners from having.

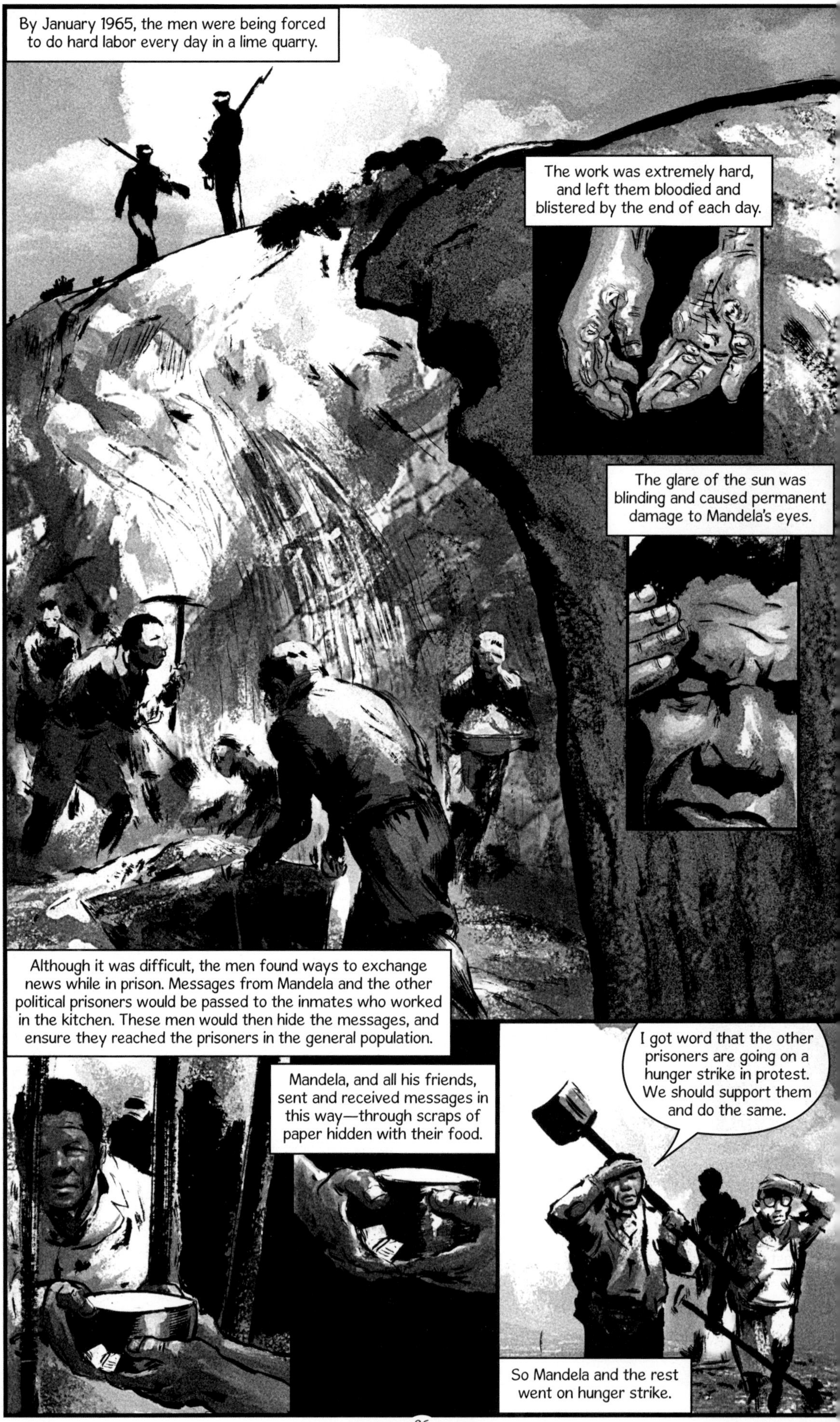
By January 1965, the men were being forced to do hard labor every day in a lime quarry.
The work was extremely hard, and left them bloodied and blistered by the end of each day.
The glare of the sun was blinding and caused permanent damage to Mandela's eyes.
Although it was difficult, the men found ways to exchange news while in prison. Messages from Mandela and the other political prisoners would be passed to the inmates who worked in the kitchen. These men would then hide the messages, and ensure they reached the prisoners in the general population.
Mandela, and all his friends, sent and received messages in this way—through scraps of paper hidden with their food.
I got word that the other prisoners are going on a hunger strike in protest. We should support them and do the same.
So Mandela and the rest went on hunger strike.

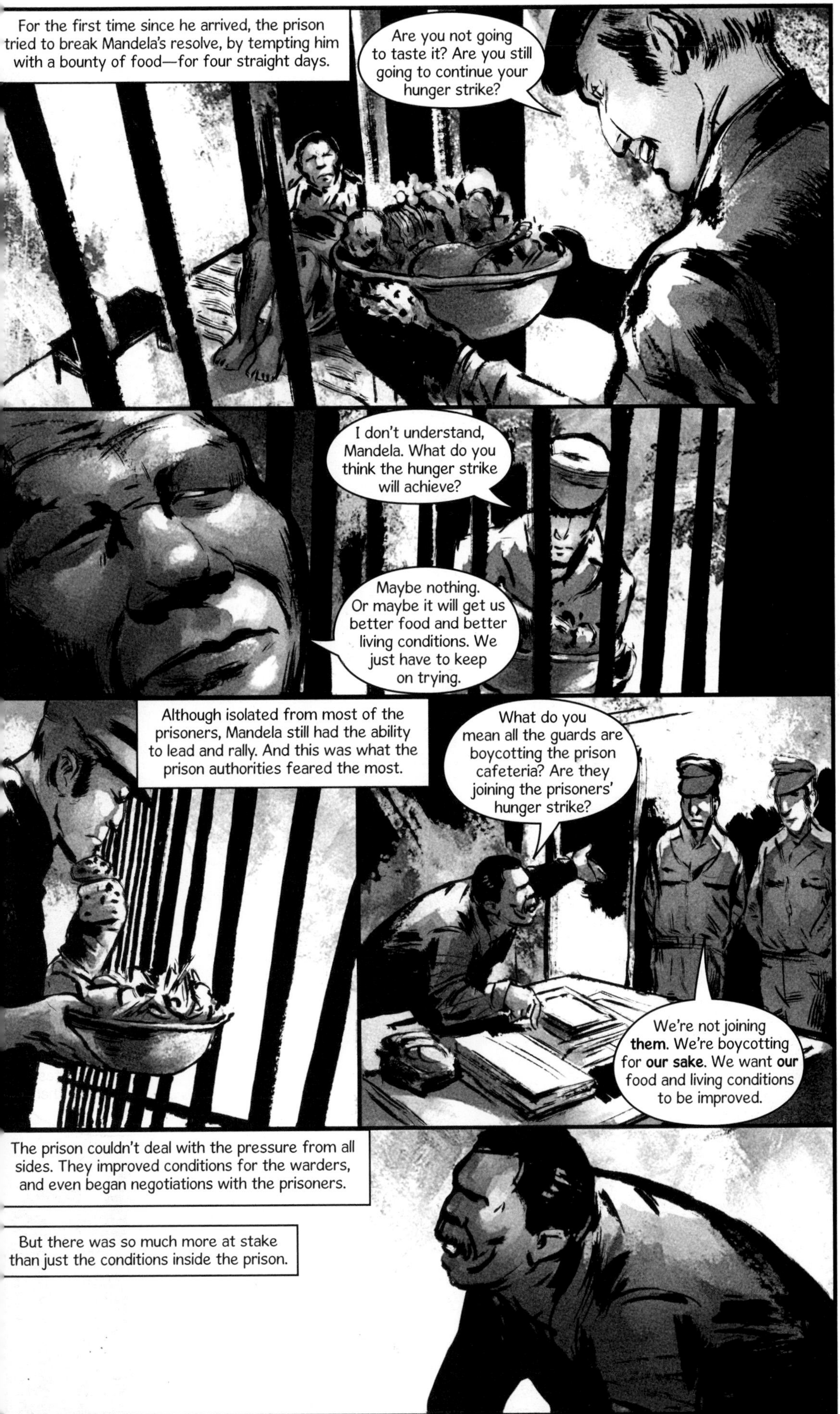
For the first time since he arrived, the prison tried to break Mandela's resolve, by tempting him with a bounty of food—for four straight days.
Are you not going to taste it? Are you still going to continue your hunger strike?
I don't understand, Mandela. What do you think the hunger strike will achieve?
Maybe nothing. Or maybe it will get us better food and better living conditions. We just have to keep on trying.
Although isolated from most of the prisoners, Mandela still had the ability to lead and rally. And this was what the prison authorities feared the most.
What do you mean all the guards are boycotting the prison cafeteria? Are they joining the prisoners' hunger strike?
We're not joining **them**. We're boycotting for **our sake**. We want **our** food and living conditions to be improved.
The prison couldn't deal with the pressure from all sides. They improved conditions for the warders, and even began negotiations with the prisoners.
But there was so much more at stake than just the conditions inside the prison.

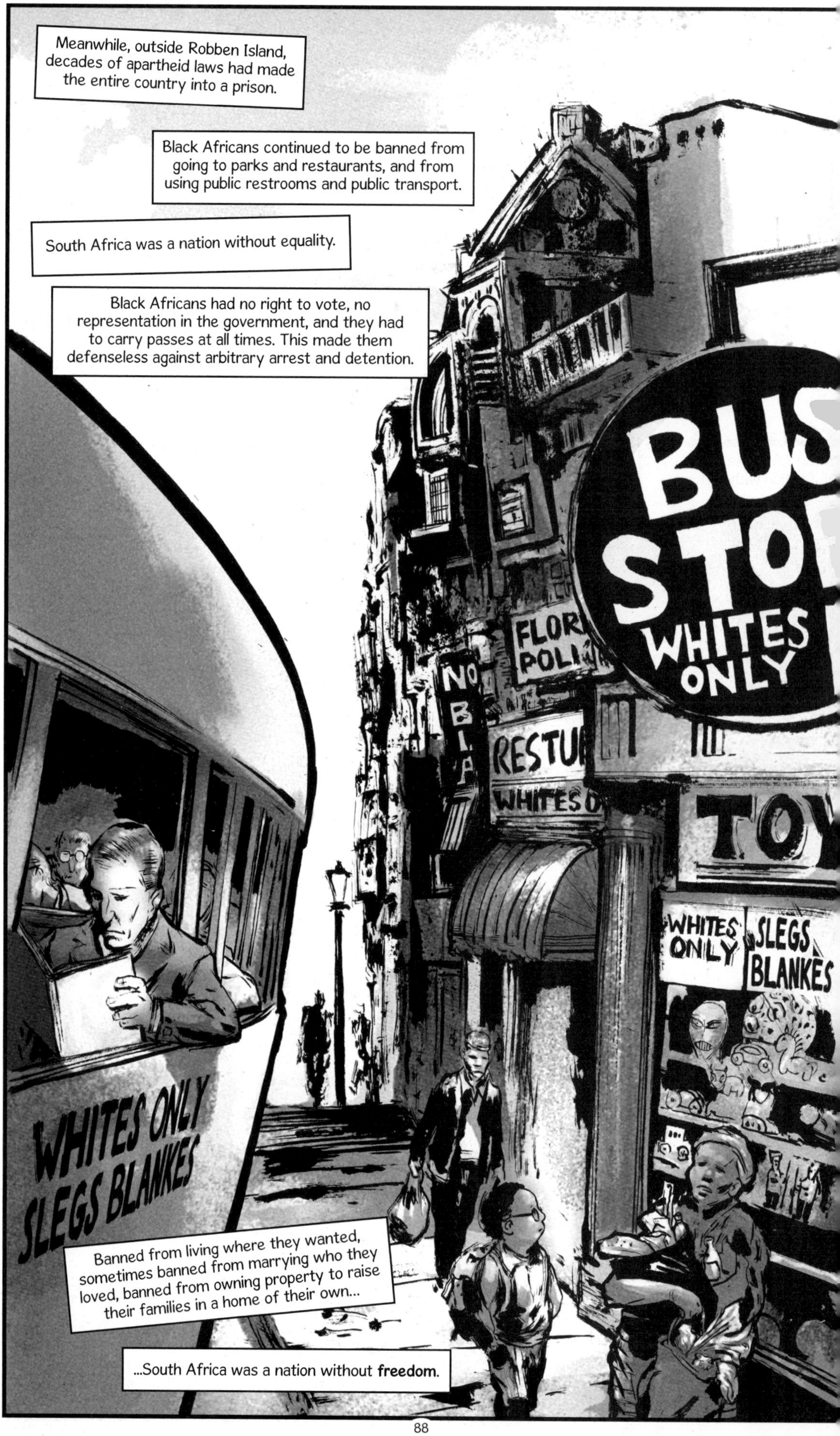

Meanwhile, outside Robben Island, decades of apartheid laws had made the entire country into a prison.
Black Africans continued to be banned from going to parks and restaurants, and from using public restrooms and public transport.
South Africa was a nation without equality.
Black Africans had no right to vote, no representation in the government, and they had to carry passes at all times. This made them defenseless against arbitrary arrest and detention.
BUS STO
WHITES ONLY
RESTU
WHITES O
WHITES ONLY
SLEGS BLANKES
WHITES ONLY
SLEGS BLANKES
Banned from living where they wanted, sometimes banned from marrying who they loved, banned from owning property to raise their families in a home of their own...
...South Africa was a nation without **freedom**.

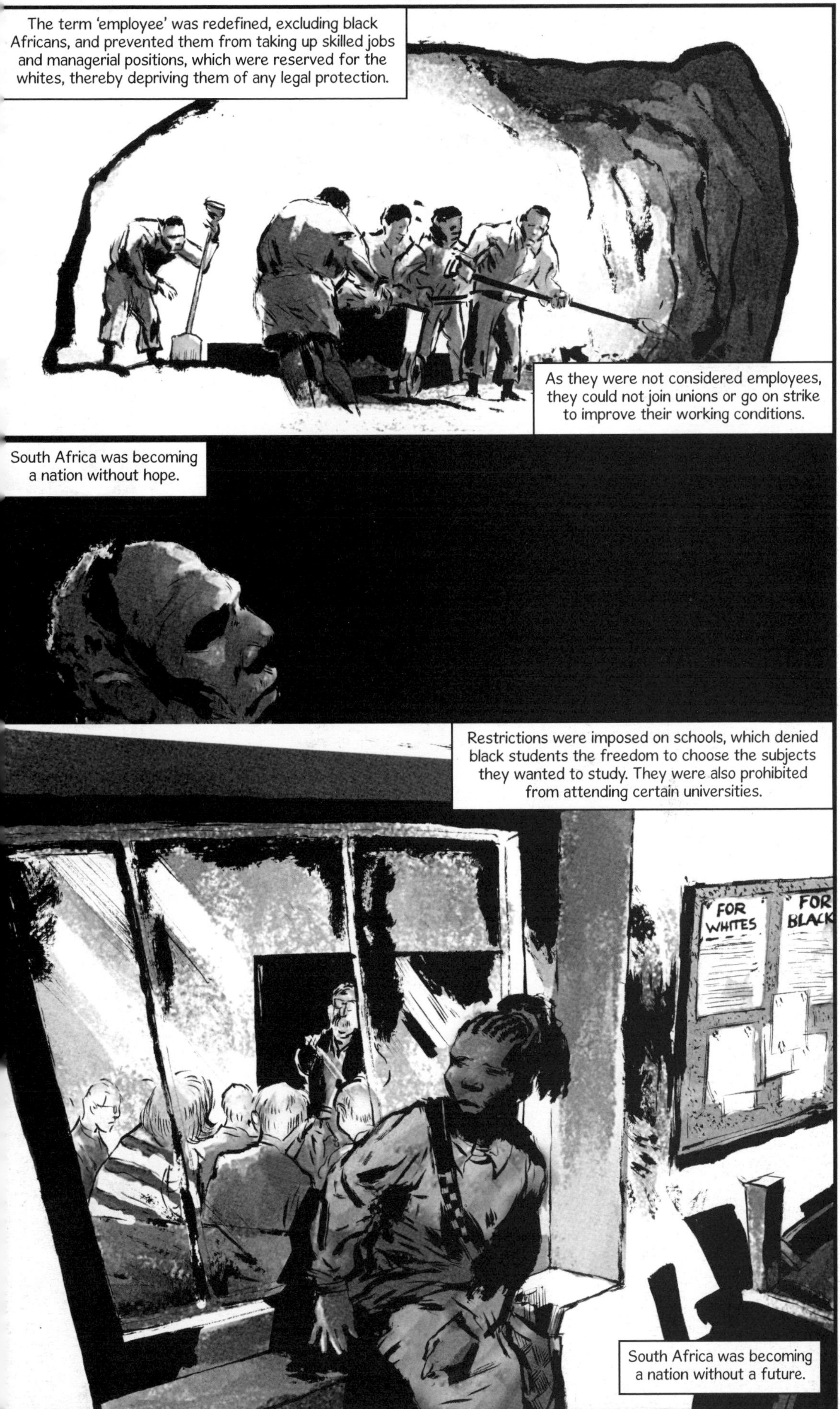
The term 'employee' was redefined, excluding black Africans, and prevented them from taking up skilled jobs and managerial positions, which were reserved for the whites, thereby depriving them of any legal protection.
As they were not considered employees, they could not join unions or go on strike to improve their working conditions.
South Africa was becoming a nation without hope.
Restrictions were imposed on schools, which denied black students the freedom to choose the subjects they wanted to study. They were also prohibited from attending certain universities.
FOR WHITES
FOR
South Africa was becoming a nation without a future.

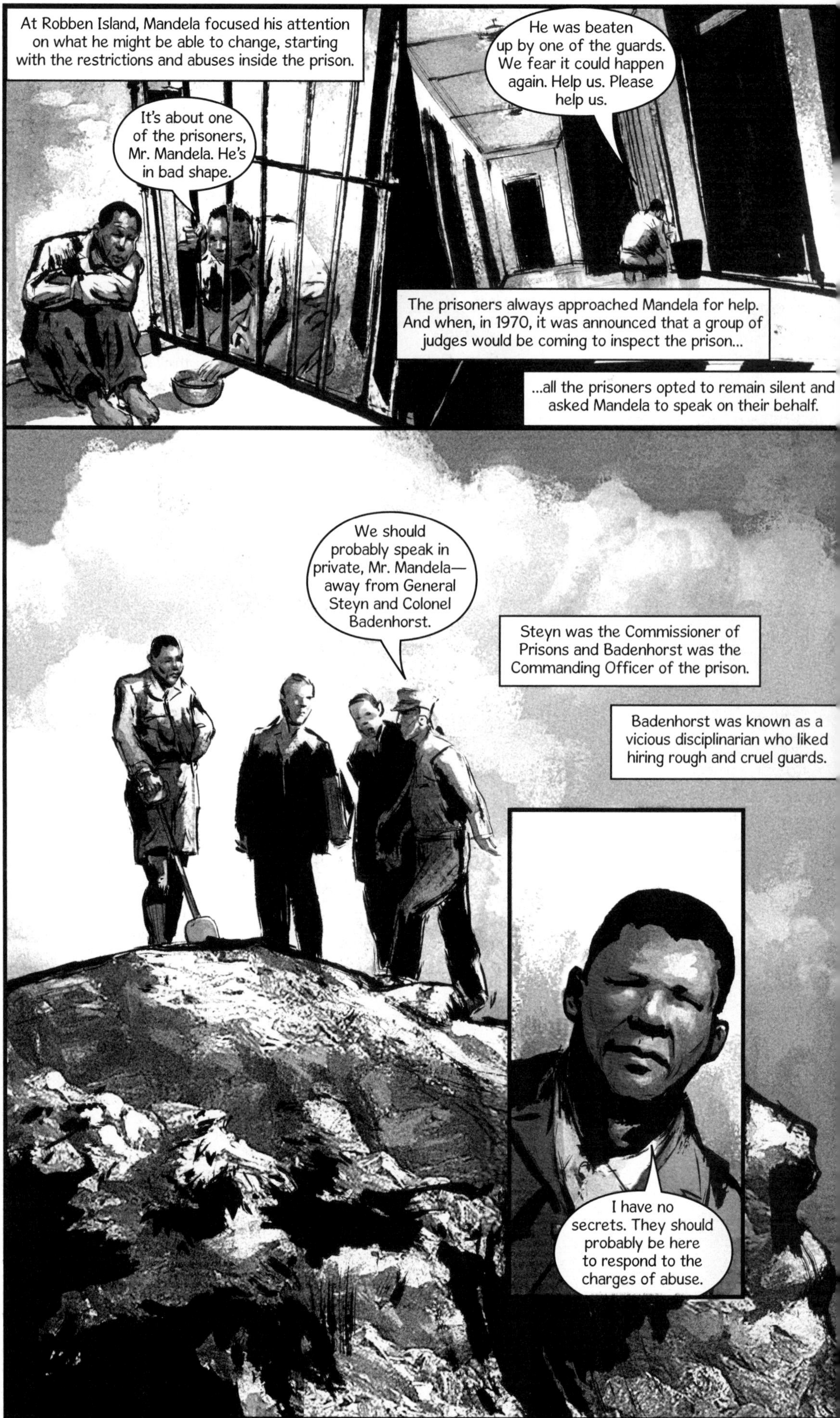

At Robben Island, Mandela focused his attention on what he might be able to change, starting with the restrictions and abuses inside the prison.
It's about one of the prisoners, Mr. Mandela. He's in bad shape.
He was beaten up by one of the guards. We fear it could happen again. Help us. Please help us.
The prisoners always approached Mandela for help. And when, in 1970, it was announced that a group of judges would be coming to inspect the prison...
...all the prisoners opted to remain silent and asked Mandela to speak on their behalf.
We should probably speak in private, Mr. Mandela—away from General Steyn and Colonel Badenhorst.
Steyn was the Commissioner of Prisons and Badenhorst was the Commanding Officer of the prison.
Badenhorst was known as a vicious disciplinarian who liked hiring rough and cruel guards.
I have no secrets. They should probably be here to respond to the charges of abuse.

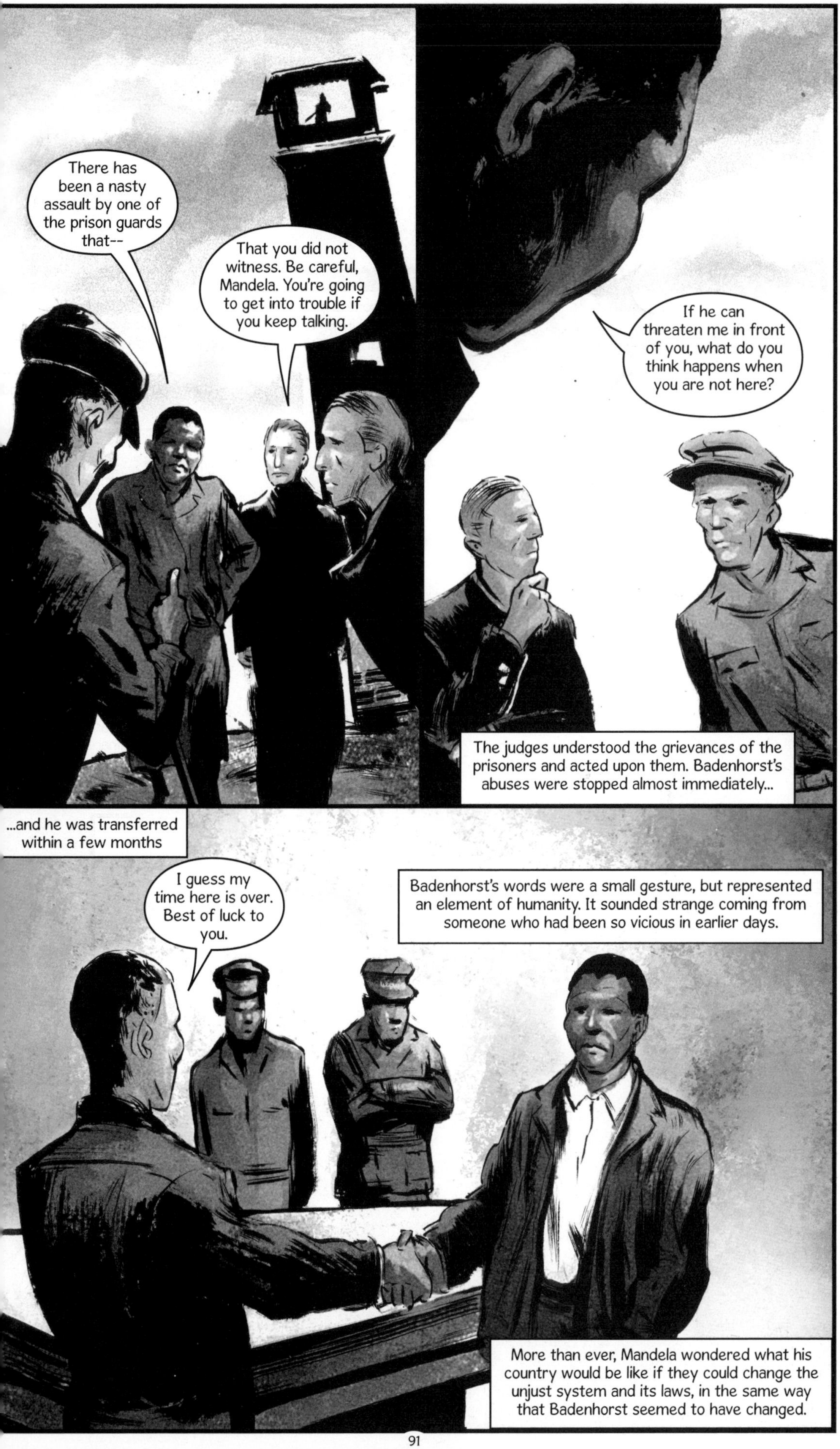
There has been a nasty assault by one of the prison guards that--
That you did not witness. Be careful, Mandela. You're going to get into trouble if you keep talking.
If he can threaten me in front of you, what do you think happens when you are not here?
The judges understood the grievances of the prisoners and acted upon them. Badenhorst's abuses were stopped almost immediately...
...and he was transferred within a few months
I guess my time here is over. Best of luck to you.
Badenhorst's words were a small gesture, but represented an element of humanity. It sounded strange coming from someone who had been so vicious in earlier days.
More than ever, Mandela wondered what his country would be like if they could change the unjust system and its laws, in the same way that Badenhorst seemed to have changed.

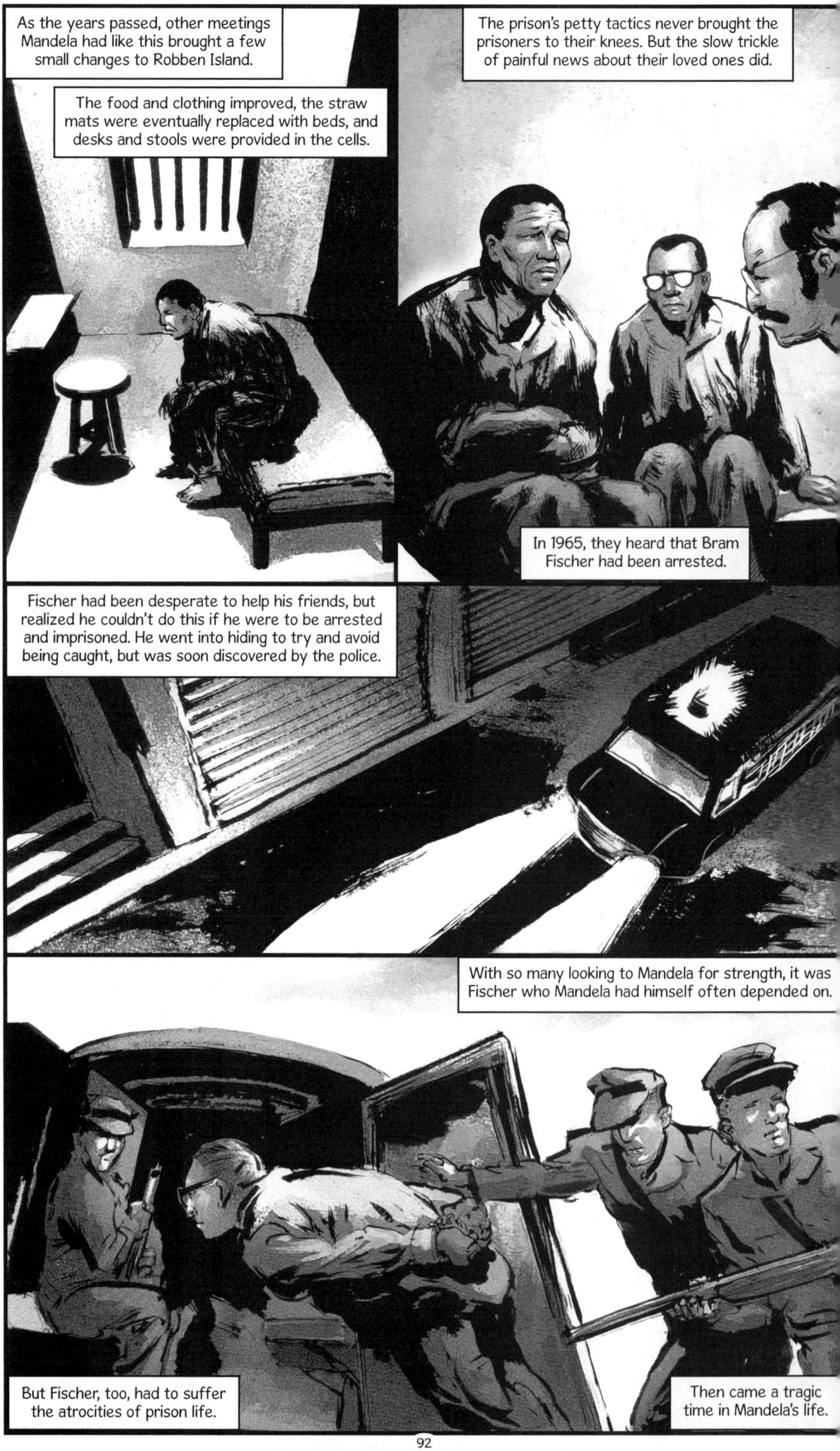
As the years passed, other meetings Mandela had like this brought a few small changes to Robben Island.
The food and clothing improved, the straw mats were eventually replaced with beds, and desks and stools were provided in the cells.
The prison's petty tactics never brought the prisoners to their knees. But the slow trickle of painful news about their loved ones did.
In 1965, they heard that Bram Fischer had been arrested.
Fischer had been desperate to help his friends, but realized he couldn't do this if he were to be arrested and imprisoned. He went into hiding to try and avoid being caught, but was soon discovered by the police.
With so many looking to Mandela for strength, it was Fischer who Mandela had himself often depended on.
But Fischer, too, had to suffer the atrocities of prison life.
Then came a tragic time in Mandela's life.

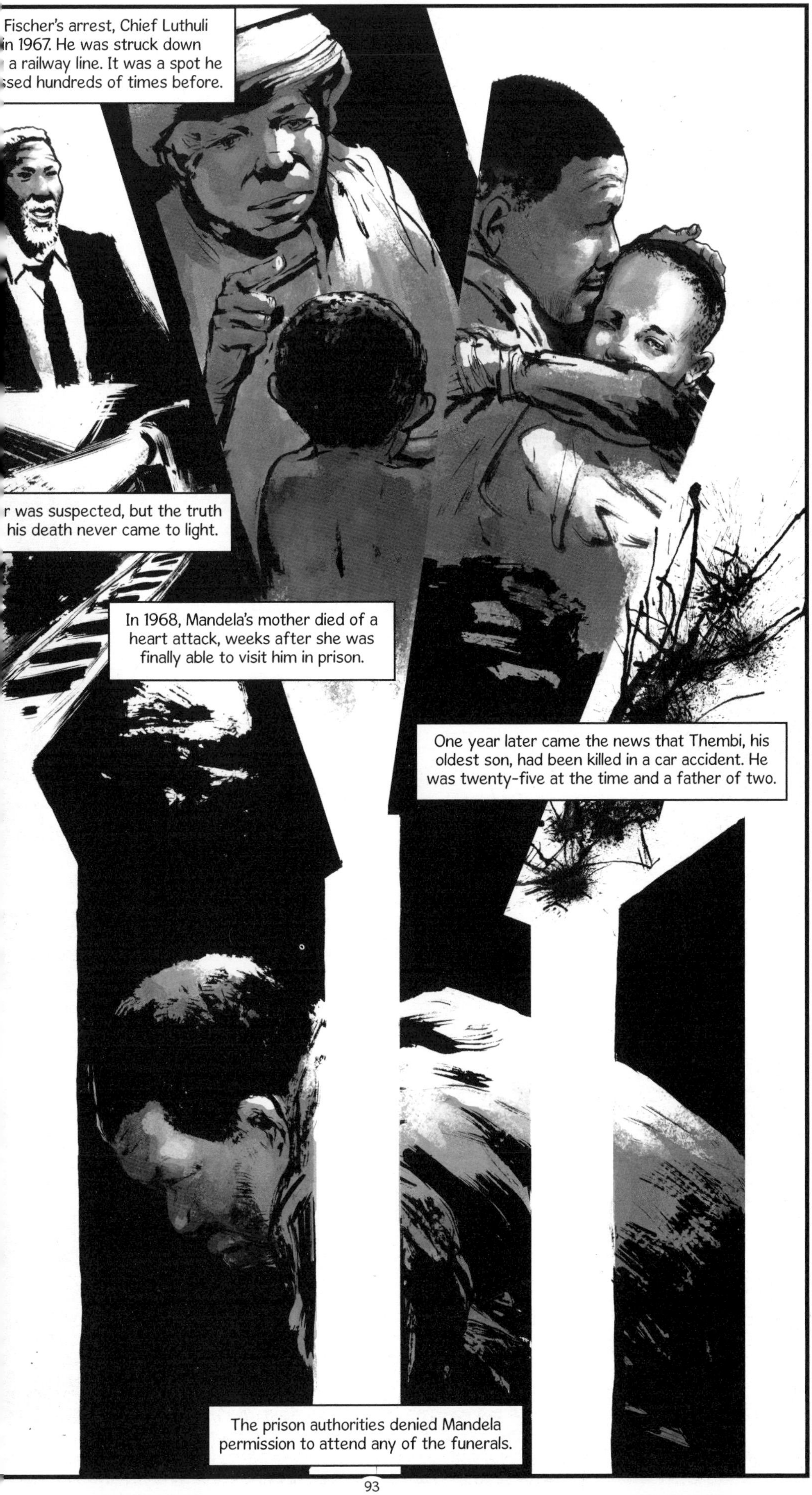
Fischer's arrest, Chief Luthuli
in 1967. He was struck down
a railway line. It was a spot he
ssed hundreds of times before.
r was suspected, but the truth
his death never came to light.
In 1968, Mandela's mother died of a heart attack, weeks after she was finally able to visit him in prison.
One year later came the news that Thembi, his oldest son, had been killed in a car accident. He was twenty-five at the time and a father of two.
The prison authorities denied Mandela permission to attend any of the funerals.

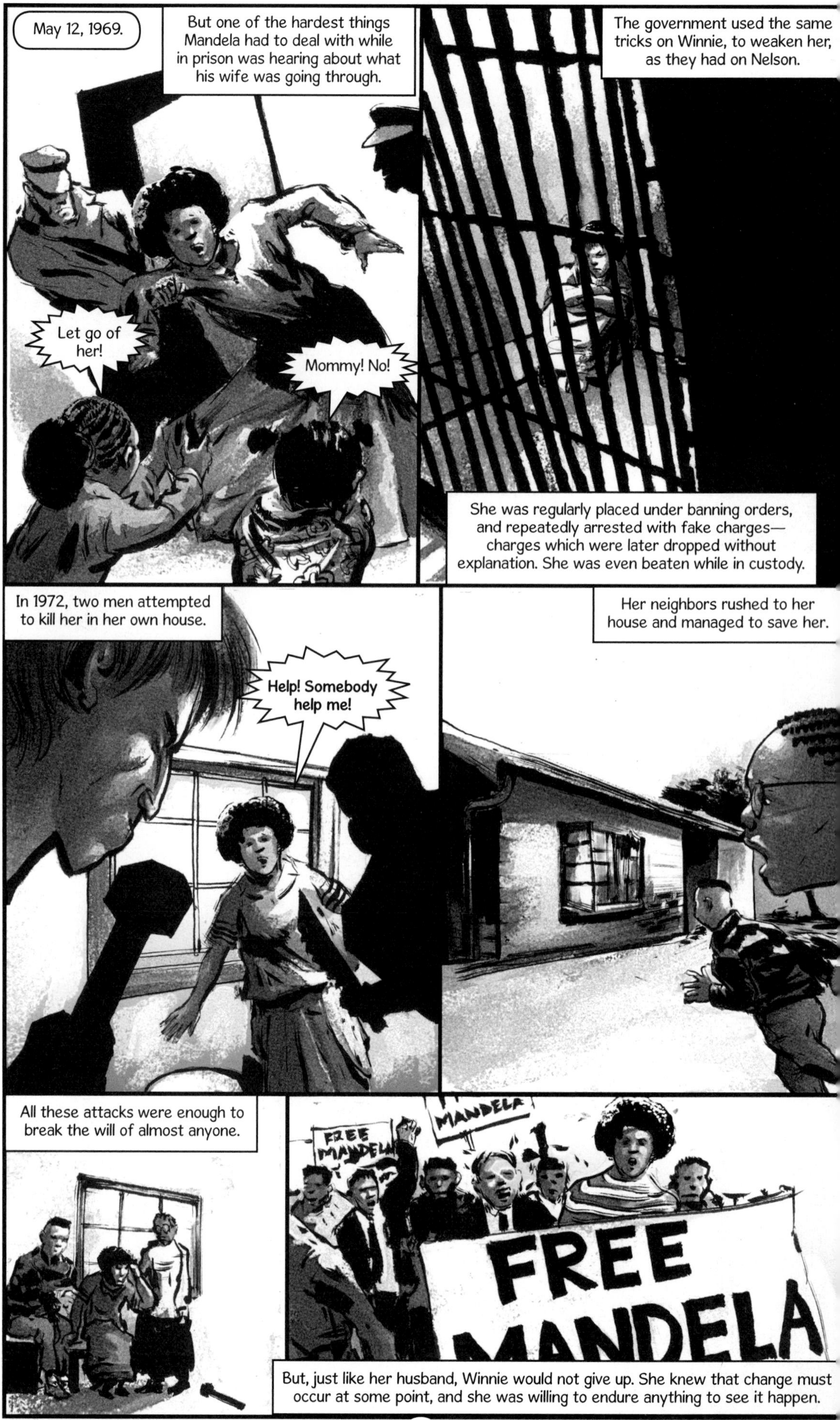
May 12, 1969.
But one of the hardest things Mandela had to deal with while in prison was hearing about what his wife was going through.
Let go of her!
Mommy! No!
The government used the same tricks on Winnie, to weaken her, as they had on Nelson.
She was regularly placed under banning orders, and repeatedly arrested with fake charges—charges which were later dropped without explanation. She was even beaten while in custody.
In 1972, two men attempted to kill her in her own house.
Help! Somebody help me!
Her neighbors rushed to her house and managed to save her.
All these attacks were enough to break the will of almost anyone.
FREE MANDELA
MANDELA
FREE MANDELA
But, just like her husband, Winnie would not give up. She knew that change must occur at some point, and she was willing to endure anything to see it happen.

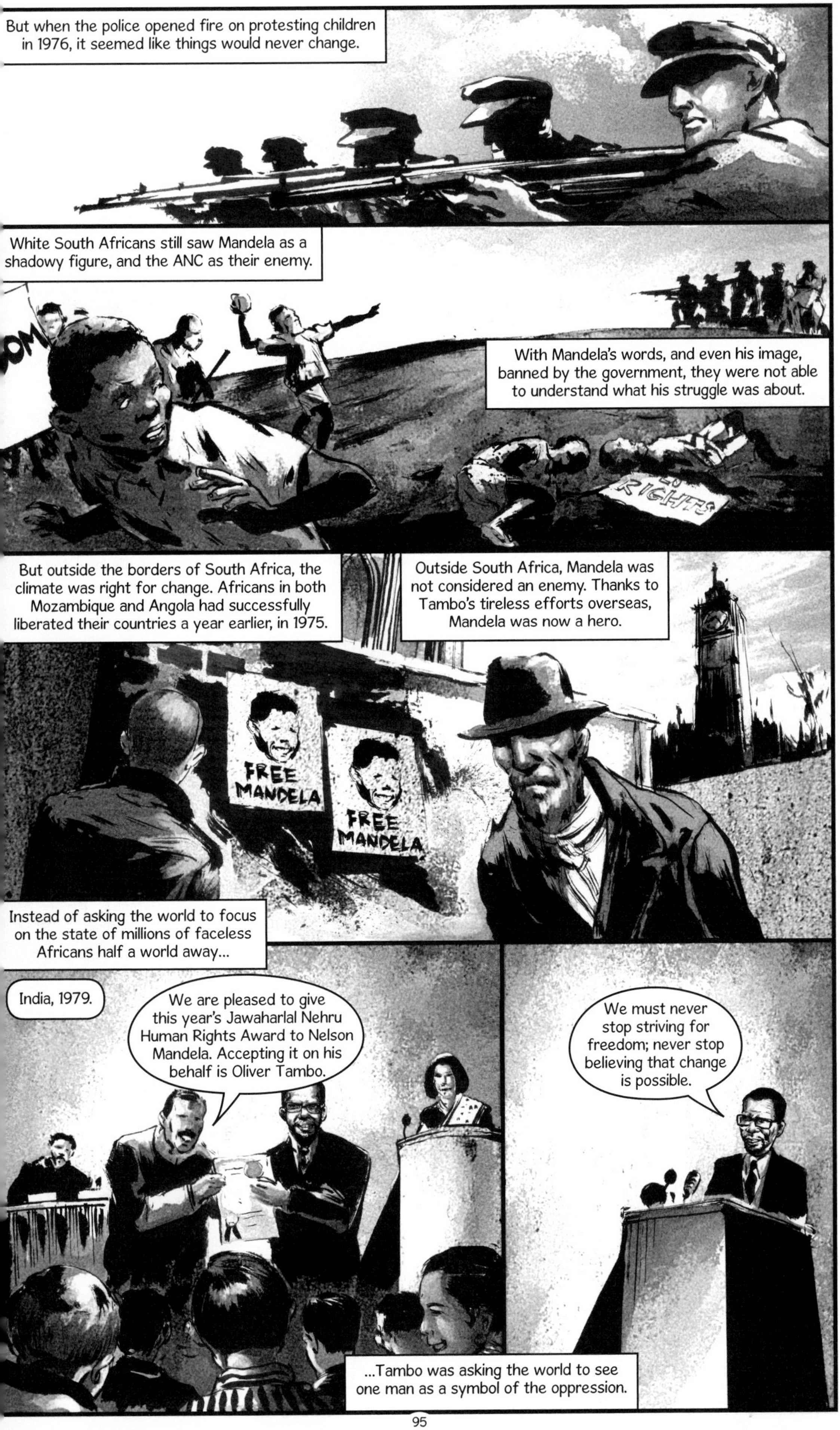
But when the police opened fire on protesting children in 1976, it seemed like things would never change.
White South Africans still saw Mandela as a shadowy figure, and the ANC as their enemy.
With Mandela's words, and even his image, banned by the government, they were not able to understand what his struggle was about.
RIGHTS
But outside the borders of South Africa, the climate was right for change. Africans in both Mozambique and Angola had successfully liberated their countries a year earlier, in 1975.
Outside South Africa, Mandela was not considered an enemy. Thanks to Tambo's tireless efforts overseas, Mandela was now a hero.
FREE MANDELA
FREE MANDELA
Instead of asking the world to focus on the state of millions of faceless Africans half a world away...
India, 1979.
We are pleased to give this year's Jawaharlal Nehru Human Rights Award to Nelson Mandela. Accepting it on his behalf is Oliver Tambo.
We must never stop striving for freedom; never stop believing that change is possible.
...Tambo was asking the world to see one man as a symbol of the oppression.

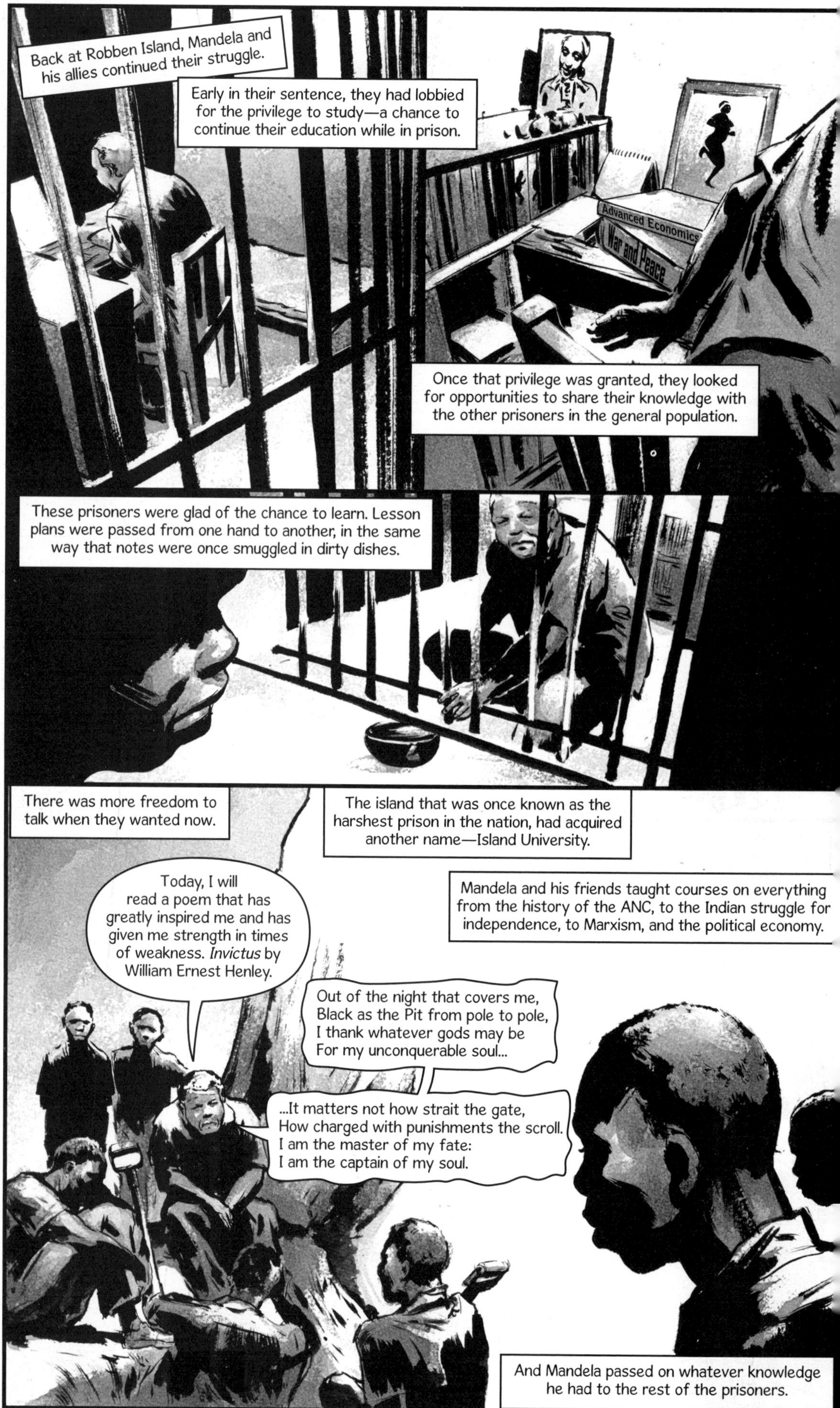

Back at Robben Island, Mandela and his allies continued their struggle.
Early in their sentence, they had lobbied for the privilege to study—a chance to continue their education while in prison.
Advanced Economics
War and Peace
Once that privilege was granted, they looked for opportunities to share their knowledge with the other prisoners in the general population.
These prisoners were glad of the chance to learn. Lesson plans were passed from one hand to another, in the same way that notes were once smuggled in dirty dishes.
There was more freedom to talk when they wanted now.
The island that was once known as the harshest prison in the nation, had acquired another name—Island University.
Mandela and his friends taught courses on everything from the history of the ANC, to the Indian struggle for independence, to Marxism, and the political economy.
Today, I will read a poem that has greatly inspired me and has given me strength in times of weakness. *Invictus* by William Ernest Henley.
Out of the night that covers me, Black as the Pit from pole to pole, I thank whatever gods may be For my unconquerable soul...
...It matters not how strait the gate, How charged with punishments the scroll. I am the master of my fate: I am the captain of my soul.
And Mandela passed on whatever knowledge he had to the rest of the prisoners.

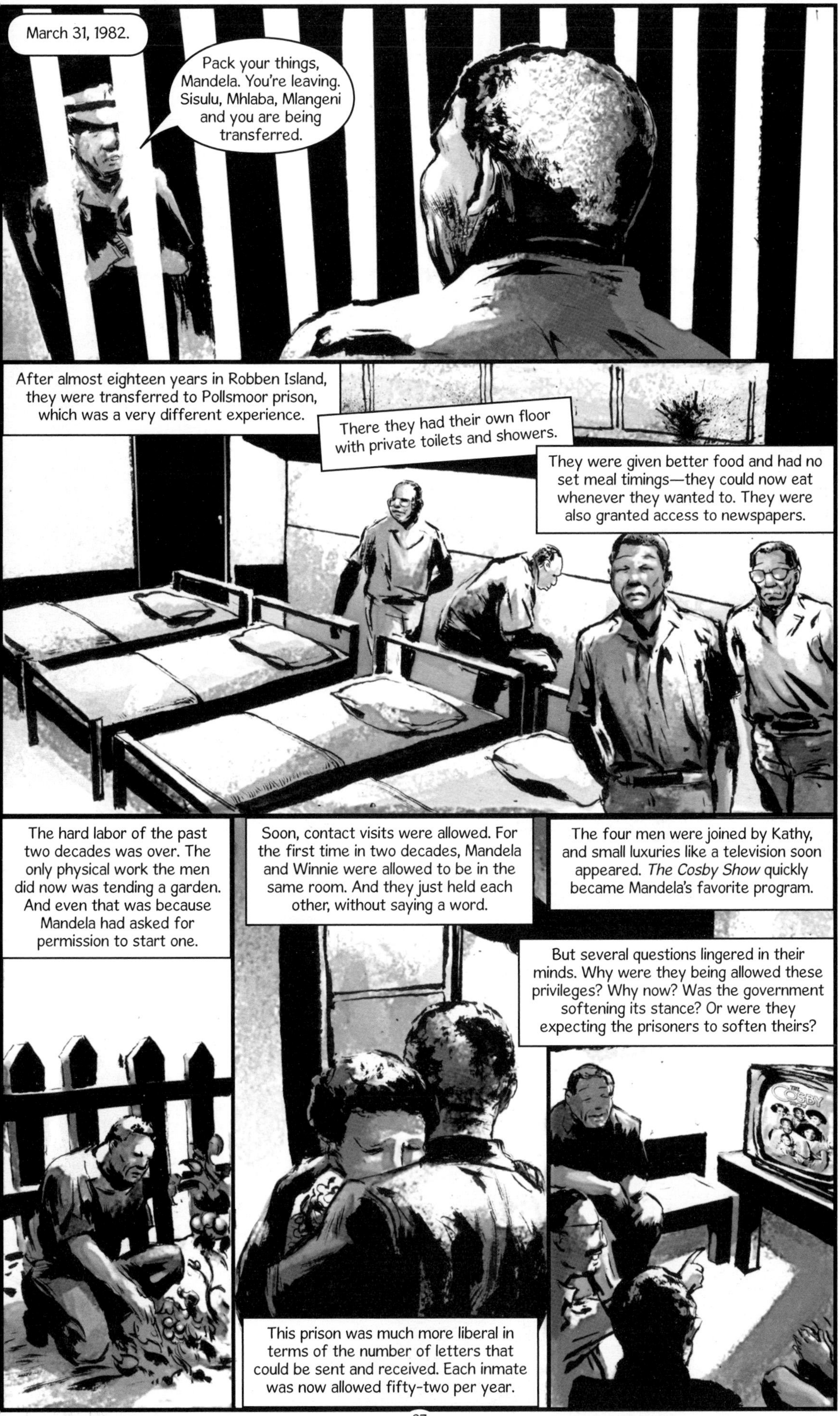
March 31, 1982.
Pack your things, Mandela. You're leaving. Sisulu, Mhlaba, Mlangeni and you are being transferred.
After almost eighteen years in Robben Island, they were transferred to Pollsmoor prison, which was a very different experience.
There they had their own floor with private toilets and showers.
They were given better food and had no set meal timings—they could now eat whenever they wanted to. They were also granted access to newspapers.
The hard labor of the past two decades was over. The only physical work the men did now was tending a garden. And even that was because Mandela had asked for permission to start one.
Soon, contact visits were allowed. For the first time in two decades, Mandela and Winnie were allowed to be in the same room. And they just held each other, without saying a word.
This prison was much more liberal in terms of the number of letters that could be sent and received. Each inmate was now allowed fifty-two per year.
The four men were joined by Kathy, and small luxuries like a television soon appeared. *The Cosby Show* quickly became Mandela's favorite program.
But several questions lingered in their minds. Why were they being allowed these privileges? Why now? Was the government softening its stance? Or were they expecting the prisoners to soften theirs?

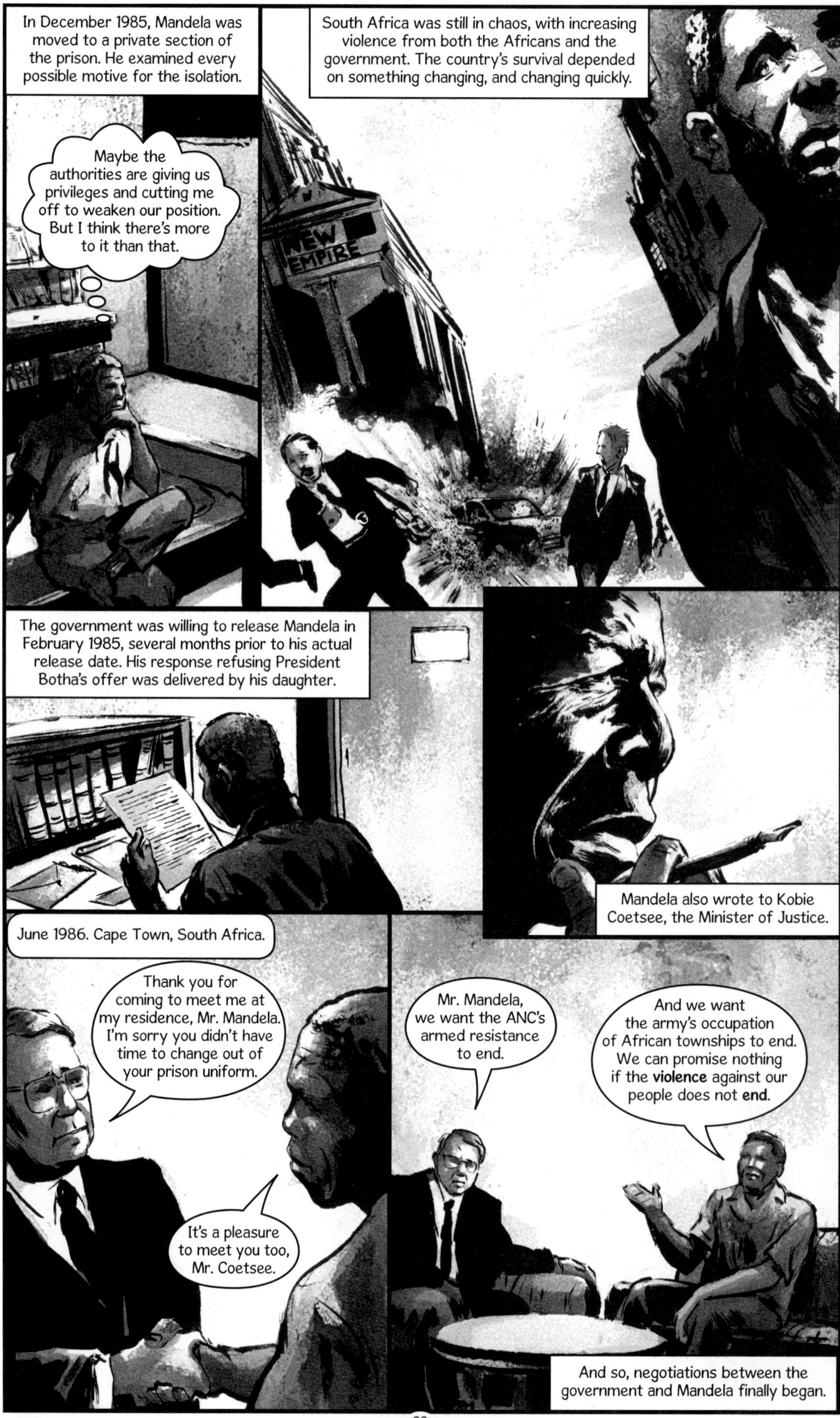
In December 1985, Mandela was moved to a private section of the prison. He examined every possible motive for the isolation.
Maybe the authorities are giving us privileges and cutting me off to weaken our position. But I think there's more to it than that.
South Africa was still in chaos, with increasing violence from both the Africans and the government. The country's survival depended on something changing, and changing quickly.
NEW EMPIRE
The government was willing to release Mandela in February 1985, several months prior to his actual release date. His response refusing President Botha's offer was delivered by his daughter.
Mandela also wrote to Kobie Coetsee, the Minister of Justice.
June 1986. Cape Town, South Africa.
Thank you for coming to meet me at my residence, Mr. Mandela. I'm sorry you didn't have time to change out of your prison uniform.
It's a pleasure to meet you too, Mr. Coetsee.
Mr. Mandela, we want the ANC's armed resistance to end.
And we want the army's occupation of African townships to end. We can promise nothing if the **violence** against our people does not **end**.
And so, negotiations between the government and Mandela finally began.

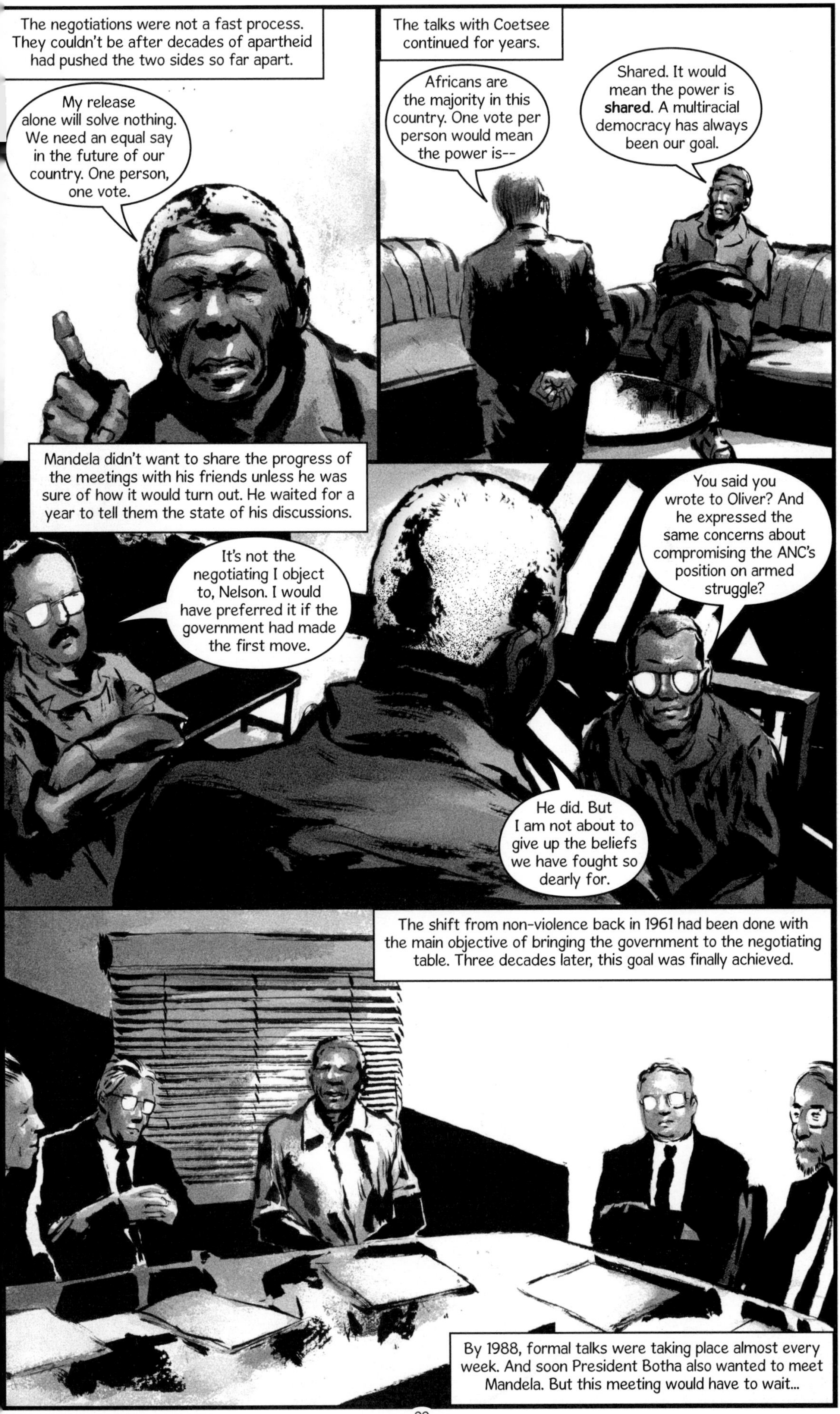
The negotiations were not a fast process. They couldn't be after decades of apartheid had pushed the two sides so far apart.
My release alone will solve nothing. We need an equal say in the future of our country. One person, one vote.
The talks with Coetsee continued for years.
Africans are the majority in this country. One vote per person would mean the power is--
Shared. It would mean the power is **shared**. A multiracial democracy has always been our goal.
Mandela didn't want to share the progress of the meetings with his friends unless he was sure of how it would turn out. He waited for a year to tell them the state of his discussions.
It's not the negotiating I object to, Nelson. I would have preferred it if the government had made the first move.
You said you wrote to Oliver? And he expressed the same concerns about compromising the ANC's position on armed struggle?
He did. But I am not about to give up the beliefs we have fought so dearly for.
The shift from non-violence back in 1961 had been done with the main objective of bringing the government to the negotiating table. Three decades later, this goal was finally achieved.
By 1988, formal talks were taking place almost every week. And soon President Botha also wanted to meet Mandela. But this meeting would have to wait...

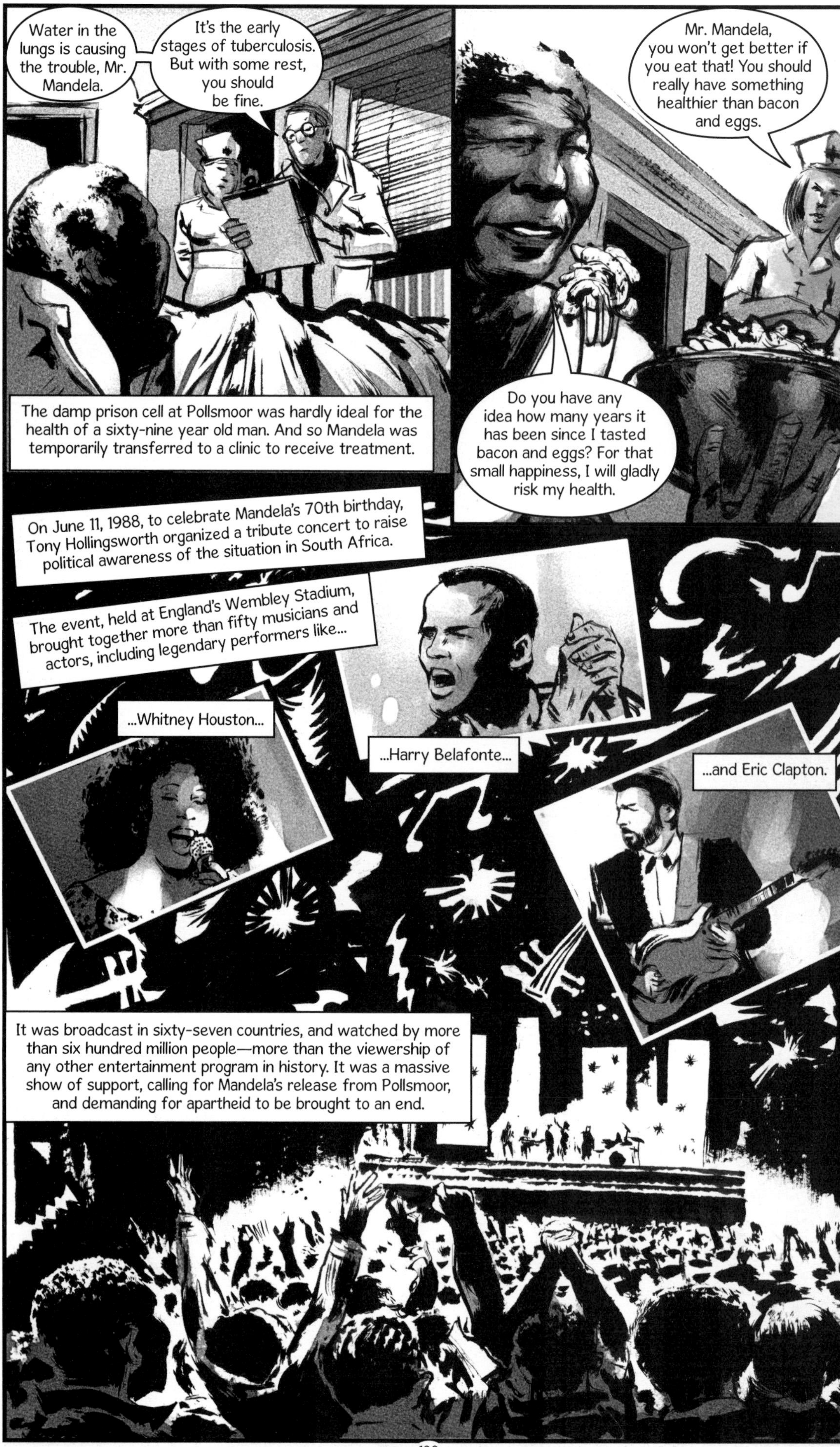
Water in the lungs is causing the trouble, Mr. Mandela.
It's the early stages of tuberculosis. But with some rest, you should be fine.
The damp prison cell at Pollsmoor was hardly ideal for the health of a sixty-nine year old man. And so Mandela was temporarily transferred to a clinic to receive treatment.
Mr. Mandela, you won't get better if you eat that! You should really have something healthier than bacon and eggs.
Do you have any idea how many years it has been since I tasted bacon and eggs? For that small happiness, I will gladly risk my health.
On June 11, 1988, to celebrate Mandela's 70th birthday, Tony Hollingsworth organized a tribute concert to raise political awareness of the situation in South Africa.
The event, held at England's Wembley Stadium, brought together more than fifty musicians and actors, including legendary performers like...
...Whitney Houston...
...Harry Belafonte...
...and Eric Clapton.
It was broadcast in sixty-seven countries, and watched by more than six hundred million people—more than the viewership of any other entertainment program in history. It was a massive show of support, calling for Mandela's release from Pollsmoor, and demanding for apartheid to be brought to an end.

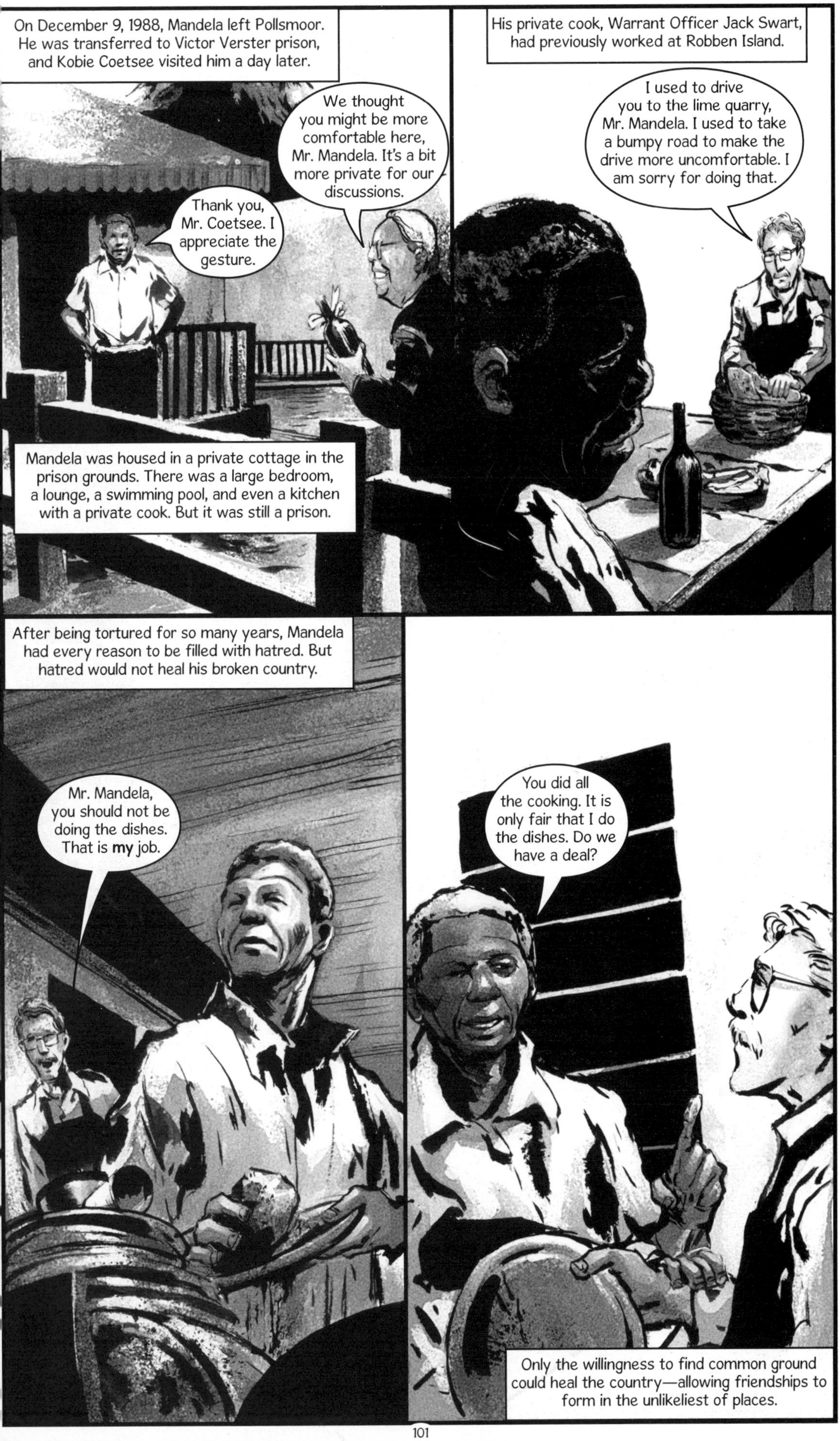
On December 9, 1988, Mandela left Pollsmoor. He was transferred to Victor Verster prison, and Kobie Coetsee visited him a day later.
We thought you might be more comfortable here, Mr. Mandela. It's a bit more private for our discussions.
Thank you, Mr. Coetsee. I appreciate the gesture.
Mandela was housed in a private cottage in the prison grounds. There was a large bedroom, a lounge, a swimming pool, and even a kitchen with a private cook. But it was still a prison.
His private cook, Warrant Officer Jack Swart, had previously worked at Robben Island.
I used to drive you to the lime quarry, Mr. Mandela. I used to take a bumpy road to make the drive more uncomfortable. I am sorry for doing that.
After being tortured for so many years, Mandela had every reason to be filled with hatred. But hatred would not heal his broken country.
Mr. Mandela, you should not be doing the dishes. That is **my** job.
You did all the cooking. It is only fair that I do the dishes. Do we have a deal?
Only the willingness to find common ground could heal the country—allowing friendships to form in the unlikeliest of places.

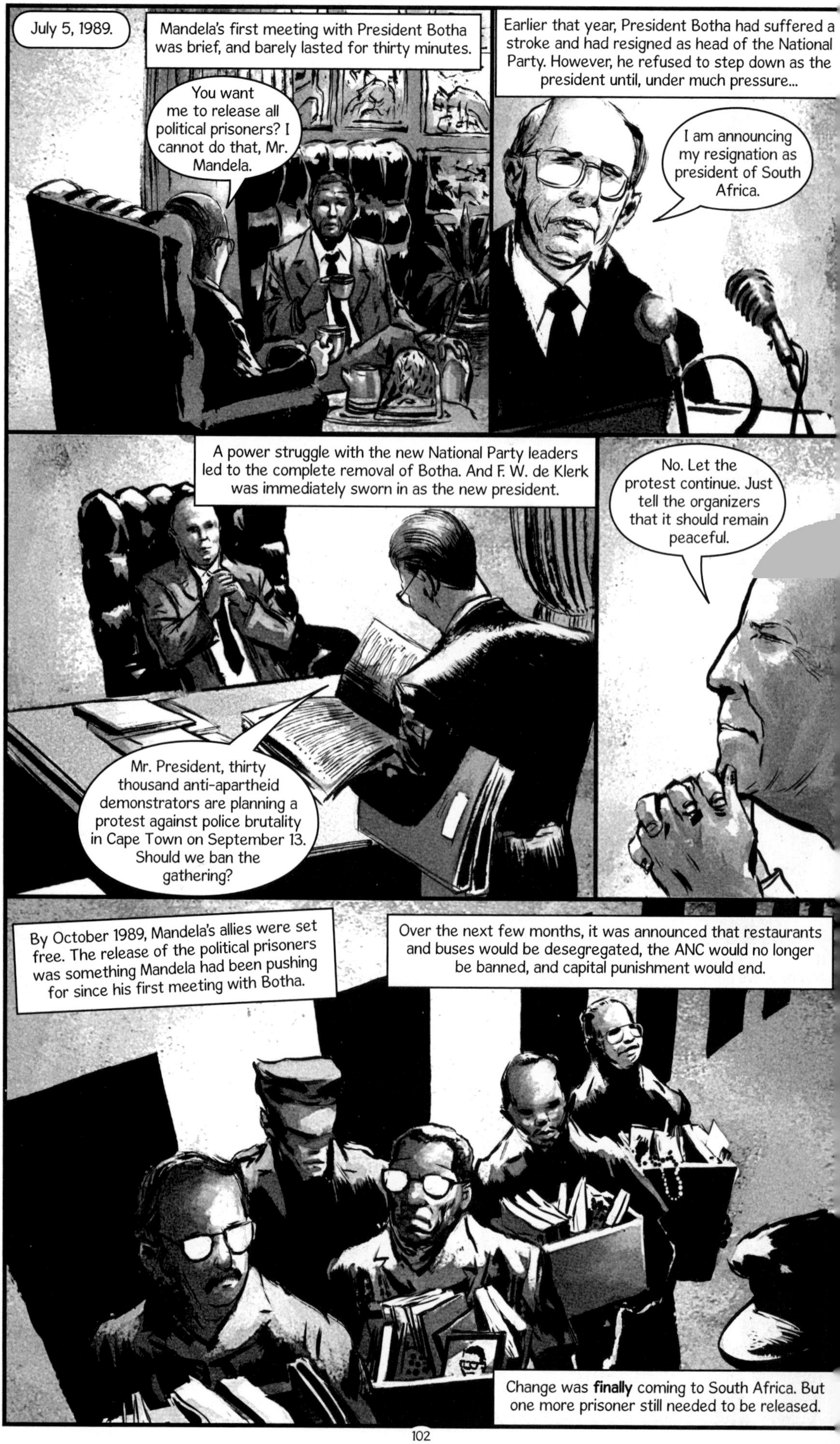

July 5, 1989.
Mandela's first meeting with President Botha was brief, and barely lasted for thirty minutes.
You want me to release all political prisoners? I cannot do that, Mr. Mandela.
Earlier that year, President Botha had suffered a stroke and had resigned as head of the National Party. However, he refused to step down as the president until, under much pressure...
I am announcing my resignation as president of South Africa.
A power struggle with the new National Party leaders led to the complete removal of Botha. And F. W. de Klerk was immediately sworn in as the new president.
Mr. President, thirty thousand anti-apartheid demonstrators are planning a protest against police brutality in Cape Town on September 13. Should we ban the gathering?
No. Let the protest continue. Just tell the organizers that it should remain peaceful.
By October 1989, Mandela's allies were set free. The release of the political prisoners was something Mandela had been pushing for since his first meeting with Botha.
Over the next few months, it was announced that restaurants and buses would be desegregated, the ANC would no longer be banned, and capital punishment would end.
Change was **finally** coming to South Africa. But one more prisoner still needed to be released.

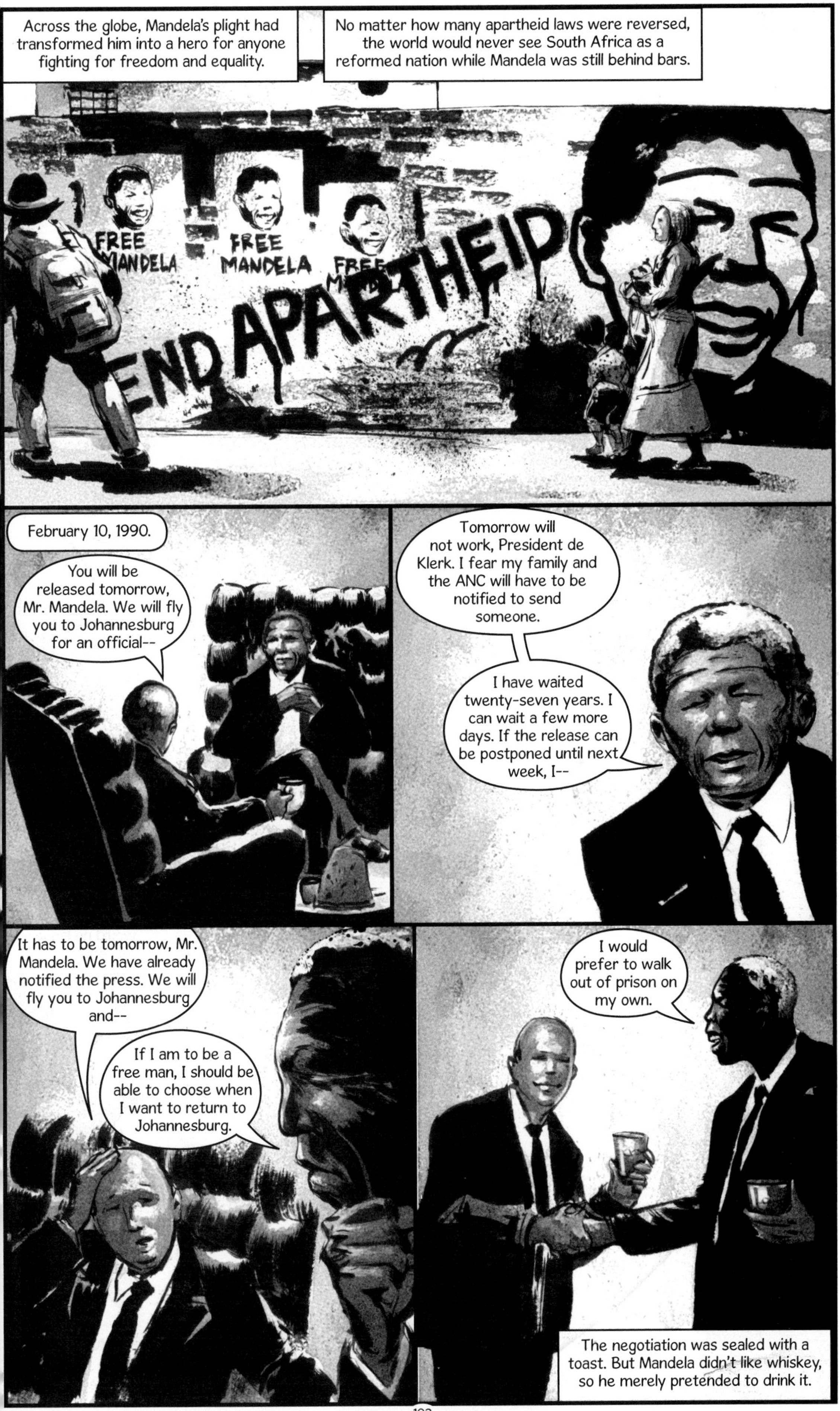
Across the globe, Mandela's plight had transformed him into a hero for anyone fighting for freedom and equality.
No matter how many apartheid laws were reversed, the world would never see South Africa as a reformed nation while Mandela was still behind bars.
FREE MANDELA
FREE MANDELA
END APARTHEID
February 10, 1990.
You will be released tomorrow, Mr. Mandela. We will fly you to Johannesburg for an official--
Tomorrow will not work, President de Klerk. I fear my family and the ANC will have to be notified to send someone.
I have waited twenty-seven years. I can wait a few more days. If the release can be postponed until next week, I--
It has to be tomorrow, Mr. Mandela. We have already notified the press. We will fly you to Johannesburg and--
If I am to be a free man, I should be able to choose when I want to return to Johannesburg.
I would prefer to walk out of prison on my own.
The negotiation was sealed with a toast. But Mandela didn't like whiskey, so he merely pretended to drink it.

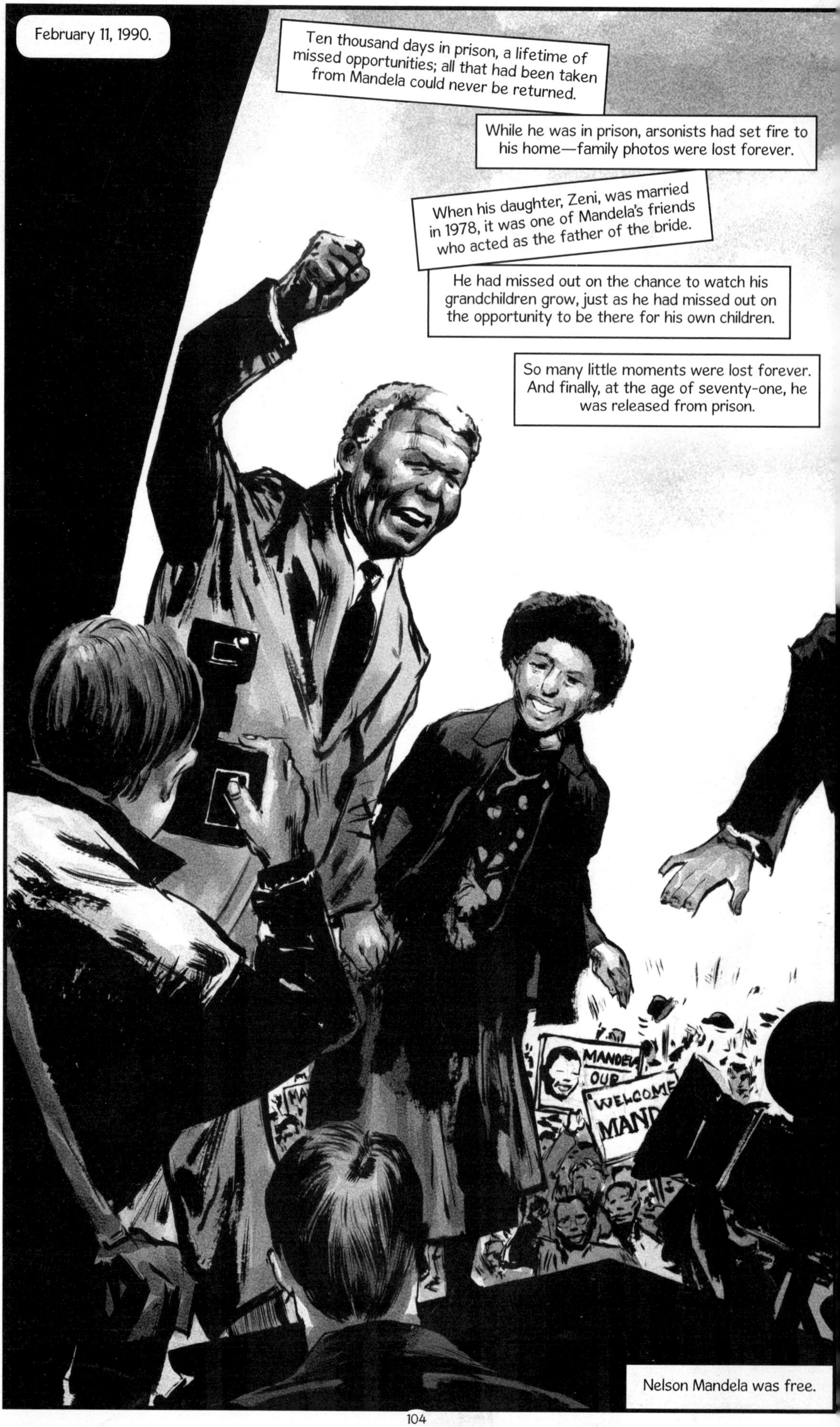
February 11, 1990.
Ten thousand days in prison, a lifetime of missed opportunities; all that had been taken from Mandela could never be returned.
While he was in prison, arsonists had set fire to his home—family photos were lost forever.
When his daughter, Zeni, was married in 1978, it was one of Mandela's friends who acted as the father of the bride.
He had missed out on the chance to watch his grandchildren grow, just as he had missed out on the opportunity to be there for his own children.
So many little moments were lost forever. And finally, at the age of seventy-one, he was released from prison.
WELCOME
Nelson Mandela was free.

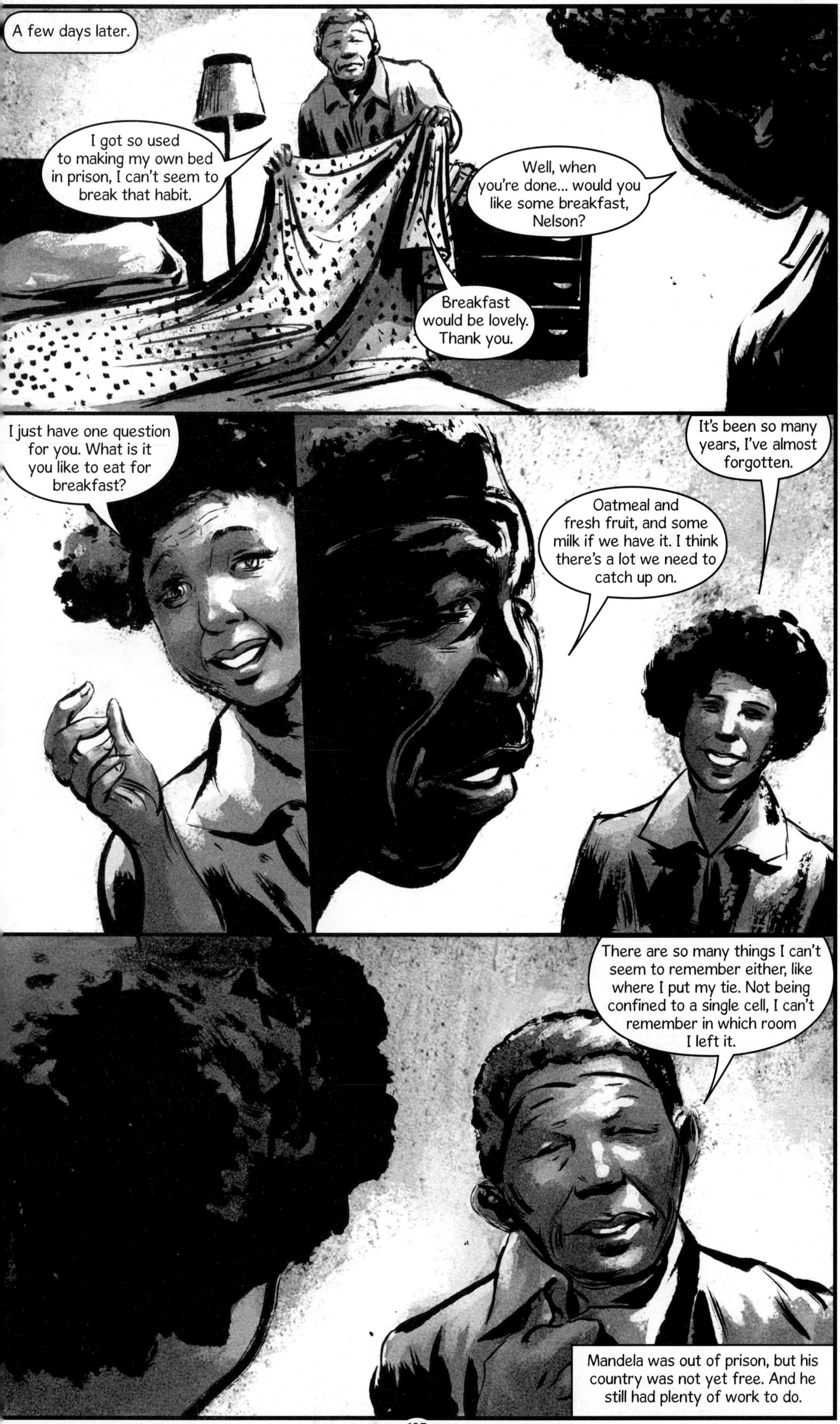
A few days later.
I got so used to making my own bed in prison, I can't seem to break that habit.
Well, when you're done... would you like some breakfast, Nelson?
Breakfast would be lovely. Thank you.
I just have one question for you. What is it you like to eat for breakfast?
It's been so many years, I've almost forgotten.
Oatmeal and fresh fruit, and some milk if we have it. I think there's a lot we need to catch up on.
There are so many things I can't seem to remember either, like where I put my tie. Not being confined to a single cell, I can't remember in which room I left it.
Mandela was out of prison, but his country was not yet free. And he still had plenty of work to do.

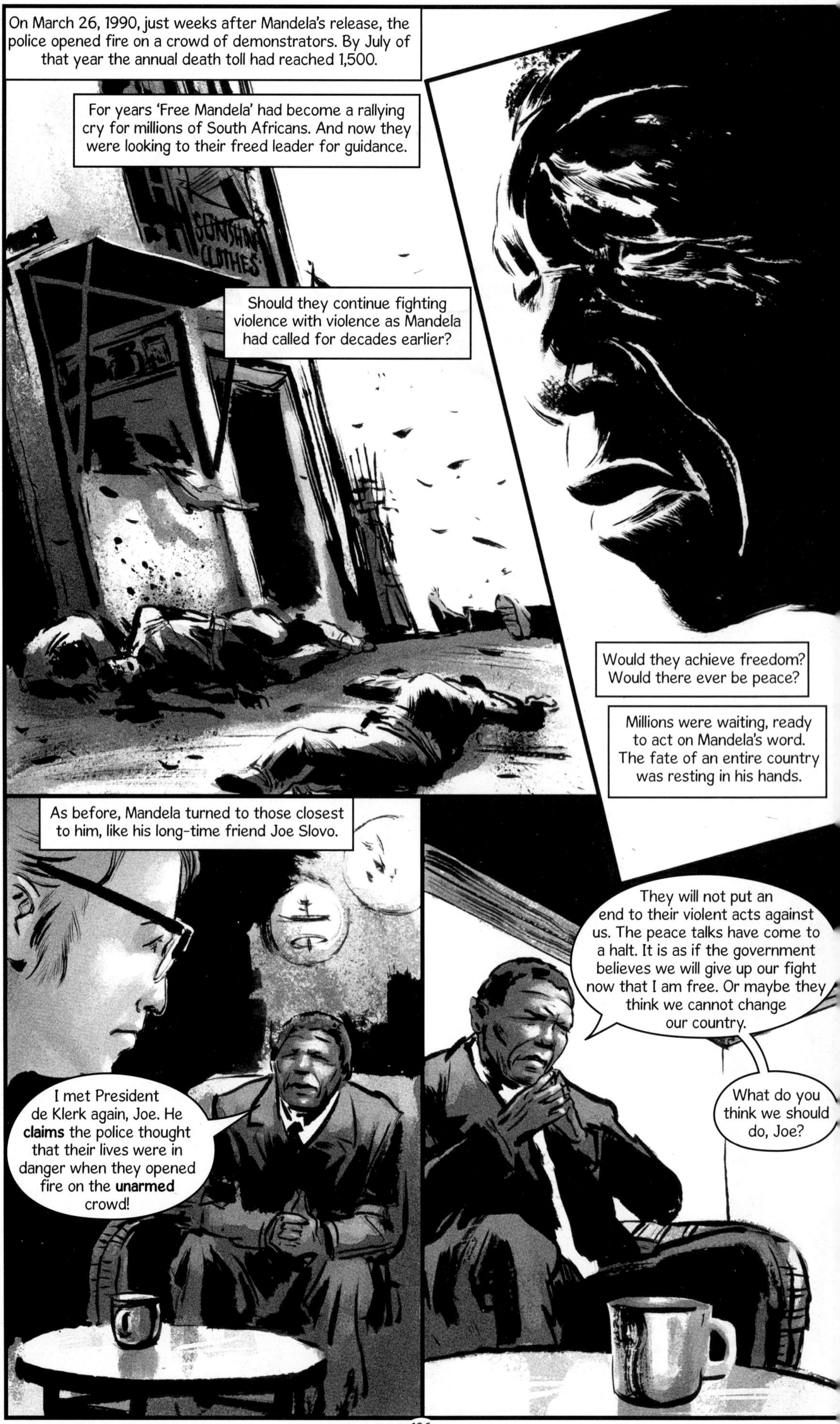
On March 26, 1990, just weeks after Mandela's release, the police opened fire on a crowd of demonstrators. By July of that year the annual death toll had reached 1,500.
For years 'Free Mandela' had become a rallying cry for millions of South Africans. And now they were looking to their freed leader for guidance.
Should they continue fighting violence with violence as Mandela had called for decades earlier?
Would they achieve freedom? Would there ever be peace?
Millions were waiting, ready to act on Mandela's word. The fate of an entire country was resting in his hands.
As before, Mandela turned to those closest to him, like his long-time friend Joe Slovo.
I met President de Klerk again, Joe. He **claims** the police thought that their lives were in danger when they opened fire on the **unarmed** crowd!
They will not put an end to their violent acts against us. The peace talks have come to a halt. It is as if the government believes we will give up our fight now that I am free. Or maybe they think we cannot change our country.
What do you think we should do, Joe?

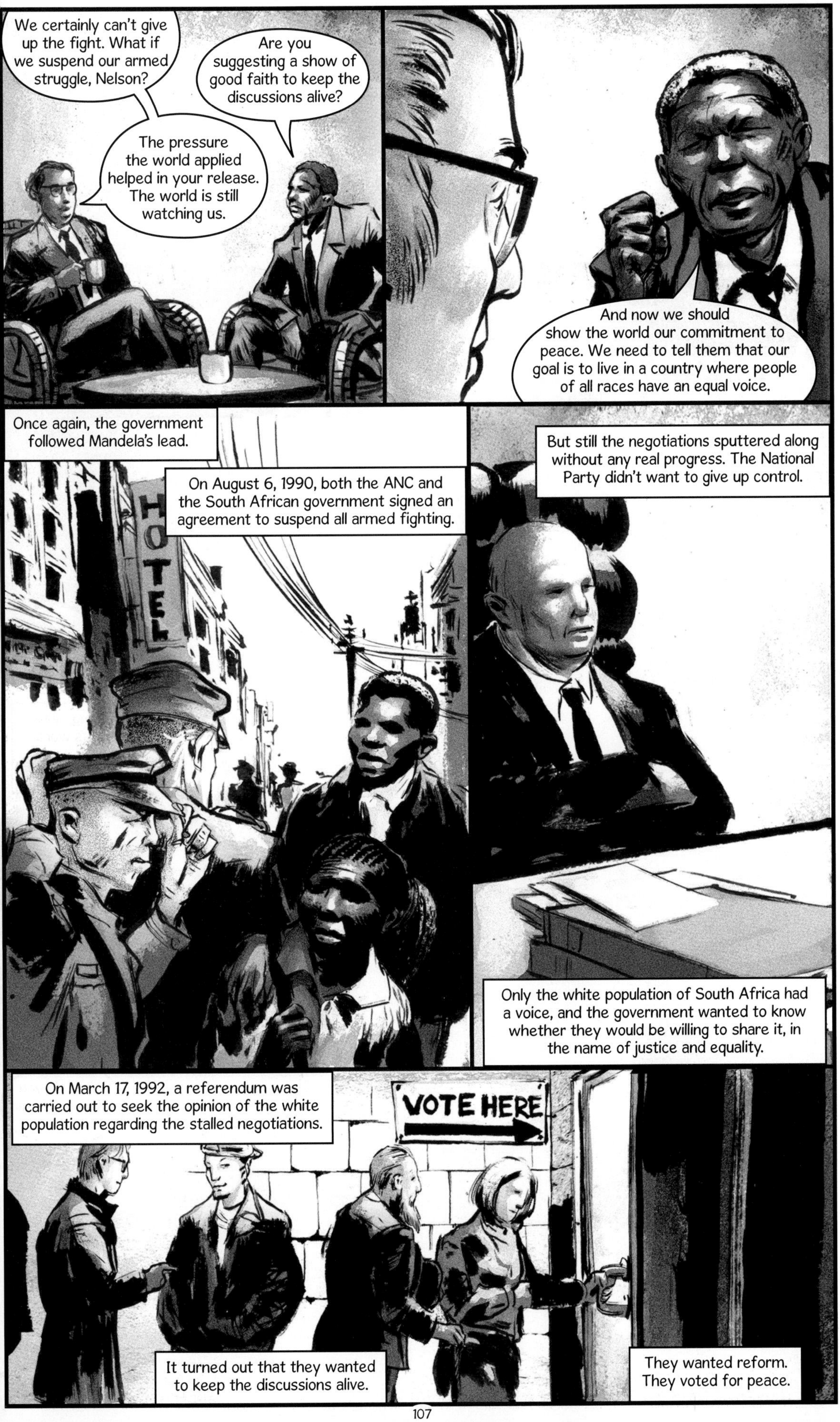
We certainly can't give up the fight. What if we suspend our armed struggle, Nelson?
Are you suggesting a show of good faith to keep the discussions alive?
The pressure the world applied helped in your release. The world is still watching us.
And now we should show the world our commitment to peace. We need to tell them that our goal is to live in a country where people of all races have an equal voice.
Once again, the government followed Mandela's lead.
HOTEL
On August 6, 1990, both the ANC and the South African government signed an agreement to suspend all armed fighting.
But still the negotiations sputtered along without any real progress. The National Party didn't want to give up control.
Only the white population of South Africa had a voice, and the government wanted to know whether they would be willing to share it, in the name of justice and equality.
On March 17, 1992, a referendum was carried out to seek the opinion of the white population regarding the stalled negotiations.
VOTE HERE
It turned out that they wanted to keep the discussions alive.
They wanted reform. They voted for peace.

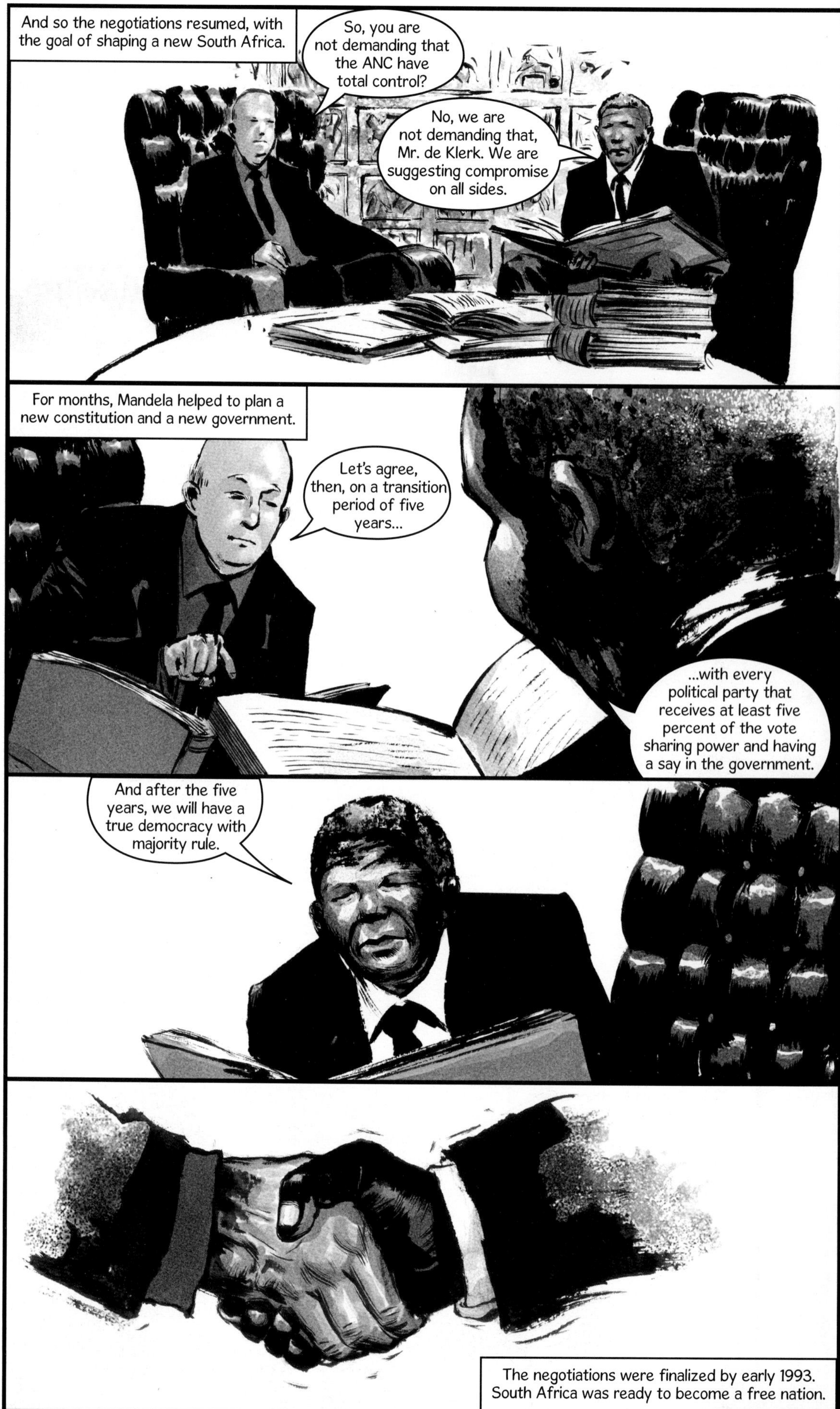
And so the negotiations resumed, with the goal of shaping a new South Africa.
So, you are not demanding that the ANC have total control?
No, we are not demanding that, Mr. de Klerk. We are suggesting compromise on all sides.
For months, Mandela helped to plan a new constitution and a new government.
Let's agree, then, on a transition period of five years...
...with every political party that receives at least five percent of the vote sharing power and having a say in the government.
And after the five years, we will have a true democracy with majority rule.
The negotiations were finalized by early 1993. South Africa was ready to become a free nation.

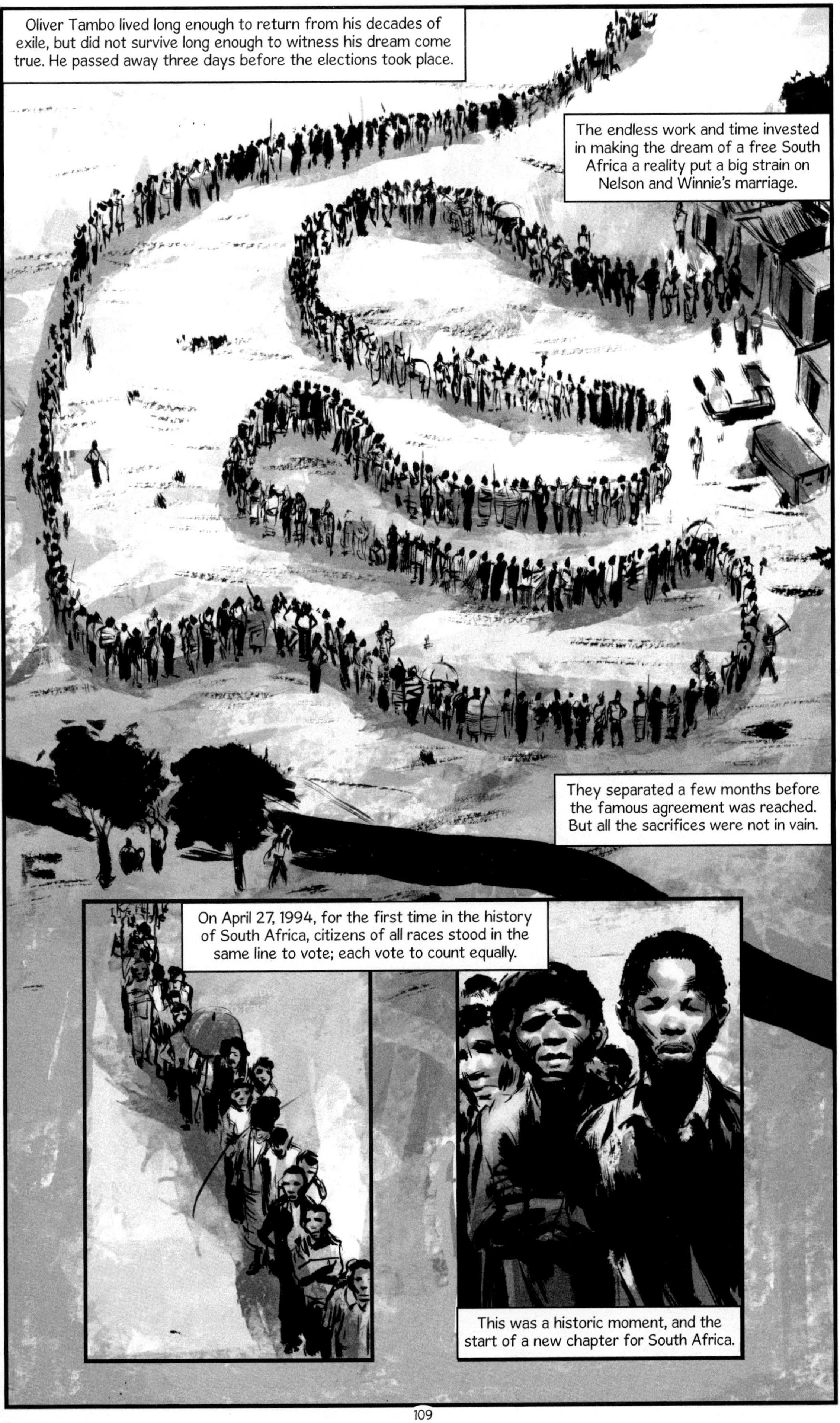

Oliver Tambo lived long enough to return from his decades of exile, but did not survive long enough to witness his dream come true. He passed away three days before the elections took place.
The endless work and time invested in making the dream of a free South Africa a reality put a big strain on Nelson and Winnie's marriage.
They separated a few months before the famous agreement was reached. But all the sacrifices were not in vain.
On April 27, 1994, for the first time in the history of South Africa, citizens of all races stood in the same line to vote; each vote to count equally.
This was a historic moment, and the start of a new chapter for South Africa.

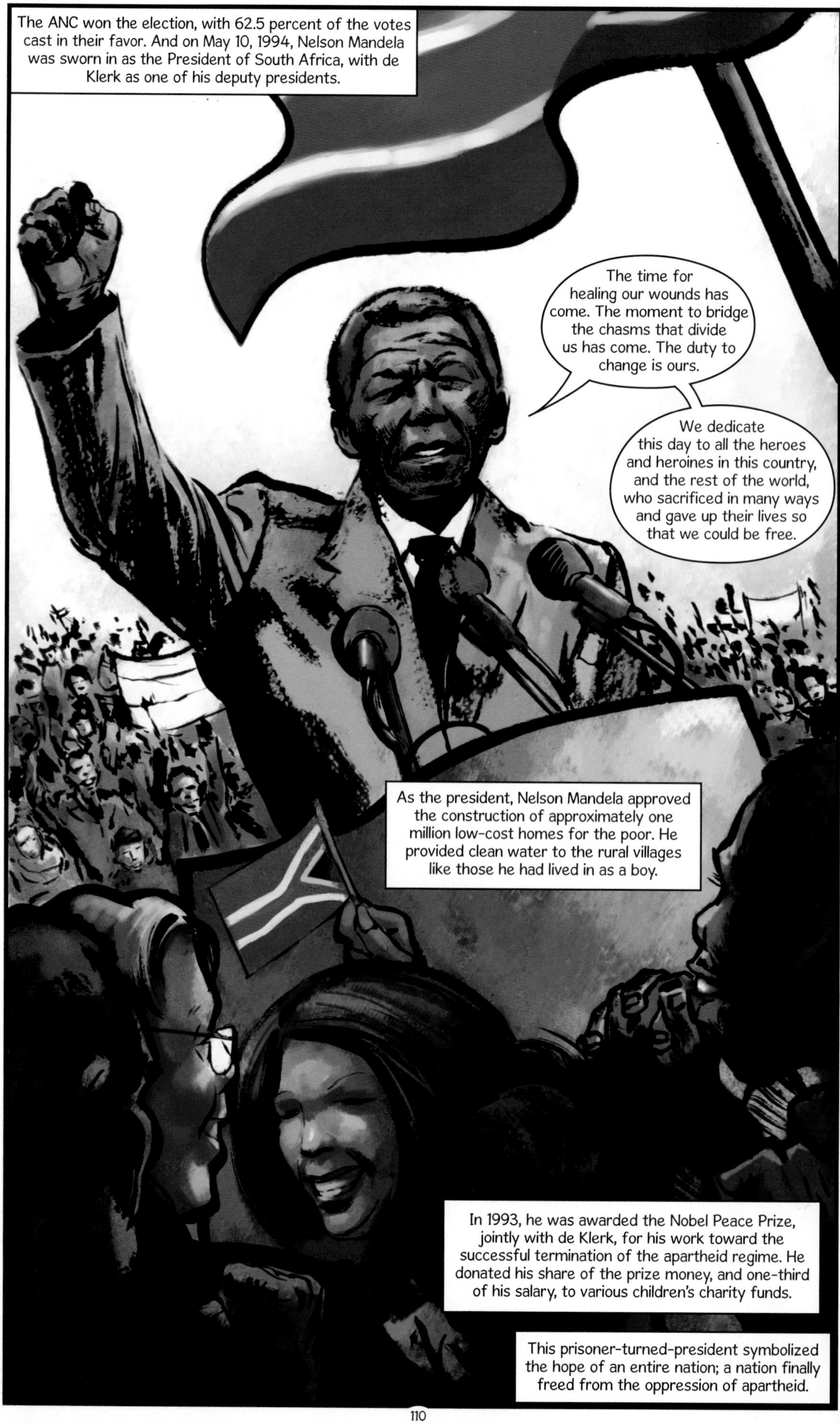
The ANC won the election, with 62.5 percent of the votes cast in their favor. And on May 10, 1994, Nelson Mandela was sworn in as the President of South Africa, with de Klerk as one of his deputy presidents.
The time for healing our wounds has come. The moment to bridge the chasms that divide us has come. The duty to change is ours.
We dedicate this day to all the heroes and heroines in this country, and the rest of the world, who sacrificed in many ways and gave up their lives so that we could be free.
As the president, Nelson Mandela approved the construction of approximately one million low-cost homes for the poor. He provided clean water to the rural villages like those he had lived in as a boy.
In 1993, he was awarded the Nobel Peace Prize, jointly with de Klerk, for his work toward the successful termination of the apartheid regime. He donated his share of the prize money, and one-third of his salary, to various children's charity funds.
This prisoner-turned-president symbolized the hope of an entire nation; a nation finally freed from the oppression of apartheid.

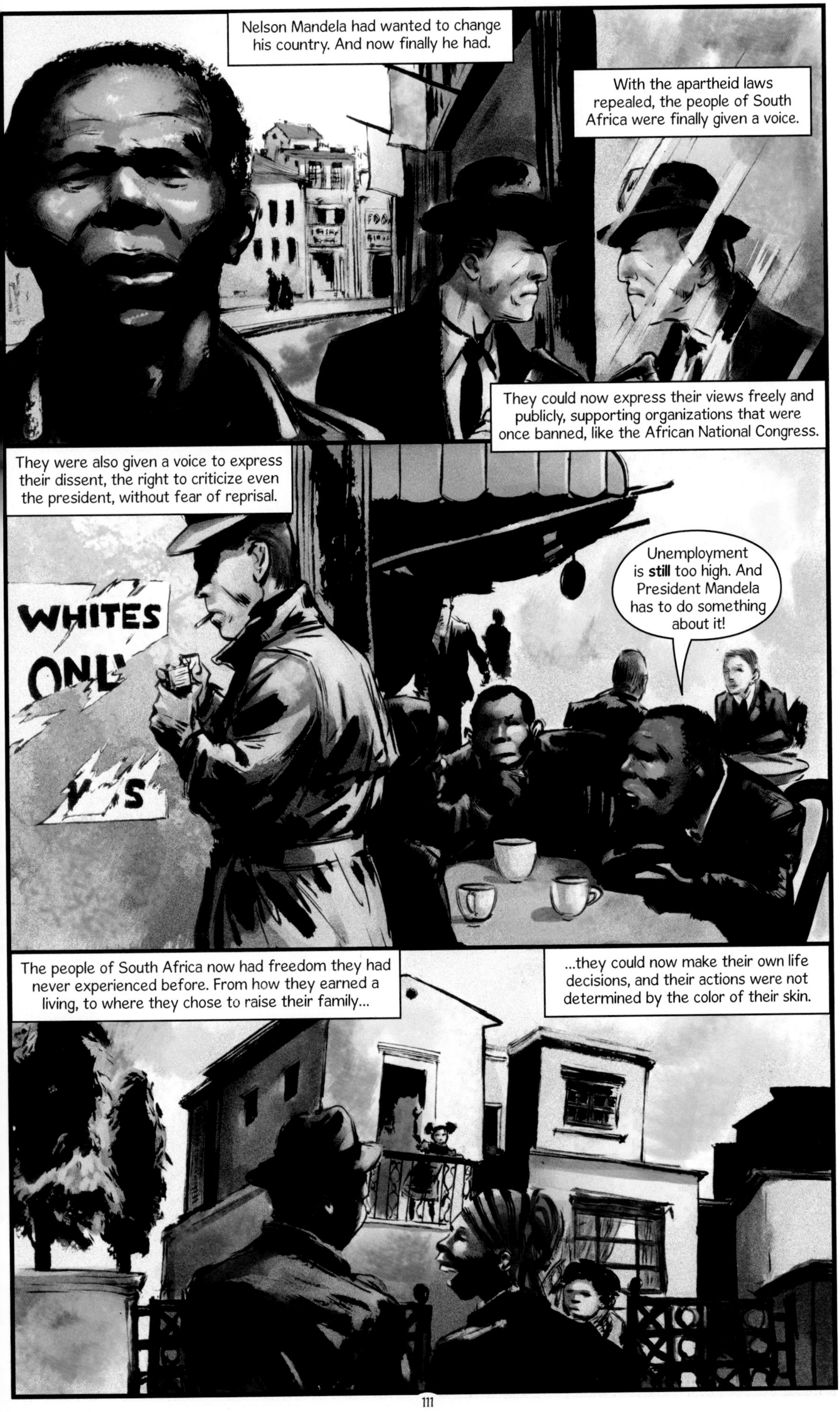
Nelson Mandela had wanted to change his country. And now finally he had.
With the apartheid laws repealed, the people of South Africa were finally given a voice.
They could now express their views freely and publicly, supporting organizations that were once banned, like the African National Congress.
They were also given a voice to express their dissent, the right to criticize even the president, without fear of reprisal.
WHITES
ONL
Unemployment is **still** too high. And President Mandela has to do something about it!
The people of South Africa now had freedom they had never experienced before. From how they earned a living, to where they chose to raise their family...
...they could now make their own life decisions, and their actions were not determined by the color of their skin.

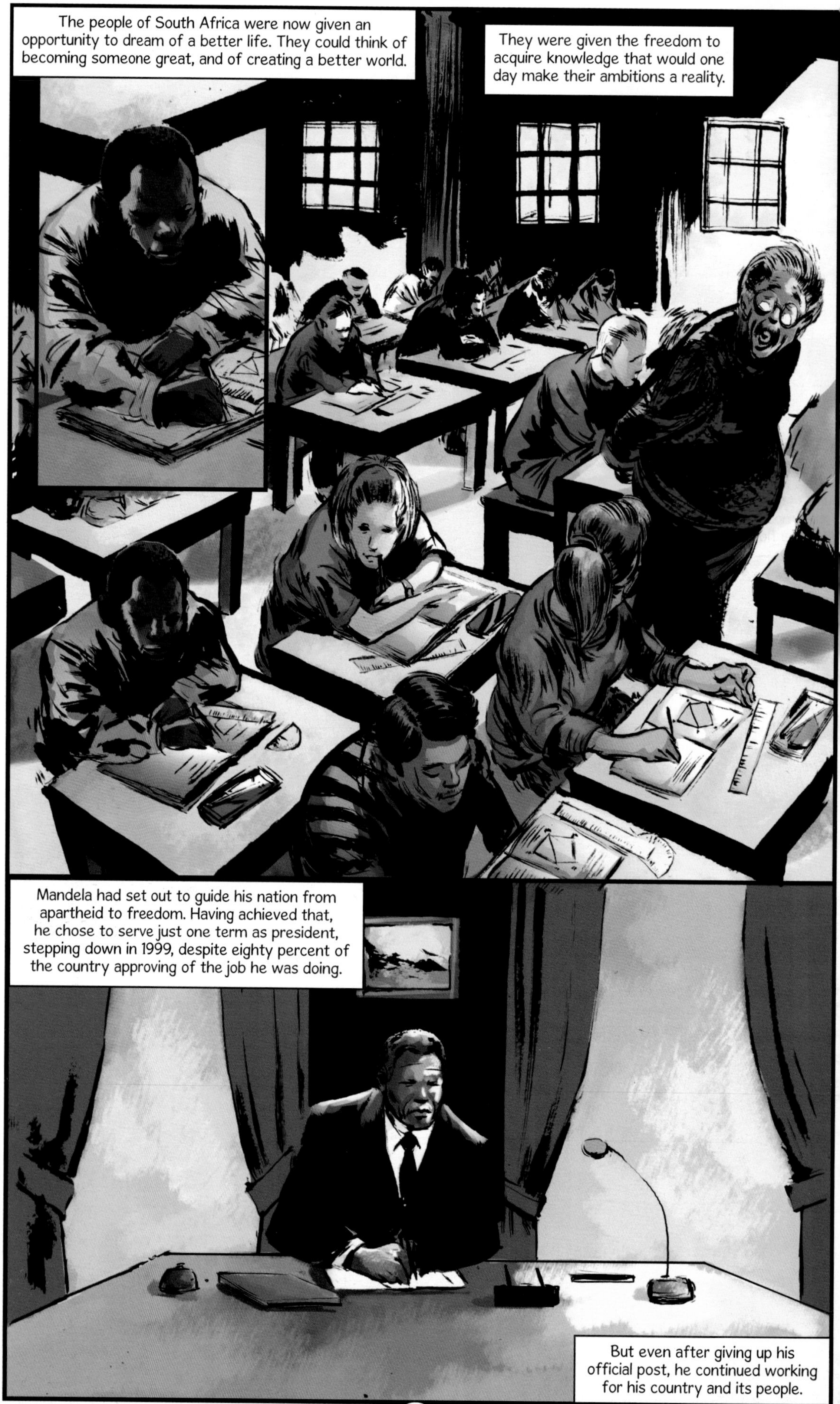
The people of South Africa were now given an opportunity to dream of a better life. They could think of becoming someone great, and of creating a better world.
They were given the freedom to acquire knowledge that would one day make their ambitions a reality.
Mandela had set out to guide his nation from apartheid to freedom. Having achieved that, he chose to serve just one term as president, stepping down in 1999, despite eighty percent of the country approving of the job he was doing.
But even after giving up his official post, he continued working for his country and its people.

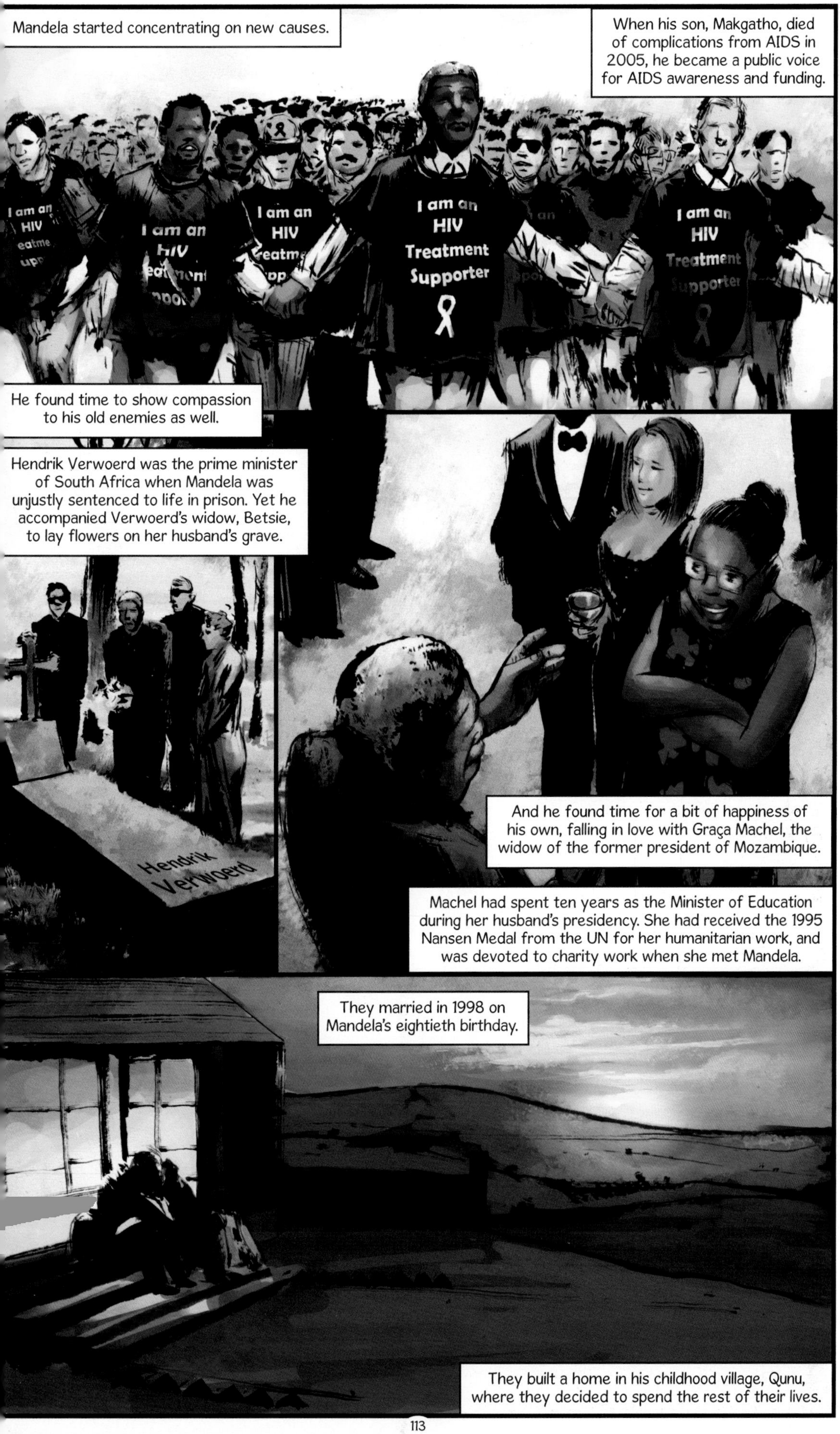
Mandela started concentrating on new causes.
When his son, Makgatho, died of complications from AIDS in 2005, he became a public voice for AIDS awareness and funding.
I am an HIV Treatment Supporter
He found time to show compassion to his old enemies as well.
Hendrik Verwoerd was the prime minister of South Africa when Mandela was unjustly sentenced to life in prison. Yet he accompanied Verwoerd's widow, Betsie, to lay flowers on her husband's grave.
Hendrik Verwoerd
And he found time for a bit of happiness of his own, falling in love with Graça Machel, the widow of the former president of Mozambique.
Machel had spent ten years as the Minister of Education during her husband's presidency. She had received the 1995 Nansen Medal from the UN for her humanitarian work, and was devoted to charity work when she met Mandela.
They married in 1998 on Mandela's eightieth birthday.
They built a home in his childhood village, Qunu, where they decided to spend the rest of their lives.

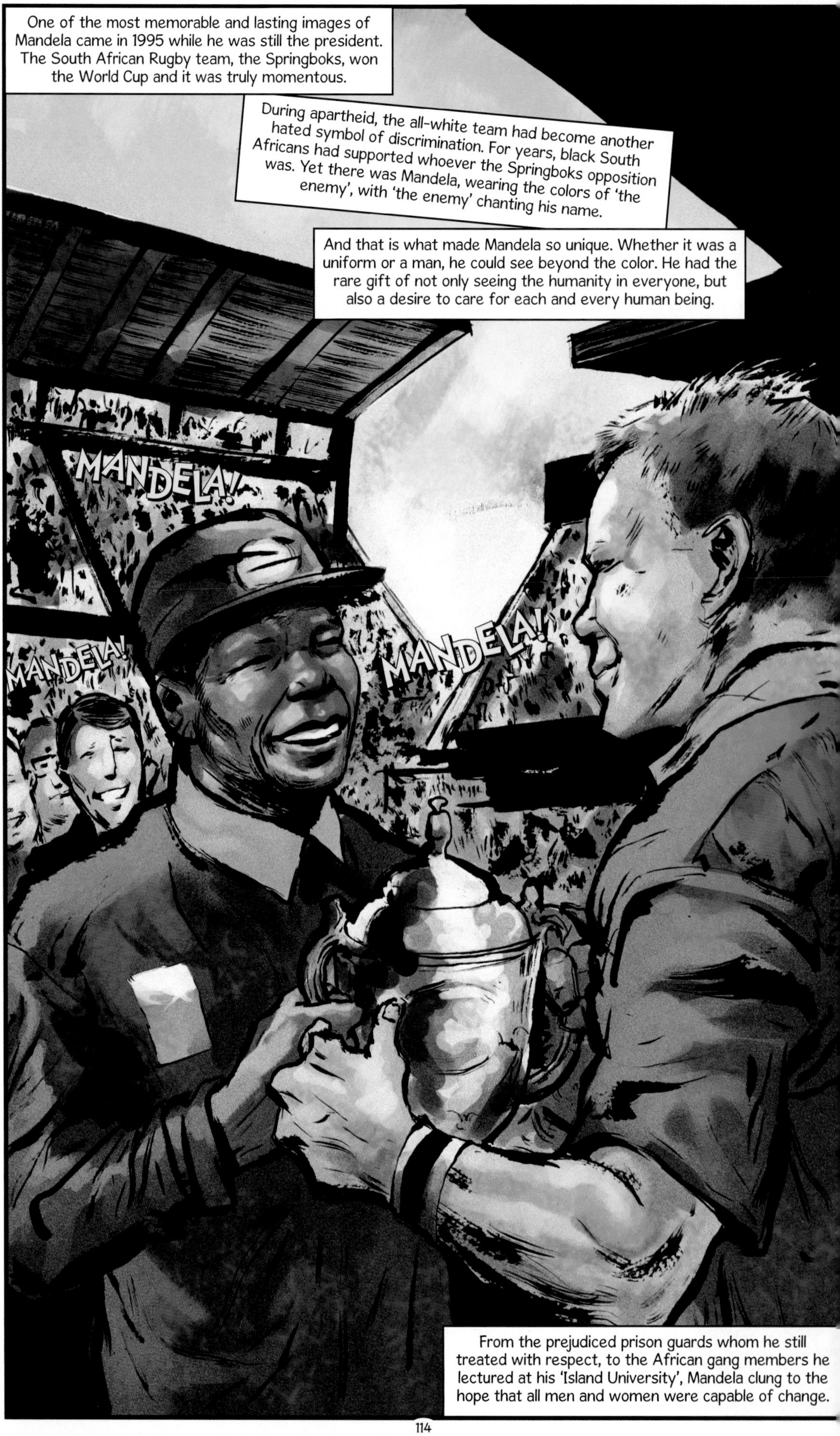
One of the most memorable and lasting images of Mandela came in 1995 while he was still the president. The South African Rugby team, the Springboks, won the World Cup and it was truly momentous.
During apartheid, the all-white team had become another hated symbol of discrimination. For years, black South Africans had supported whoever the Springboks opposition was. Yet there was Mandela, wearing the colors of 'the enemy', with 'the enemy' chanting his name.
And that is what made Mandela so unique. Whether it was a uniform or a man, he could see beyond the color. He had the rare gift of not only seeing the humanity in everyone, but also a desire to care for each and every human being.
MANDELA!
MANDELA!
MANDELA!
From the prejudiced prison guards whom he still treated with respect, to the African gang members he lectured at his 'Island University', Mandela clung to the hope that all men and women were capable of change.

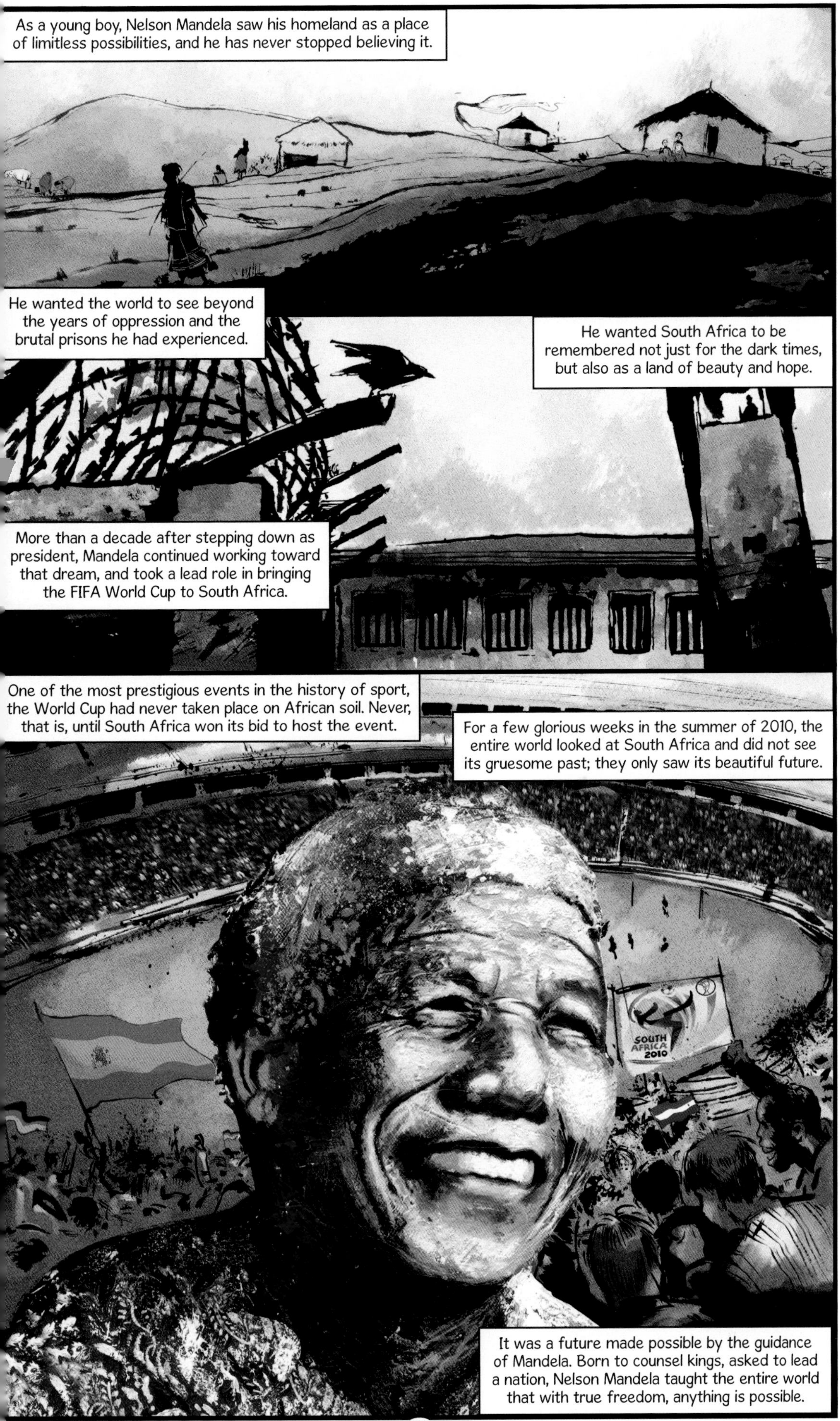
As a young boy, Nelson Mandela saw his homeland as a place of limitless possibilities, and he has never stopped believing it.
He wanted the world to see beyond the years of oppression and the brutal prisons he had experienced.
He wanted South Africa to be remembered not just for the dark times, but also as a land of beauty and hope.
More than a decade after stepping down as president, Mandela continued working toward that dream, and took a lead role in bringing the FIFA World Cup to South Africa.
One of the most prestigious events in the history of sport, the World Cup had never taken place on African soil. Never, that is, until South Africa won its bid to host the event.
For a few glorious weeks in the summer of 2010, the entire world looked at South Africa and did not see its gruesome past; they only saw its beautiful future.
SOUTH AFRICA 2010
It was a future made possible by the guidance of Mandela. Born to counsel kings, asked to lead a nation, Nelson Mandela taught the entire world that with true freedom, anything is possible.

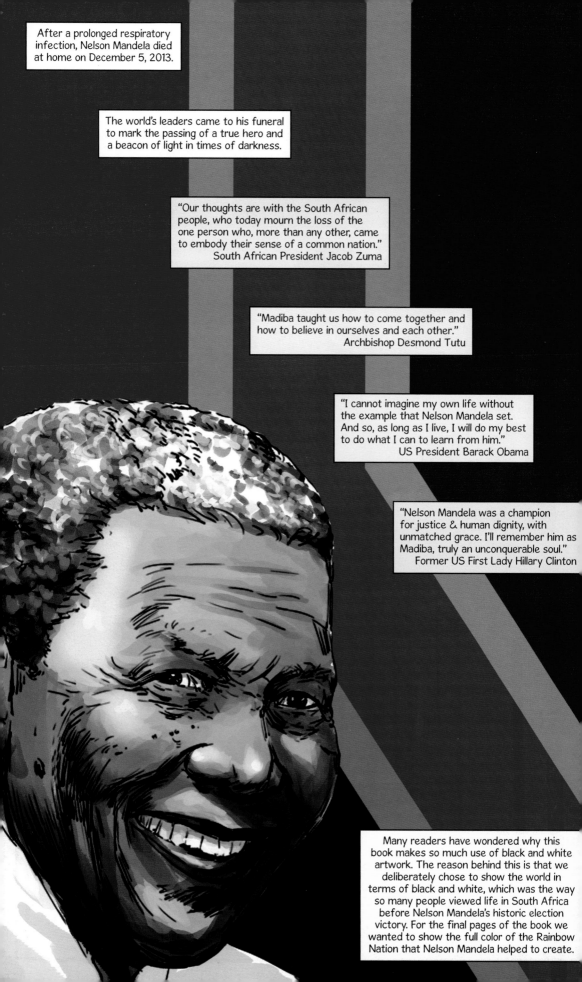

After a prolonged respiratory infection, Nelson Mandela died at home on December 5, 2013.

The world's leaders came to his funeral to mark the passing of a true hero and a beacon of light in times of darkness.

"Our thoughts are with the South African people, who today mourn the loss of the one person who, more than any other, came to embody their sense of a common nation."
South African President Jacob Zuma

"Madiba taught us how to come together and how to believe in ourselves and each other."
Archbishop Desmond Tutu

"I cannot imagine my own life without the example that Nelson Mandela set. And so, as long as I live, I will do my best to do what I can to learn from him."
US President Barack Obama

"Nelson Mandela was a champion for justice & human dignity, with unmatched grace. I'll remember him as Madiba, truly an unconquerable soul."
Former US First Lady Hillary Clinton

Many readers have wondered why this book makes so much use of black and white artwork. The reason behind this is that we deliberately chose to show the world in terms of black and white, which was the way so many people viewed life in South Africa before Nelson Mandela's historic election victory. For the final pages of the book we wanted to show the full color of the Rainbow Nation that Nelson Mandela helped to create.

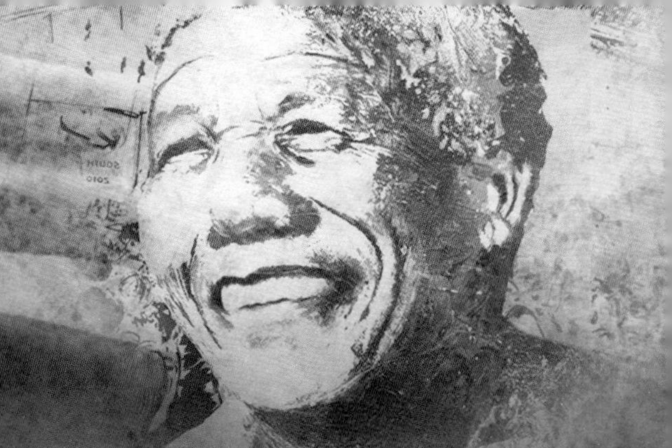

Glossary

AmaMfengu: One of the many African tribes native to South Africa. Members of this tribe moved to Nelson Mandela's village when he was a boy.

Apartheid: A system of unjust laws set up by the government of South Africa between 1948 and 1993, that involved discrimination against 'non-whites'. Apartheid helped keep the white minority in power.

Arsonists: Criminals who set fire to property.

Boycott: To abstain from, or prevent dealings with, as an expression of protest.

Che Guevara: A leader in the Cuban revolution, Guevara advocated that the people of oppressed nations should use guerrilla warfare to win their freedom; a strategy that involved taking up arms and striking out against the government at its weakest points. He fought against oppression in Africa and South America. His teachings were among those that Nelson Mandela consulted when he fought to free South Africa.

Desegregation: Elimination of the laws and rules that keep different races apart.

Discrimination: Unfair treatment based on the race, gender, class, or group to which a person belongs.

Kaffir: A racial insult used against black people. It originally meant a heathen, or someone who does not believe in god.

Mao Tse-tung: As a member of China's Communist Party, Mao Tse-tung (also known as Mao Zedong) helped bring a revolution to China by uniting the poor peasants in the countryside. After overthrowing the government, he served as president of the People's Republic of China. There is controversy surrounding the implementation of Mao's philosophies as they did not always yield positive results.

Martial Law: The temporary rule by military authorities in times of unrest.

Parole: Early release from prison for good behavior.

Sanction: An economic penalty adopted by a group of countries against another nation that is guilty of breaking international law or violating moral principles.

State of Emergency: A situation where the government suspends laws and the rights of people, often done in an attempt to stop protests.

Thembu: One of the many African tribes native to South Africa. After Nelson Mandela's father died, he lived with Chief Jongintaba Dalindyebo and his family, all of whom were members of the Thembu tribe.

Xhosa people: Inhabitants of south-east South Africa who speak Bantu languages belonging to different tribes, having related but distinct heritages. Nelson Mandela was born to the Xhosa nation.

This Time For South Africa

There's still lots more to say about the story of South Africa. Read on to find out more interesting and fun details about Nelson Mandela's 'Rainbow Nation'.

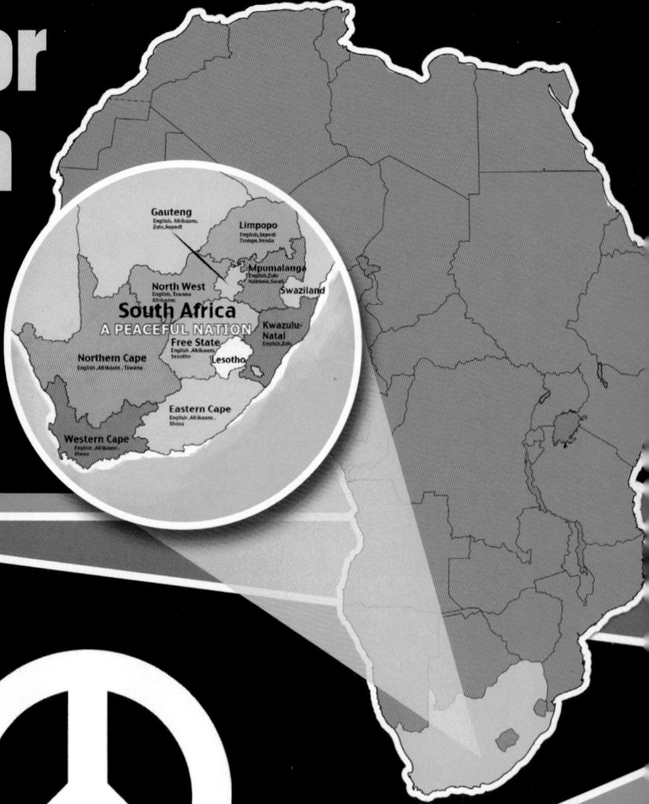
Gauteng
Limpopo
Mpumalanga
Swaziland
North West
South Africa
A PEACEFUL NATION
Kwazulu-Natal
Free State
Lesotho
Northern Cape
Eastern Cape
Western Cape

DISARMAMENT

South Africa was the first country in the world to voluntarily shut down its nuclear weapons programme, which began during the apartheid era. South Africa used the left over nuclear fuel to produce new technology for detecting cancer and heart disease. The symbol on the right stands for peace and is now the logo for the Campaign for Nuclear Disarmament.

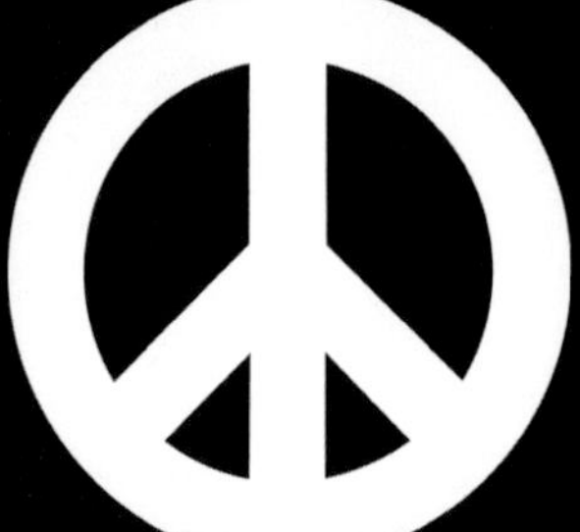

ANCIENT HISTORY

The Vredefort Dome near Parys in South Africa is the sight of the world's oldest meteor scar. South Africa is also home to the oldest remains of modern humans ever found. They are well over 160,000 years old. As if that isn't enough, scientists have also discovered traces of a strange blue-green algae dating back 3,500 million years.

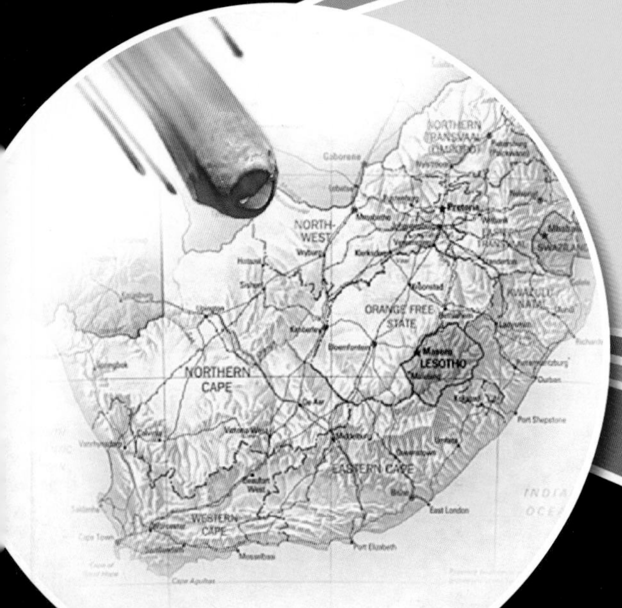
NORTH-WEST
ORANGE FREE STATE
LESOTHO
NORTHERN CAPE
EASTERN CAPE
WESTERN CAPE
Pretoria
Durban
Port Shepstone
East London
Port Elizabeth

ICONIC STREET

Vilakazi Street in Soweto is the only street in the world ever to house two Nobel Peace prize winners. Nelson Mandela lived there and so does Archbishop Desmond Tutu.

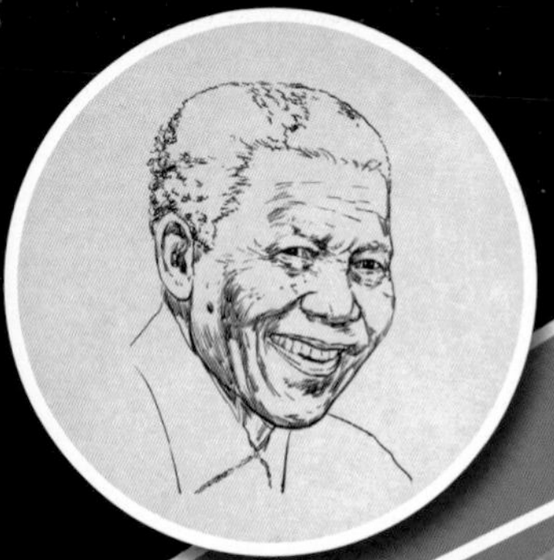

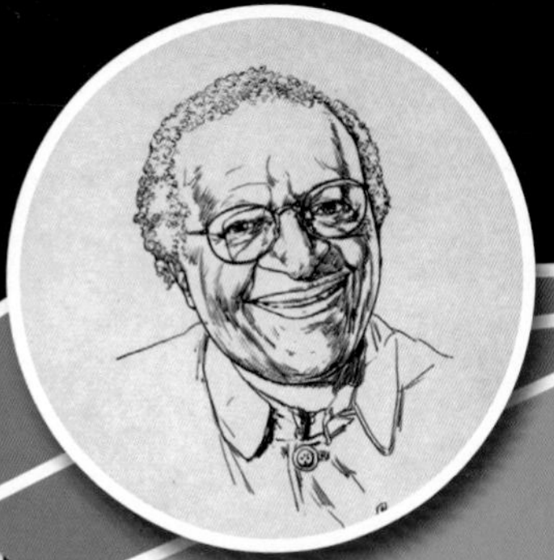

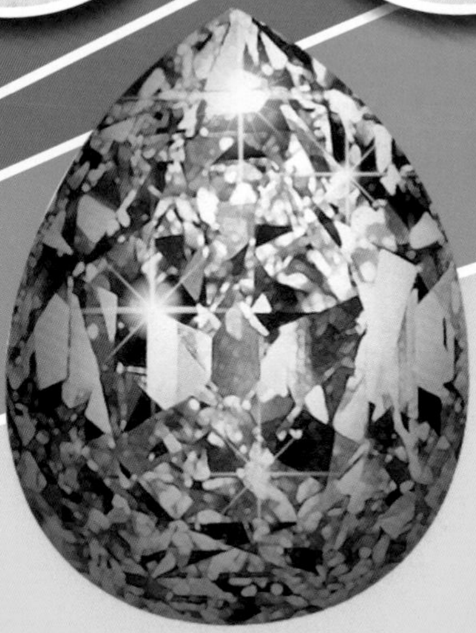

HOW MANY CAPITALS?

Most countries have one capital city, but South Africa has three! Cape Town is the legislative capital where all the laws are created and enacted. Pretoria is the administrative capital where everything is managed, and Bloemfontein is the judicial capital of the country where justice is carried out.

DIAMONDS ARE FOREVER

The world's largest diamond was found in the Transvaal, South Africa, back in 1905. It was called the Cullinan and uncut it weighed 3106.75 carats. It was later cut into the Great Star of Africa, the Lesser Star of Africa and 104 other diamonds that now form part of the British crown jewels.

ZAKUMI THE LEOPARD

South Africa was the first African country to host the FIFA World Cup. Zakumi is the name of the official mascot used for the 2010 tournament. The 'za' in 'Zakumi' is the international abbreviation for South Africa and 'kumi' means 'ten' in various different South African languages.

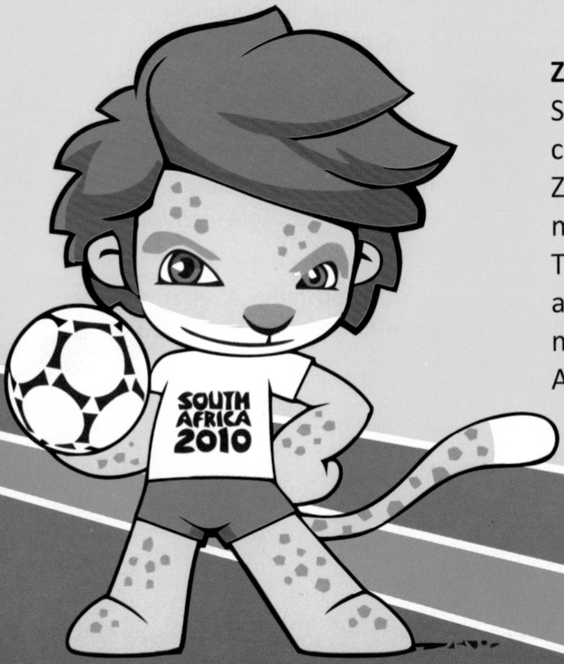
SOUTH
AFRICA
2010

ABOUT THE AUTHOR

Lewis Helfand was born on April 27, 1978 in Philadelphia, and grew up in nearby Narberth, Pennsylvania. Although interested in cartoons and animation from a young age, Lewis turned to writing by the time he was twelve. After finishing high school, he remained in the Philadelphia area with the intention of pursuing a degree in English.

Four years later, with a degree in Political Science and a passion for comic books, Lewis began working for local publishers, proofreading books and newspaper articles. By the age of twenty-four, Lewis had been editing phone books for a year and a half, and felt no closer to his lifelong goal of writing comic books. So one day he decided to quit his job.

Lewis then spent the next two months working day and night to write and draw his first comic book, *Wasted Minute*. It tells the story of a world without crime where superheroes are forced to work regular jobs. To cover the cost of self-publishing, he began working odd jobs in offices and restaurants, and started exhibiting at local comic-book conventions. With the first issue received well, he was soon collaborating with other artists, and released four more issues over the next few years.

Outside the field of comic books, Lewis works as a freelance writer and reporter for a number of national print and online publications. He has covered everything from sports and travel to politics and culture, for magazines such as *Renaissance*, *American Health and Fitness*, and *Computer Bits*.

Lewis is one of Campfire's most prolific writers, having adapted many Western classics, written several biographies, and scripted the original titles *400 B.C.* and *Photo Booth*.